Small Business Microsoft® Office 97 For Dummies®

Cheat Sheet

Word's Standard Toolbar

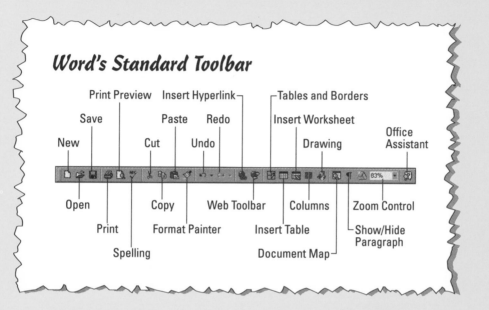

New
Save
Print Preview
Cut
Paste
Insert Hyperlink
Undo
Redo
Tables and Borders
Insert Worksheet
Drawing
Office Assistant

Open
Print
Spelling
Copy
Format Painter
Web Toolbar
Insert Table
Document Map
Columns
Show/Hide Paragraph
Zoom Control

Word's Formatting Toolbar

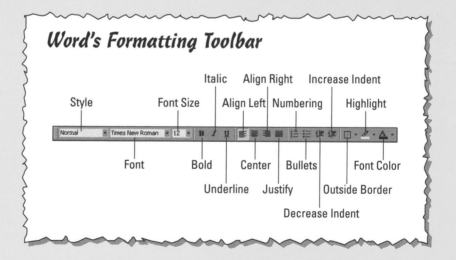

Style
Font Size
Italic
Align Right
Align Left
Numbering
Increase Indent
Highlight

Font
Bold
Underline
Center
Justify
Bullets
Decrease Indent
Outside Border
Font Color

Copyright © 1998 IDG Books Worldwide, Inc.
All rights reserved.
Cheat Sheet $2.95 value. Item 0290-5.
For more information about IDG Books,
call 1-800-762-2974.

...For Dummies: #1 Computer Book Series for Beginners

COMPUTER
BOOK SERIES
FROM IDG

Small Business Microsoft® Office 97 For Dummies®

Cheat Sheet

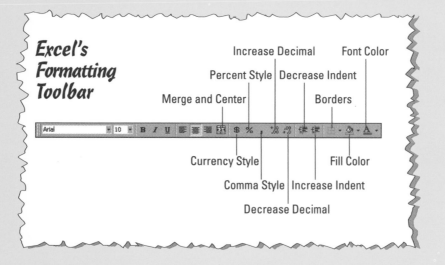

Excel's Formatting Toolbar

- Increase Decimal
- Font Color
- Percent Style
- Decrease Indent
- Merge and Center
- Borders
- Currency Style
- Fill Color
- Comma Style
- Increase Indent
- Decrease Decimal

Common Office 97 Commands

Command	Keyboard Shortcut	Function
New	Ctrl+N	Creates a new document
Open	Ctrl+O	Opens a document
Save	Ctrl+S	Saves a document
Print	Ctrl+P	Prints a document
Spelling	F7	Checks spelling
Cut	Ctrl+X	Cuts selected text or graphic
Copy	Ctrl+C	Copies selected text or graphic
Paste	Ctrl+V	Pastes item from clipboard
Undo	Ctrl+Z	Undoes the last operation

Command	Keyboard Shortcut	Function
Redo	Ctrl+Y	Reverses the last Undo
Bold	Ctrl+B	Bolds text
Italic	Ctrl+I	Italicizes text
Underline	Ctrl+U	Underlines text
Align Left	Ctrl+L	Aligns text to the left
Align Right	Ctrl+R	Aligns text to the right
Center	Ctrl+E	Centers text horizontally
Justify	Ctrl+J	Justifies text across the column or page
Select All	Ctrl+A	Selects all text and art in a document
Find	Ctrl+F	Opens the Find dialog box
Replace	Ctrl+H	Opens the Replace dialog box

...For Dummies: #1 Computer Book Series for Beginners

SMALL BUSINESS MICROSOFT® OFFICE 97 FOR DUMMIES®

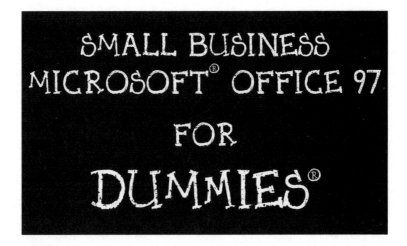

SMALL BUSINESS MICROSOFT® OFFICE 97 FOR DUMMIES®

by Dave Johnson and Todd Stauffer

IDG BOOKS WORLDWIDE

IDG Books Worldwide, Inc.
An International Data Group Company

Foster City, CA ♦ Chicago, IL ♦ Indianapolis, IN ♦ Southlake, TX

Small Business Microsoft® Office 97 For Dummies®

Published by
IDG Books Worldwide, Inc.
An International Data Group Company
919 E. Hillsdale Blvd.
Suite 400
Foster City, CA 94404
www.idgbooks.com (IDG Books Worldwide Web site)
www.dummies.com (Dummies Press Web site)

Library of Congress Catalog Card No.: xx-xxxxx

ISBN: 0-7645-0290-5

Printed in the United States of America

10 9 8 7 6 5 4 3 2 1

1O/QV/QR/ZY/IN

Distributed in the United States by IDG Books Worldwide, Inc.

Distributed by Macmillan Canada for Canada; by Transworld Publishers Limited in the United Kingdom; by IDG Norge Books for Norway; by IDG Sweden Books for Sweden; by Woodslane Pty. Ltd. for Australia; by Woodslane Enterprises Ltd. for New Zealand; by Longman Singapore Publishers Ltd. for Singapore, Malaysia, Thailand, and Indonesia; by Simron Pty. Ltd. for South Africa; by Toppan Company Ltd. for Japan; by Distribuidora Cuspide for Argentina; by Livraria Cultura for Brazil; by Ediciencia S.A. for Ecuador; by Addison-Wesley Publishing Company for Korea; by Ediciones ZETA S.C.R. Ltda. for Peru; by WS Computer Publishing Corporation, Inc., for the Philippines; by Unalis Corporation for Taiwan; by Contemporanea de Ediciones for Venezuela; by Computer Book & Magazine Store for Puerto Rico; by Express Computer Distributors for the Caribbean and West Indies. Authorized Sales Agent: Anthony Rudkin Associates for the Middle East and North Africa.

For general information on IDG Books Worldwide's books in the U.S., please call our Consumer Customer Service department at 800-762-2974. For reseller information, including discounts and premium sales, please call our Reseller Customer Service department at 800-434-3422.

For information on where to purchase IDG Books Worldwide's books outside the U.S., please contact our International Sales department at 415-655-3200 or fax 415-655-3295.

For information on foreign language translations, please contact our Foreign & Subsidiary Rights department at 415-655-3021 or fax 415-655-3281.

For sales inquiries and special prices for bulk quantities, please contact our Sales department at 415-655-3200 or write to the address above.

For information on using IDG Books Worldwide's books in the classroom or for ordering examination copies, please contact our Educational Sales department at 800-434-2086 or fax 817-251-8174.

For press review copies, author interviews, or other publicity information, please contact our Public Relations department at 415-655-3000 or fax 415-655-3299.

For authorization to photocopy items for corporate, personal, or educational use, please contact Copyright Clearance Center, 222 Rosewood Drive, Danvers, MA 01923, or fax 508-750-4470.

About the Authors

Todd Stauffer and Dave Johnson share microphones (although they use their own "spit guards") on America's hippest computer talk radio show. They speak for America when they say "Stop it with the Nieman Marcus cookie story already."

Dave Johnson has been writing about computers since his first book, *The Desktop Studio: Multimedia with the Amiga* was published in 1990. Since then, he's seen the Amiga join the ranks of betamax and *Three's Company,* prompting him to take up a new underdog: the Apple Newton MessagePad. To pass the time until the Newton takes up residence in the hereafter, he's written extensively for magazines like *Computer Shopper, Windows Magazine,* and *PC Computing.* He's helped author such books as Que's *Platinum Edition Using Windows 95* and IDG Books' *Windows 95 Bible.* His latest book is *Internet Explorer 4: Browsing and Beyond.*

Dave is the "Office@Home" columnist and contributing editor for *Peak Computing Magazine.* He reviews cars for the Colorado Springs Gazette and is secure enough as a person to beg his wonderful editor in an open forum like this: "Please, Julie! No more trucks! Just let me drive one sports car!"

As a former Air Force officer, Dave has flown satellites (by remote control — people don't sit in those things), trained space operators, and managed a munitions facility for Strategic Air Command. If you have any tricky questions, send Dave an e-mail, and he'll let you have Todd's home phone number.

Todd Stauffer is the author of eight other computer book titles, including *Using Your Mac, Using HTML 3.2 2nd Edition,* and *Creating Your Own AOL Web Pages* (with Andy Shafran), as well as contributing to *Netscape Navigator 3 Starter Kit, Platinum Edition, Using Windows 95,* and *SE Using the Internet with Your Mac.* He's the co-host of the nationally-televised "Disk Doctors" show on JEC Knowledge TV and a contributor to magazines like *WebSight Magazine, NetProfessional,* and *Windows Sources.* He's currently the Mac OS Chat columnist for *Peak Computing Magazine.*

In his spare time, Todd is busy starting a production company to focus on radio, public speaking, and seminars. The pursuit of his first love, professional volleyball, was severely handicapped by his failure to practice any sports in high school and college but golf.

ABOUT IDG BOOKS WORLDWIDE

Welcome to the world of IDG Books Worldwide.

IDG Books Worldwide, Inc., is a subsidiary of International Data Group, the world's largest publisher of computer-related information and the leading global provider of information services on information technology. IDG was founded more than 25 years ago and now employs more than 8,500 people worldwide. IDG publishes more than 275 computer publications in over 75 countries (see listing below). More than 60 million people read one or more IDG publications each month.

Launched in 1990, IDG Books Worldwide is today the #1 publisher of best-selling computer books in the United States. We are proud to have received eight awards from the Computer Press Association in recognition of editorial excellence and three from *Computer Currents'* First Annual Readers' Choice Awards. Our best-selling *...For Dummies*® series has more than 30 million copies in print with translations in 30 languages. IDG Books Worldwide, through a joint venture with IDG's Hi-Tech Beijing, became the first U.S. publisher to publish a computer book in the People's Republic of China. In record time, IDG Books Worldwide has become the first choice for millions of readers around the world who want to learn how to better manage their businesses.

Our mission is simple: Every one of our books is designed to bring extra value and skill-building instructions to the reader. Our books are written by experts who understand and care about our readers. The knowledge base of our editorial staff comes from years of experience in publishing, education, and journalism — experience we use to produce books for the '90s. In short, we care about books, so we attract the best people. We devote special attention to details such as audience, interior design, use of icons, and illustrations. And because we use an efficient process of authoring, editing, and desktop publishing our books electronically, we can spend more time ensuring superior content and spend less time on the technicalities of making books.

You can count on our commitment to deliver high-quality books at competitive prices on topics you want to read about. At IDG Books Worldwide, we continue in the IDG tradition of delivering quality for more than 25 years. You'll find no better book on a subject than one from IDG Books Worldwide.

John Kilcullen
CEO
IDG Books Worldwide, Inc.

Steven Berkowitz
President and Publisher
IDG Books Worldwide, Inc.

**Eighth Annual
Computer Press
Awards ≥1992**

**Ninth Annual
Computer Press
Awards ≥1993**

**Tenth Annual
Computer Press
Awards ≥1994**

**Eleventh Annual
Computer Press
Awards ≥1995**

Acknowledgments

The authors would like to diligently acknowledge everyone who made a contribution to this book, including the both of us. We've done a splendid job and we couldn't have done it otherwise. We'd also like to briefly mention that buffalo-style chicken wings played rather a large role.

Others would like to think they had something to do with it, and it is out of a grave and humble respect for our contractual obligations that we type their names:

Tim Gallan proved to be a great project editor, constantly rolling with the punches, helping us through the tough times, and consoling us in our darkest moments. (Okay, so we talked to this guy like twice via e-mail.) Tim, we didn't mean to add your name to the e-mail bomber manifesto list, and if it affected your ability to use the Internet in any way, we're sorry.

Jill Pisoni, thanks for the opportunity to write this book. As an acquisitions editor, you're without equal.*

Jill Brummett, thanks for having the same first name as Jill Pisoni, eliminating our need to memorize the name of another faceless voicemail recipient over at IDG World Headquarters. Your service in the copy editing of this book was invaluable, if infuriating. Yes, the edited copy is considerably more politically correct. But the original manuscript was destined to procure for us a guest spot on Jerry Springer, which was (and remains) our only goal in writing this book.

Brian Gill, you're the best agent either of us has ever had. (You're also the only agent either of us has ever had, and frankly, we were hoping for someone who wasn't always running off getting married and having extended honeymoons. Isn't there anyone older in your firm?) Thanks for realizing we'd work well together and helping make it happen.

Kris, thanks for being the ever-considerate wife and copy editor, and thanks again for not throwing me out on my ears for talking endlessly about Sandra Bullock and Kristin Hersh. —*DJ*

To Sandra Bullock and Kristin Hersh, thanks for just being there for me. Well, "there" in the sense that I actually kind of pretended that you were there for me. —*DJ*

To Donna Ladd, thanks for helping me through yet another book crunch and listening as I inevitably complained about all the awful things Dave and IDG did every step of the way. Thanks, also, for keeping it between us. —*TS*

---

* This comment should in no way be taken in the context of any other books we've written in which we called some other acquisitions editor "unequaled" or "the best." This is a stand-alone comment.

Dedication

Writes Dave:

I was going to dedicate this one to Newt, but my parents would probably disown me if I dedicated yet another book to one of my cats before them.

Mom and Dad, this book is for you. I love you both very much, even though I live altogether too far away.

Writes Todd:

Because I have already largely thanked Dave's parents in other books, I looked around for another dedication possibility — fearing it would embarrass my partner, Donna Ladd, who's been immensely helpful and understanding throughout this entire process. I finally decided to dedicate the book to her cat, Daisy, who has done next to nothing for me.

Publisher's Acknowledgments

We're proud of this book; please register your comments through our IDG Books Worldwide Online Registration Form located at http://my2cents.dummies.com.

Some of the people who helped bring this book to market include the following:

Acquisitions, Development, and Editorial

Project Editor: Tim Gallan

Acquisitions Editor: Jill Pisoni

Media Development Manager: Joyce Pepple

Permissions Editor: Heather H. Dismore

Copy Editor: Jill Brummett

Technical Editors: Jamie Marcum, Joell Smith

Editorial Manager: Leah P. Cameron

Editorial Assistant: Donna Love

Production

Project Coordinator: Regina Snyder

Layout and Graphics: Lou Boudreau, J. Tyler Connor, Maridee V. Ennis, Angela F. Hunckler, Todd Klemme, Jane E. Martin, Drew R. Moore, Anna Rohrer, Janet Seib, Brent Savage

Proofreaders: Henry Lazarek, Kelli Botta, Christine Berman, Robert Springer, Janet M. Withers

Indexer: Christine Spina

General and Administrative

IDG Books Worldwide, Inc.: John Kilcullen, CEO; Steven Berkowitz, President and Publisher

IDG Books Technology Publishing: Brenda McLaughlin, Senior Vice President and Group Publisher

Dummies Technology Press and Dummies Editorial: Diane Graves Steele, Vice President and Associate Publisher; Mary Bednarek, Acquisitions and Product Development Director; Kristin A. Cocks, Editorial Director

Dummies Trade Press: Kathleen A. Welton, Vice President and Publisher; Kevin Thornton, Acquisitions Manager; Maureen F. Kelly, Editorial Coordinator

IDG Books Production for Dummies Press: Beth Jenkins, Production Director; Cindy L. Phipps, Manager of Project Coordination, Production Proofreading, and Indexing; Kathie S. Schutte, Supervisor of Page Layout; Shelley Lea, Supervisor of Graphics and Design; Debbie J. Gates, Production Systems Specialist; Robert Springer, Supervisor of Proofreading; Debbie Stailey, Special Projects Coordinator; Tony Augsburger, Supervisor of Reprints and Bluelines; Leslie Popplewell, Media Archive Coordinator

Dummies Packaging and Book Design: Patti Crane, Packaging Specialist; Lance Kayser, Packaging Assistant; Kavish + Kavish, Cover Design

♦

The publisher would like to give special thanks to Patrick J. McGovern, without whom this book would not have been possible.

♦

Contents at a Glance

Cartoons at a Glance

By Rich Tennant

page 319

page 281

page 185

page 5

Fax: 508-546-7747 • E-mail: the5wave@tiac.net

Table of Contents

Introduction

• •

*M*ost books begin with an overview of why you should spend your hard-earned money to take this collection of paper, plastic, and printing ink home with you. We'd like to begin a little differently. We'd like to kick off this book with a poem:

Doctor Seuss for the Office

By Paul B. Rice, II

I work on the 4th floor.
There is a printer in my office on the 4th floor.
I can't print to the printer in my office on the 4th floor.
The guy in the next office prints to the printer in my office on the 4th floor.
I have to print to the printer on the 8th floor.
The people on the 8th floor can't print to the printer on the 8th floor.
They print to the printer in my office on the 4th floor.

In our experience, most of the problems people encounter in the office are a result of not knowing how to take advantage of the tools you already have — like Microsoft Office. *Small Business Microsoft Office 97 For Dummies* is designed to discuss Office 97 — both the Professional and Small Business Editions — a little differently than many books on the bookstore shelves. Sure, we talk about the mechanics of using Office. But we also talk about how to actually apply this suite of applications to everyday small business situations. Plus, we asked business experts to weigh in with their opinions throughout the book. Even if you already have a guide to using Office, we dare say that you need this book. Actually, you need 4 or 5 copies of this book — one for each room of your house. And it makes a great gift item, too.

Who Should Buy This Book

Perhaps you're new to Microsoft Office. Or maybe you have some familiarity with the program, but you're trying to apply it to your small business. Either way, *Small Business Microsoft Office 97 For Dummies* is for you. It doesn't matter how sketchy your computer background is — even absolute beginners can benefit from this book.

Go ahead and flip through the chapters that follow (but leave a finger here so that you can come back and read the other elegant prose we put in the introduction). You'll notice that we discuss all the major office applications — even the scary ones like Excel and Access — and show you in plain English (as opposed to those other Office books that look good until you get them home and discover they're written in plain French) how to master the basics and do productive work with your computer.

One of the best reasons to buy this book is that in addition to demonstrating the basics of each Office program, we show you how to apply these tools to everyday small business functions. Need to create a Web site? Business card? Print envelopes? Take an e-mail poll of your coworkers? It's all in here.

How This Book Is Organized

To get you going as quickly and efficiently as possible, we've divided this book into five exciting, heart-pounding parts. We recommend that you keep various copies of this book in different rooms of your home or small business, and whenever you have a question, reach for the closest copy and open to the appropriate part. You'll find your answer quickly and then can get back to playing computer games.

Part I: Learning the Ropes

Consider it boot camp for Microsoft Office. In this part of the book, you find out how to use each one of the Office 97 applications. We cover what is probably the best word processor ever written — Microsoft Word — plus Excel, PowerPoint, and Access. The Small Business Edition includes two programs that are new to the Office family: Automap and Publisher. We discuss the basics of these apps as well. If you're really new to Office — or looking for instructions on how to use a particular feature — this is the first place to go.

Part II: Making Your Business Look Bigger

This part dives into ways to use Office to make your customers think you're as big as GigantaCorp. Look here for tips on creating printed documents like business cards and newsletters. We also cover how to create contact management systems with Outlook and knock your boss's socks off with cool and exciting financial reports. There's even advice on creating and maintaining a Web site.

Part III: Making Your Business Work Better

Your company may not be as big as GigantaCorp, but you may still need to coordinate with a bunch of coworkers, vendors, and clients. Is there an easy way to do that? You bet there is — and it's here in Part III. Look here to learn how to set up an ad hoc intranet (an internal Internet for posting notices, human resources information, and ground rules for the Christmas party), how to share files among cubicle-mates, and track changes to documents so you know exactly who to blame.

Part IV: The Part of Tens

You're busy — we know that. We don't want to take up a lot of your time, and that's why we're typing as fast as we can. If you want to track down tips and tricks that can help you work faster and smarter, the Part of Tens is the place for you. Here we've amassed helpful tips in bite-sized chunks.

The Appendix

That silver round thing in the back of the book is a CD-ROM (but you already knew that). The appendix discusses how to install and use the software we've included.

Icons Used in This Book

You've probably seen the icons used in other *...For Dummies* books that help point out important or particularly useful information. Keep an eye out for these icons throughout the book:

Tips are tricks or shortcuts that should help you to work more effectively.

If you can keep this nugget in the back of your mind, it can save you time later.

Danger, Will Robinson. Be careful or you might hurt yourself, your data, or the cat next door.

Don't get too wound up about this one. It points out information that's fun to know but not immediately useful for operating the program.

When we want you to, um, take note of something (usually something nonserious), we use this icon.

A Few Conventions

Throughout this book, we often refer to menu commands in the Office 97 suite of applications. When we do, we use this sort of structure:

File⇨Open

That bit of text means "Choose the Open command from the File menu." What about the underlined characters in File and Open? Those are hot keys, which you access by pressing in combination with the Alt key. In other words, you can also initiate the Open command by pressing Alt+F+O.

When we refer to Web pages and e-mail addresses, we use this typeface: `http://shutup101.com/office97/`

Need Extra Help?

Any errata, frequently asked questions, or other issues that crop up after the printing of this book will be quickly identified, addressed, and destroyed with aplomb and agility on the Web site we've created to extend this book into cyberspace. If you have a question, concern or issue with _Small Business Microsoft Office 97 For Dummies,_ stop by `http://shutup101.com/office97/` and ask for Dave or Todd. You can send us e-mail questions, comments, and praise through that page as well.

Part I
Learning the Ropes

In this part . . .

We cover all of the major applications in Office 97. We realize that some of you may not have PowerPoint or Access, but we include coverage anyway, just in case you decide to obtain these software packages and try to use them to do some work. When you're done with this part, you'll be able to format a Word document, get Excel to add a column of numbers, run a query in Access, create a presentation in PowerPoint, create professional-looking documents in Publisher, send and receive e-mail with Outlook, and even put Automap to good use.

Chapter 1

Everything You Need to Know about Office 97

In This Chapter

▶ Verifying that you bought the wrong version of Office (just kidding)

▶ Getting organized with your computer's help

▶ Getting to know the dancing paperclip

▶ Coaxing a little info out of Microsoft Help

Chances are good that you didn't come across your current version of Microsoft Office 97 by accident. Either you're required to use it for work, or you got a copy with your new computer system. In both cases, the most important thing to figure out is which version of Office 97 you have on your computer. From there, you can figure out how exactly you use the beast.

Microsoft actually offers two consumer versions of Office 97 — the Professional Edition and the Small Business Edition. You may already have one edition or the other. Which edition you use determines not only how you read this book (and what you can skip), but also how you organize your work and what tools you have at your disposal.

Actually, a third version of Microsoft Office exists, called the Developer Edition. It's apparently designed almost exclusively to foil book authors who like nice, neat, two-option systems. The Developer edition adds to the Professional Edition, offering extra controls for developing database programs for corporate Information Systems types. Another version specialized for CPA penguins is rumored to be forthcoming.

Discovering the Professional Edition versus the Small Business Edition

Although you may not believe that Microsoft has your best interests at heart, the fact is that they've done their homework. The Small Business Edition of Office 97 has the right programs for running a home office or telecommuting (working a few days a week from home). In fact, Microsoft has done extensive research that leads them to believe that folks in their home offices would much rather use Publisher to create newsletters, for example, than use Access to create incredibly complicated databases. Similar research also indicates that most folks would rather have large, hairy spiders crawl all over them while they sleep than use Access to create incredibly complicated databases.

So, Microsoft came up with the Small Business Edition, a suite of Microsoft programs that unfortunately comes without room service. It's designed to be cheaper than Microsoft Office Professional Edition, and less intimidating by offering easier and more widely used programs. All this makes the Small Business Edition pretty popular with the companies that build and sell Windows computers — especially that *cheaper* part.

How do you know if you have the Small Business Edition? You can look at the CD-ROM — the name of the edition is on the label. You can also select the Start➪Programs. If you see a bunch of Microsoft programs (like Microsoft Excel, Microsoft Word, and so on) just sitting there in the menu, you probably have the Small Business Edition. If you see a Microsoft Office folder, you probably have the Professional Edition. Figure 1-1 shows what you see if you have the Small Business Edition.

What makes the two editions different? Well, for one thing, if everyone went out and bought a copy of Microsoft Office Professional Edition today, Bill Gates would be a trillionaire in less than the four minutes of commercials that run between segments on MS/NBC (the joint NBC/Microsoft news cable channel). If everyone bought the Small Business Edition, Gates could retire the United States national debt by the time that his toddler daughter hits him up for prom money.

Microsoft Office is a *suite* of individual programs designed to work together, as opposed to a *single* program with more than one type of functionality. Office includes many different programs. Each program is a completely separate and individual program, as opposed to a program like Microsoft Works, which offers word processing, spreadsheet, and database tools in the same program.

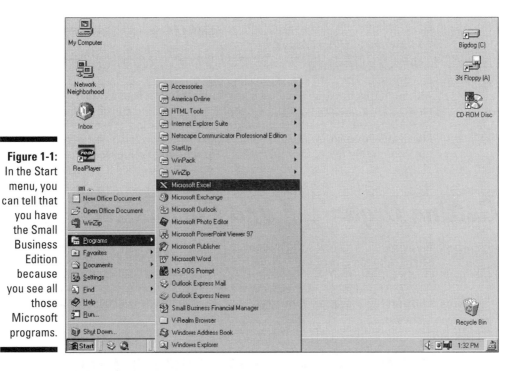

Figure 1-1:
In the Start
menu, you
can tell that
you have
the Small
Business
Edition
because
you see all
those
Microsoft
programs.

The other major difference between the two editions revolves around the programs included with each edition. The Small Business Edition features

- ✔ Microsoft Word
- ✔ Microsoft Excel
- ✔ Microsoft Outlook
- ✔ Microsoft Publisher
- ✔ Microsoft Small Business Financial Manager
- ✔ Microsoft Automap Streets Plus

The Professional Edition features a slightly different but no less wacky mix of programs:

- ✔ Microsoft Word
- ✔ Microsoft Excel
- ✔ Microsoft Outlook
- ✔ Microsoft PowerPoint

> ✔ Microsoft Access
> ✔ Microsoft Office Manager
> ✔ Bookshelf Basics

Although this book focuses on using the Small Business Edition to solve most of your problems, special chapters are devoted to things like working with Microsoft Access to create databases or creating presentations with Microsoft PowerPoint. Even though both these things are very cool, they're not completely necessary for all small and home businesses.

Getting Organized and Customized

If you received Microsoft Office with your new PC, more than likely the Microsoft Office programs already appear in your Start menu. This makes the job of starting them a simple one. To start any program, you can choose Start⇨Program⇨Microsoft Office⇨Microsoft *Whatever* or choose Start⇨Program⇨Microsoft *Whatever*, depending on how the software was installed.

Finding out about the SBE CD-ROM

The Small Business Edition is often referred to as the *Office SBE* because of the computing world's love affair with TLAs (Three-Letter Acronyms). That's just an FYI, but this is interesting from the POV of your CPU. SBE has its own CD-ROM, enabling you to act as a PC EMT, if one of your programs is DOA. But enough of this — IOU an explanation. ASAP.

The SBE CD-ROM is the digital repository of every file that has something to do with Microsoft Office Small Business Edition and is pretty easy to get around in. Hopefully, you won't have much cause for using the CD-ROM because many PC vendors preinstall Office on your machine for you. You may be upgrading your Office setup or adding Office for the first time, however. In this case, here's how you gain access to all Office SBE programs:

1. **Insert the CD-ROM in your CD-ROM drive.**

2. **Double-click My Computer.**

   The My Computer dialog box appears.

3. **Double-click the CD-ROM icon.**

Windows AutoRun kicks in, and the Windows start-up theme sound plays. Then a pretty, graphical screen appears to give you access to everything that comes on the SBE CD-ROM, as shown in Figure 1-2.

More about acronyms

Todd likes to call things like SBE an acronym, but the cold, harsh reality of life is that acronyms are, by definition, words formed from the combination of initial letters of other words. Thus, RADAR is an acronym for *Radio* *Detection and Ranging*, but SBE, lacking that important vowel between the *S* and the *B*, is simply an abbreviation — not a word. Don't be too hard on Todd; he means well.

Figure 1-2:
The Office SBE CD-ROM offers a straight-forward multimedia presentation of the Setup programs for each individual program.

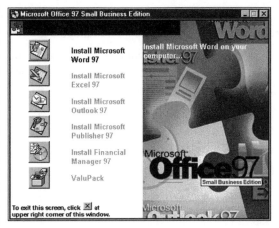

Being able to selectively install the programs that you want from the CD-ROM can be beneficial, without question. But it can also be a pain. (We think it'd be nice if there were a separate installation program. Microsoft, however, doesn't seem to care what we think.) To access the Setup program for any program, just click the program icon.

The Setup program for each Office program is useful for more than just installing the program. It can also be used to Add or Remove components of each Office program, as described in the following aptly named section "Adding and removing programs."

Adding and removing programs

The Microsoft Office suite can be rather demanding on your computer — especially when it begins storing its files on your computer's hard drive. A *full installation* of the Small Business Edition (an installation that makes it possible to use all the Microsoft-included goodies) weighs in at around 160 MB in our unscientific estimate. That's a lot of hard drive space.

Fortunately, you're free to determine what, if anything, gets left behind during the Office Small Business Edition installation.

If you already installed the Small Business Edition or if it was preinstalled on your computer, you can add and remove parts of the installation by accessing the Add/Remove programs Properties sheet:

1. **Choose Start⇨Settings⇨Control Panel to open the Windows control panel.**

2. **In the control panel, double-click Add/Remove Programs.**

   The Add/Remove Programs properties sheet appears.

3. **Choose the program that you want to add or subtract from, and then click the Add/Remove button, as shown in Figure 1-3.**

   Next, Windows launches the Setup Wizard for the program you chose. Most of them act like the Microsoft Excel Wizard, shown in Figure 1-4.

4. **To uninstall some of the components, but not all of them, click the Add/Remove button.**

   The Maintenance dialog box appears.

5. **Use the Maintenance dialog box to choose which parts of the program to uninstall.**

   To remove a complete component, deselect the check box next to that component.

6. **When you deselect the check boxes next to everything you want to remove, click the Continue button.**

   The Setup Wizard removes the components.

Figure 1-3:
The Add/
Remove
Programs
properties
sheet is
where you
trim Office
fat by
uninstalling
bits of
Office that
you don't
want.

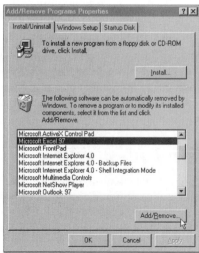

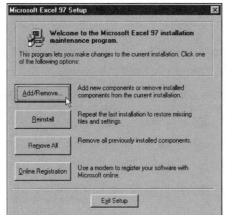

Figure 1-4:
The
Maintenance
dialog box
enables
you to
individually
select
components
for
annihilation
or reprieve.

In the Maintenance dialog box you have another option: You can click the Select All button. Doing so selects every component of an Office program, which allows you to uninstall the entire thing. And, to be honest, that's probably a really good idea. (See Chapter 2 for more on using a manual typewriter for all your business needs.)

You may not believe this, but to add components to your setup, you simply select their check boxes in the appropriate Maintenance dialog box. The cool part is that when you go to install or reinstall removed components, you can highlight the component and then click the Options button. Doing so lets you install only the bits of that component that you think are really important.

Setting the document folder

Here's another headache common to computing: Where do you save your files? Fortunately, this one has been largely solved by most of the programs in Microsoft Office. You can use any of the following systems:

✔ You can use the My Document folder provided by Windows to save all your documents in one place.

✔ You can use each program's folder to store your documents so that Word documents are saved right next to the Word program files, and so on.

✔ You can create your own folders on the Desktop or on your hard drive where you save documents.

✔ Like a small but forceful contingent of users who focus on the non-linear nature of time and insist that humanity offers a collective conscience in which nothing is lost, you can choose to save nothing.

In all cases — but especially the last one — we sincerely recommend a backup plan. In any of the three more earthy ways of saving computer files, Microsoft Office programs are flexible enough to accommodate you. As an extra bonus, you get to manually set this Save mechanism in each program when using the Small Business Edition. Whoopie!

Here's how you configure your default documents folder in Microsoft Word:

1. **Open the program by choosing it from the Start menu.**

   By way of example, we use Microsoft Word.

2. **In the program menu, choose Tools⇨Options.**

   The Options properties sheet appears.

3. **In the Options properties sheet, click the File Locations tab, shown in Figure 1-5.**

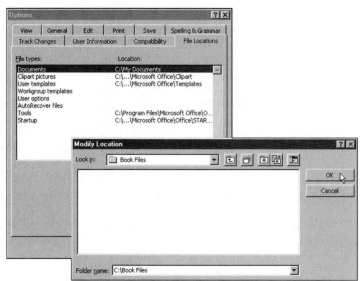

Figure 1-5:
Changing
the location
for your
saved
documents
in each
Office
program is
similar to
the process
shown
here for
Microsoft
Word.

4. **Either double-click the Documents file type or click it once and then click the Modify button.**

   The Modify Location dialog box appears.

5. **In the Modify Location dialog box, open the folder where you want this program to store its documents or where you usually want them stored.**

6. **After you open the folder, click OK.**

   The default Save folder is now set. Whenever you go to save a new file, the Save As dialog box opens to your preset folder.

You may find that this process is similar but not exactly the same in the various Office programs. In Microsoft Excel, you choose Tools⇨Options, but then you click the General tab and type a file path (like C:\My Documents). Outlook allows you to specify an archive folder (where e-mail messages and contact information are stored) in the Options properties sheet and the AutoArchive tab. Publisher defaults to the Microsoft Publisher folder on your hard drive.

If you use PowerPoint, you can specify the default file save location from the downright wacky Advanced tab in the Options properties sheet. And if you liked that, you'll love Access: Look in Tools⇨Options and then click the General tab.

Note: Where you save your work is largely a matter of personal taste, but keep some things in mind. If you have a network drive or part of your hard disk that gets backed up regularly (like to a tape backup drive or a Zip drive), you may want to store all your data there. Likewise, you can keep your data files stored separately from programs for easier and shorter backup sessions — particularly if you only back up the data. After all, you can always reinstall the programs from CD-ROM if anything really bad happens. You may also need to keep data on your office's network drive so that others can get to your work, but have a second, private part of your own hard drive that you can store personal or sensitive information on.

Getting Help

Although we're not absolutely convinced that Microsoft should be promoting the notion of talking to paperclips in the workplace (even if the workplace is your basement or garage), we do appreciate the new help system offered in Office 97. More than ever, the help is engaging, intelligent, and easy to access. In fact, the Office 97 system does an admirable job of walking you through any trouble you have with the basics of an Office 97 program.

Microsoft Office actually employs a number of different kinds of help to make things easier on us. Though not every program uses every type of help, the following types are fairly universal in the Office bundle:

✔ **Office Assistant:** By default, the Office Assistant shows up as a paperclip in a small window, although you can change the appearance and set options for how often you see the Assistant. It's designed to offer tips and advice based on the tasks you are trying to accomplish. It also gives access to the other types of help.

✔ **Intellisense:** This help technology requires even less interaction from you because it basically describes the different *intelligent* helpers that are running in the background while you work. For example, Microsoft Word constantly checks your grammar while you write, only offering a suggestion when it comes across something that seems out of sorts.

✔ **Hypertext Help:** The heart of the Microsoft Office Help system is still the hypertext help, which works like pages on the World Wide Web to enable you to read about a particular task or command. This help is available throughout the Office suite and is often the most complete.

✔ **Wizards:** Wizards walk you through some predefined tasks and allow you to quickly accomplish things that may have proven much more difficult without the help. Examples include creating a mail merge (where addresses and salutations are automatically added to a form letter) and building the design for a brochure, as shown in Figure 1-6.

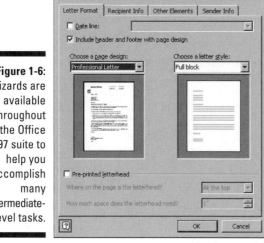

Figure 1-6:
Wizards are available throughout the Office 97 suite to help you accomplish many intermediate-level tasks.

Each of these help methods is useful in its own right, although in most of the Office 97 programs they've actually been merged together in a way that makes them even easier to deal with.

When we first started our computer writing careers over a decade ago, we honestly never expected to say "Click little Power Pup (one of the Office Assistant personalities) for help with your sales contact database." Today, we're still embarrassed to be saying such a thing, but we know it serves an important purpose.

Office Assistant

Maybe you've broken out on your own and left behind the office support staff. Maybe, like much of the corporate world, your bosses have decided that support staff isn't necessary because they bought you a shiny new PC. Great, but why don't they hire someone to *work* the silly PC? Wouldn't it be nice if you had an assistant?

Well, too bad. Instead, Microsoft has come up with a clever way to mock you and your lack of office help. It's called the Office Assistant, and it appears by default when you start a new Office program. The Assistant generally has a number of things to say, and if you leave it active while you work, you'll eventually get sick of it and wish you knew how to turn it off. Figure 1-7 shows the Office Assistant at work.

Fortunately, we tell you exactly how to turn it off. In the meantime, though, you may want to check out the Assistant and see if you think it's helpful. Through most of the programs in Microsoft Office, the Assistant is a common thread, floating over everything even as you switch between tasks and programs. In this way, it serves as a convenient one-stop repository for help and tips.

Figure 1-7:
By default,
the Office
Assistant
appears as
a paperclip.

Tips

The first contact you have with the Assistant is probably in the form of a tip. The Assistant is designed to offer a new tip whenever you open one of the Office programs that uses the Assistant. The tips appears in a *thought bubble* similar to those you may see in a Sunday comic strip. To turn off this tip, click the Close button in the thought bubble, as shown in Figure 1-8.

Figure 1-8:
The Office
Assistant
communicates
using comic
strip-like
thought
bubbles.

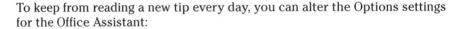

Want to see that tip again? Here's how you do it:

1. **Click the Assistant to get its attention.**

   A thought bubble appears, allowing you to choose the type of help you need.

2. **Click the Tips button.**

   The tip reappears.

3. **Click Close when you're finished with the tip, or click Forward and Back to scroll through other tips you've seen.**

   You can also press the F1 key to get the Assistant's attention.

To keep from reading a new tip every day, you can alter the Options settings for the Office Assistant:

1. **Click the Assistant to get its attention.**

   The What Would You Like to Do thought bubble appears.

2. **Click the Options button in that thought bubble.**

   The Office Assistant properties sheet appears.

3. **In the Office Assistant properties sheet, select the Options tab.**

   Note the Tip-related options at the bottom of the screen.

4. **Select or deselect the check box next to each option.**

   A deselected check box means that the option is inactive. To get rid of daily tips, for example, deselect the check box next to Show the Tip of the Day at Startup (so that no check mark appears).

5. **Click OK to put your option changes into effect.**

   The Office Assistant now behaves according to your changes.

Advice

Aside from tips, the Office Assistant also offers advice while you work, depending on what exactly it is that you're trying to accomplish. By watching the data or text you type as you work in an Office program, the Assistant pops up advice that points you to more help within the Microsoft Help system or within a Wizard.

When the Office Assistant offers advice, you can

   ✔ Click the button next to the advice to open the associated Wizard or Help screen.

   ✔ Click the option that allows you to work without help.

   ✔ Just keep working and ignore the Office Assistant.

If you don't want more advice, access the Assistant Options, and deselect Help with wizards.

Here's another way that the Assistant likes to give advice: If it notices that you're not doing something the most efficient way, a little light bulb appears in the Assistant window. Click the light bulb, and you get a quick tip about the current task. Why two different methods for alerting you? Because the Assistant only interrupts your work (with a thought bubble) if it wants you to use a Wizard. A simple tip only merits a light bulb icon.

Search for help

The Office Assistant offers a third help option: It enables you to search for the help you need while performing a particular task. This is probably the most useful and, at the same time, maybe the most underused type of help. In fact, we recommend searching for help topics even before you pick up this book as a reference. You may save lots of time by using Microsoft's built-in guidance. Plus, this gives you a good chance to play with the cute little Assistant again.

To search for a help topic:

1. **Click the Assistant to get its attention.**

2. **In the text box labeled What Would You Like to Do, type a phrase that describes what you're trying to accomplish (see Figure 1-9).**

3. **Click the Search button.**

   The Assistant responds with a number of choices.

4. **Choose the help topic that seems closest to the question you asked or click the See More button for more help topics.**

   The Microsoft Help system appears, giving you access to the help topic you chose.

Figure 1-9:
Searching
for help is
an excellent
way to
quickly find
an answer
to a question
you have
about an
Office
program.

What would you like to do?

- Get Help without the Office Assistant
- Ways to get assistance while you work
- Troubleshoot the Office Assistant
- Turn the Office Assistant sound on or off
- Choose a different Office Assistant

Turn off Assistant

Search

Tips   Options   Close

When asking the paperclip (or other Assistant personality) for help, use action words and specific nouns that describe the process that you want to accomplish. The more targeted you are, the better the paperclip's chance to help. And trust us — you don't want to be around the paperclip when it's frustrated.

Notice that Microsoft Help, once activated, appears in its own window. You can easily switch back and forth between your Microsoft Office program and the Microsoft Help system, so you can work as you discover new things. We discuss Microsoft Help a bit more in the following section, "Other Assistant options."

Other Assistant options

You can make a couple other behavior changes in the Office Assistant. The best part is that you don't need input from the Human Resources Legal Department to do so. Just point and make your demands (well, pretty darn close to that). Actually, we've heard that the paperclips are unionizing. Stay tuned; we'll let you know.

To open the Office Assistant options, click the Assistant once to get its attention and then click the Options button. A couple of new options appear that you can set.

Want the Assistant to look different? In the Office Assistant property sheet, choose the Gallery tab (see Figure 1-10). Now, use the Back and Next buttons to scroll through the different happy faces you can put on your Assistant. When you find one you like, click OK.

Figure 1-10: Options that help you to discipline your Office Assistant.

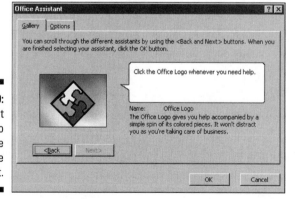

Here are the options available to you when you click the Options tab:

- **Capabilities:** In the top half of the Office Assistant dialog box are general characteristics you can set for your Assistant. Do you want it to make sounds? Do you want it to display alerts (like Do you want to save your work messages)?

- **Show tips about:** The middle of the dialog box offers options regarding the sorts of tips that you want the Assistant to display.

- **Other tips options:** These we covered earlier in the Tips section of this chapter. Here you can determine if and when tips appear. Also, notice the Reset My Tips button, which tells the Assistant to forget which tips it has shown you in the past. This is a great option if you have bad long-term memory or if you inherited your computer from someone else and want to see what tips they already read.

When you're done altering, reprimanding, or otherwise putting your Assistant on notice, click the OK button. That made you feel pretty powerful, eh?

Here's what you've really been waiting for. Want to hide the Office Assistant from view? You can do this two ways: You can simply select the Assistant's Close box to hide it or right-click the Assistant to bring up a number of options, including Hide Assistant. (You can also choose to edit other options for your Assistant by right-clicking the Assistant. And, you can use the Animate button to make the Assistant instantly do silly things.) To get the Assistant back, just press F1 or click the Question Mark button on the program toolbar.

Microsoft Help

Although not nearly as newfangled and cute as the Office Assistant, Microsoft Help is the soul of the help available to you in Microsoft programs and Windows itself. This Help system uses a combination of searching, contents lists, and hypertext so that you can maneuver to the topics that you want to find.

You can access Microsoft Help in at least two different ways:

- **Search for a topic by using the Assistant.** The Assistant responds with related help topics.

- **Choose Help⇨Contents and Index from the Office program menu.** You can choose a help topic from the Contents screen.

Help screens

Like World Wide Web pages, Microsoft Help uses *hypertext* — clickable text that takes you to something else with information about a particular topic. Sometimes called *hot text* or *links,* hypertext is text that's been linked to more information. Most of the hypertext in Microsoft Help simply pops up a small window that contains additional information or a definition of the hypertext, as shown in Figure 1-11.

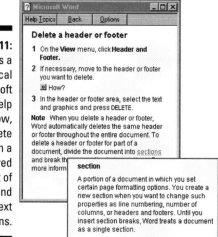

Figure 1-11: Here's a typical Microsoft Help window, complete with a numbered list of steps and hypertext definitions.

Most help screens offer step-by-step instructions for accomplishing a task, hypertext definitions, and the occasional tip or advice for getting something done more quickly. These help screens are a little like having a continuing education teacher available at all times, except that Microsoft Help is much less likely to try to convince you to buy its recently published books.

Hypertext need not be text. You also find some clickable icons and images that pop up definitions in the Windows Help system.

Contents

Often you move directly from the Office Assistant to a useful help topic. Every once in a while, however, the Assistant may not pick up on the exact vibe of curiosity that you're sending its way. Maybe you're not even sure exactly what sort of help you're looking for. In this case, you may be better off using the Contents screen.

If you're already viewing a help screen, you click the Help Topics button to get to the Contents screen. Otherwise, you can go directly to the Contents screen by choosing Help⇨Contents and Index from the program's Help menu.

Chapter 2
Making Things Happen in Word

*I*n the olden days, or as Todd says, "Yonder a few years back, when I was a young'un," people used typewriters to create business documents. This method had some real drawbacks. Errors required you to apply a big blotch of correction fluid, or even retype from scratch, hoping that you didn't make another mistake. Making personalized variations of a form letter was also a tedious endeavor. Given the large manual typewriters used prior to 1960, building Web pages was altogether tricky.

Those old clunkers had advantages, too. Because making corrections was so difficult, documents rarely had to be letter perfect before being approved for distribution (oh, how I long for the old days!). You didn't have to read a book to learn how to use the newest typewriters because they were, for the most part, just typewriters. The most impressive features you'd ever expect to see were low- torque carriage returns.

Despite the maze of features found in Word, though, don't pine for the old times. Word may be more complex than a typewriter, but you can easily discover Word's basics, which we cover here in this chapter. The basics will work just fine until you need to learn some new tricks, and then you can add those little flourishes to your repertoire as you go.

Getting to Know Word

Word, meet our friend Ed. Ed, Word. (If your name isn't Ed, we apologize, but we couldn't convince the publisher to customize the book for each reader. Instead, we're going with a fairly common name and hoping to not alienate everyone else.)

If you're brand new to word processing, don't fret. In this section, we'll talk about all the things you need to know to get started creating fancy looking documents that'll earn you a big, fat raise. In return, we only ask for 15 percent of your new revenues. Pay particular attention to the toolbar, which give you access to almost every important feature in Word. But first, let's look at getting the program started to begin with.

Starting Word

Ironically, you can't begin typing until you start the program. Here are two ways to get to Word:

✔ Choose Start⇨Programs⇨Microsoft Office⇨Microsoft Word.

✔ Click the Word icon in the Microsoft Office Manager.

Doing one of those opens a blank copy of Word, ready for you to imbue it with your colorful typing. If you want to open an existing document, you can do that in several ways:

✔ Even without starting Word, choose Start⇨Documents⇨*myfile*, where *myfile* is the name of a recent document you created in Word. Figure 2-1 shows the Documents menu, filled with Word, and Excel documents, as well as other files. Word automatically starts, and opens the document you select.

✔ After starting Word, open the File menu in the toolbar, and choose a recently opened document from the list at the bottom of the menu. Word automatically opens the document you choose.

✔ After starting Word, click the Open button in the toolbar. Choose the file you want from the Open File dialog box that appears.

Why navigate through file folders when you can avoid it? You can easily configure Word so that it displays more recently opened files. Just choose Tools⇨Options and select the General tab. You can set the Recently Used File List to store up to nine documents, as shown in Figure 2-2.

Dissecting Word's toolbars

Until you're familiar with Word's many tools, menus, and buttons, the main Word screen can be a little intimidating, almost as if the IRS had decided to start making software, and this was their first product. You see something like Figure 2-3 the first time you start the program.

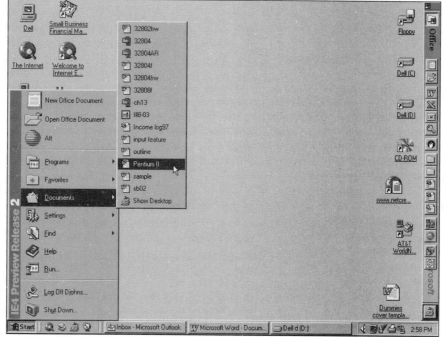

Figure 2-1:
The Documents menu lists recently opened files, including Word documents.

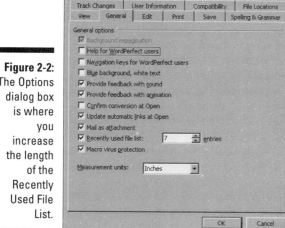

Figure 2-2:
The Options dialog box is where you increase the length of the Recently Used File List.

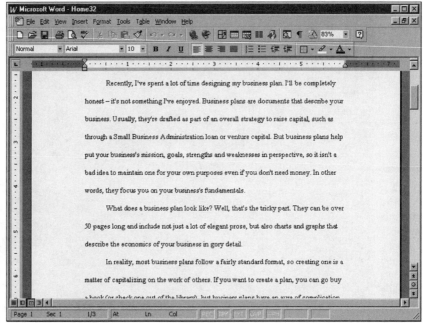

Figure 2-3:
The
Microsoft
Word main
screen.

You can accomplish most of the important stuff that Word offers from the set of toolbars at the top of the screen. You can move these toolbars around and open and close them to suit the task at hand. If you're working with tables, for example, you may want to open the Tables and Borders toolbar (it's a special toolbar designed to hold the icons and commands used for creating tabular data and adding borders to different parts of your document). You certainly don't need to waste screen space with it when you're done with the table, however. In Word, you can see the toolbar when you need it, but get rid of it when you don't need it.

To manage the toolbars, just right-click the toolbar region of the screen. You'll see a menu like the one in Figure 2-4 that lists the available toolbars. You can click specific toolbars to open or close them. Figures 2-5 and 2-6 show a couple of toolbars that you'll probably use often.

To move toolbars around, grab a toolbar by the double grab bars on the left edge, and place them where you want.

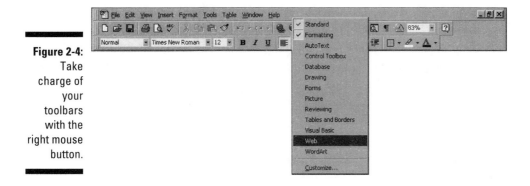

Figure 2-4:
Take
charge of
your
toolbars
with the
right mouse
button.

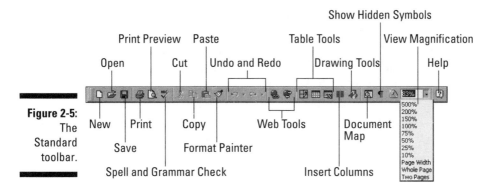

Figure 2-5:
The
Standard
toolbar.

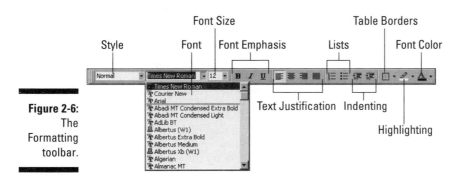

Figure 2-6:
The
Formatting
toolbar.

Editing Documents

You may take a while to get used to the concept of editing documents, which is why Dave felt that it was necessary to mention it here. Once again, Word is not a typewriter. That means you have a slew of tools available to edit and correct text, without needing to erase an entire line of text or pressing the Arrow key a dozen times to get there.

Cut, copy, and paste

No, these are not the names of cartoon characters promoting a new breakfast cereal on children's television. These terms represent the method by which you can easily make changes to your document, without rewriting it from scratch every half-hour. They are invoked from three buttons on the toolbar, shown in Figure 2-7. The Copy button is what you use to make a duplicate of selected text elsewhere in the document. Cut is what you use to move the text without leaving a trace of the original behind. Paste is what you use when you are ready to place text in its new home.

Figure 2-7:
The Cut,
Copy, and
Paste
buttons.

Copy

Cut | Paste

Copy

To copy a word, phrase, or even pages of text at a time, and make a duplicate of it to use somewhere else in the document, you follow these steps:

1. **At the start of the text you want to copy, click-and-drag across all the text you want to move.**

   When you release the mouse button, the text is selected.

2. **Click the Copy button.**

   A copy of what you selected is placed on the clipboard.

3. **Place the cursor in the part of the document where you want the copied text to appear.**

4. **Click the Paste button.**

   The selected text now appears where the cursor was.

Because you made a copy of this text on the Windows clipboard, you can paste that same text over and over again until you copy different text to the clipboard. Only one thing can occupy the clipboard at one time. That *thing* can be a character, word, paragraph, or picture. As soon as you copy something else to the clipboard, the first thing is gone.

Cut

What if you want to move text, not just duplicate it? That's when you want to use the Cut button. The procedure is identical to copying, except that instead of clicking the Copy button, you click Cut. You still need to use the Paste button to deposit the text, and you can still paste over and over.

Want to stack a bunch of text in the clipboard and paste it somewhere else all at once? Ordinarily, that won't work, but you can use the *spike* instead. Just select text, press Ctrl+F3, and repeat until you have all the text that you want loaded into the spike. Then press Ctrl+Shift+F3 to deposit the accumulated text in the desired location.

Word's a drag

An even easier way to move text around exists, and it's a lot like reaching into the page and moving things with your hands. Perhaps you want to take a paragraph from the end of your masterpiece and place it near the beginning, or move just a few words from one part of a sentence to another. All it takes is a technique known as *drag-and-drop*. Here's how to use drag-and-drop:

1. **Select the desired text.**

2. **Point the mouse anywhere in the highlighted text, click and hold the button.**

   The pointer changes shape, resembling the one in Figure 2-8.

3. **Drag the text to the new location, and then release the mouse button.**

You can use drag-and-drop to copy text, not just move it. Just hold down the Ctrl key while you click the text, and drag it to its new location. The original text is left behind.

Formatting Your Work

You probably won't be happy with the way Word initially renders your text and paragraphs. Perhaps the text is too small, or the paragraphs don't indent to your satisfaction. Whatever the case, an easy one-stop shopping way exists to design the appearance of your document, and it's found in the Format menu.

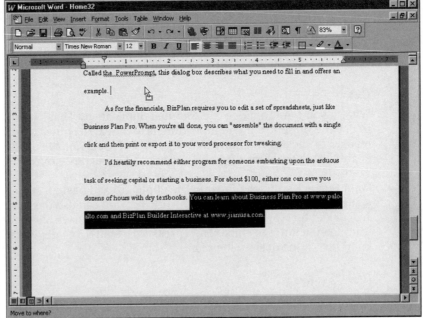

Figure 2-8:
Move text
easily with
the drag-
and-drop
technique.

Formatting paragraphs

To change the appearance of a paragraph in your document, follow these
steps:

1. **Place the cursor anywhere in the paragraph you want to modify.**

2. **Choose Format⇨Paragraph.**

   The Paragraph properties sheet appears, as shown in Figure 2-9.

3. **Make your changes, and click OK.**

The Paragraph dialog box is where you change

- ✔ Alignment (left, center, and right).
- ✔ Indenting.
- ✔ Special indenting (what you use to indent just the first line of a paragraph, for example).
- ✔ Spacing before and after a paragraph. This is the professional equivalent of adding a line between paragraphs when you were writing a
  three-page grade school paper so that you didn't have to type as much.

Formatting text

The format of your document includes more than just the paragraph style, however. The Font properties sheet has many more options, including the ability to add superscript, subscript, and strikethrough characters. For the most common format changes, you can just use the toolbar. Select the text you want to change, for example, and choose a new font from the Font drop-down menu on the toolbar. For formatting options that aren't on the toolbar, however, you visit the Format⇨Font menu, and the Font properties sheet appears, as shown in Figure 2-10.

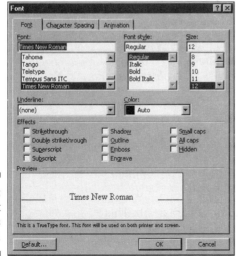

When formatting paragraphs, you only need to place the cursor in the paragraph. When formatting text, however, you select exactly the words or characters that the format change will effect.

A fast way to reach the Font and Paragraph properties sheets is by using the right mouse button. Place the mouse over the paragraph or selected text you want, and right-click. A small menu appears, and you just select the appropriate menu item.

Using Format Painter

Often, you may want to borrow the format from one section of a document and apply it to another. You don't want to use the text. You just want to take the very pretty double-spaced, 12-point text, where the first line is indented, and make another paragraph look just like it. Format Painter to the rescue! (Insert dramatic superhero music here.) To use the Format Painter, you follow these steps:

1. **Select the text that has the really cool formatting.**

2. **Click the Format Painter button (shown flexing its muscles in Figure 2-11).**

   If you want to use the same format more than once, just as if you were using the same color of paint on each new paragraph, double-click the Format Painter button. It stays pressed in until you click it again, press the Escape key, or click another toolbar icon. In the meantime, you can paint other text elements to your heart's content.

3. **Click the text you want to format.**

Having trouble filching paragraph formatting with the Format Painter? You need to either place the cursor in the paragraph or select the entire paragraph for the tool to work. If you only select a part of the paragraph, even if you just forget to highlight the last little period, the Format Painter won't work.

Figure 2-11:
Use Format
Painter to
steal the
style from
one part
of your
document,
and give it
to another.

Format Painter

Formatting the page

To change the page margins or the orientation of the paper, visit the Page Setup properties sheet. This sheet isn't where you may expect it to be (it's not in the Format menu with Font and Paragraph). You can find it at File⇨Page Setup (see Figure 2-12). The most important settings are

- ✔ **Margins:** Margin — it's not just for toast anymore. This is where you tell Word how much margin to use in this document. It's the white space (blank space) at the top, bottom, left, and right of the body text in your document.

- ✔ **Orientation:** Portrait or Landscape? *Portrait* orientation means stuff is printed on the page thinner than longer (like the pages in this book). *Landscape* orientation means text is printed on the page longways (like in an accounting ledger book).

- ✔ **Headers and footers:** You can have the same ones on every page, different on odd and even pages, and still different on the title page.

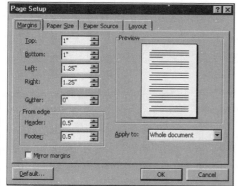

Figure 2-12:
The Page properties sheet.

Creating lists

One thing you can say about professionals (by professionals, I mean folks who dress up, drive to a big building that looks like a background scene from Logan's Run, and stare all day at important looking documents created with Microsoft Office) is that they love lists. And who can blame them? Lists turn difficult-to-follow paragraphs of raw data into bulleted collections of important information, kind of like Cliff Notes for grown-ups.

You know — Logan's Run! The one where the guy is nearly thirty, so they're going to kill him in that big chamber. But he escapes because he's a cop, and runs away with the girl in the progressively torn dress. Then they meet the old guy, who comes back to the city and splashes around in the water. If we remember correctly, they decide not to kill folks so young anymore.

Lists are very easy to create in Word. You can create them the manual way or the automatic way. To create a *numbered* list automatically, just place the cursor on a new line, and type something like this:

Advantages of outsourcing:

1. Faster ramp-up and ramp-down times

As soon as you press Enter, Word has predicted you're creating a list. It automatically places a **2** on the next line, so you can continue your list without worrying about the mechanics of creating a list. (And we all know how tough typing a **2** can be.)

You can create an automatic *bulleted* list in much the same way. Just place an asterisk on the line instead of a number. When you press Enter, Word converts the asterisk to a real bullet and places a bullet on every line afterwards.

When your list is complete, Word still places a number on the next line. Just press Enter one extra time, and the last number disappears.

This automatic list feature can be annoying, particularly when you put a number at the start of a line that isn't going to be a list. The feature is easy to disable, however. To avoid the Autolist in a particular instance, choose Edit⇨Undo Typing immediately after the list starts. Word undoes the AutoFormat.

To disable the Autolist permanently, choose Tools⇨AutoCorrect and click the AutoFormat As You Type tab. Deselect the boxes for numbered lists and bulleted lists, as shown in Figure 2-13. To the best of our knowledge, Autolist and AutoFormat did not appear in the movie Logan's Run, unless that's what the old guy named his cats.

You can also create lists manually. Just click the Numbering button or the Bullets button in the toolbar (see Figure 2-14) before starting your list, and then deselect the button when you complete your list.

Creating tables

Perhaps the most popular of the Word's built-in goodies, *tables* are both eye-catching and downright useful. You can't eat off them, but hey, nothing is perfect. Tables, like spreadsheets, are composed of rows, and columns.

A *spreadsheet* is either that thing that covers your bed or a document that is made of rows and columns. You can insert numbers and formulas in these rows and columns and perform nifty mathematical operations on them.

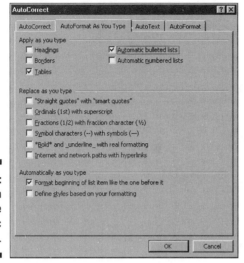

Figure 2-13:
You can disable automatic lists.

Figure 2-14:
Manually bullet or number a list using the Numbering and Bullets buttons on the toolbar.

Number List

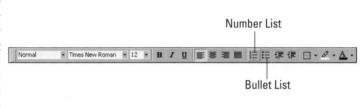

Bullet List

To add a table to your document, follow these steps:

1. **Place the cursor on the page where you want to begin a table.**

2. **Click the Table button in the toolbar.**

   A table diagram appears.

3. **Yell out, "C'mon Word, pappy needs a new mesa!"**

4. **Move the mouse to define the table size you want, as shown in Figure 2-15.**

   The numbers of rows and columns appears at the bottom (in this case, three rows, and four columns).

5. **After you identify the table size you want, click the mouse again.**

   The table will appear in Word.

Figure 2-15:
Create a
table of
almost any
size from
the toolbar.

 If you want a table that is bigger than the largest size shown on-screen (four rows, and five columns), click the diagram and continue dragging the mouse while the button is pressed in. (And hey, "mesa" means "table" in Spanish. Are you following all this?)

Editing tables

After you draw a table inside your document, you can change its appearance to suit your needs. You can do this many ways, but here are the highlights:

- **Change the width of table columns.** Click the border between columns and drag it with the mouse.

- **Add columns or rows.** Select an entire row or column and then right-click. A drop-down menu appears. Choose Insert Row or Insert Column to the table.

- **Add special effects like shaded cells or heavy borders.** Open the Tables and Borders toolbar and edit the table with the tools (see Figure 2-16).

- **Let Word automatically format your table.** Right-click the table and choose Table AutoFormat from the drop-down menu. You can then preview the styles and choose one that best displays the table data.

Figure 2-16:
The Tables
and
Borders
toolbar.

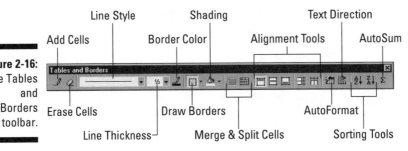

Letting Word Work for You

You've already seen some ways that Word automatically performs actions for you, like Table AutoFormat and automatic lists. These just scratch the surface, though. Word has a collection of Auto technologies designed to reduce the amount of typing and correcting you need to do to complete a document.

AutoCorrect: Leave the typing to us

AutoCorrect changes commonly typed text as you type it, preventing spelling errors or expanding a shorthand set of characters into a unique phrase.

Type **(c)**, for example, and Word changes it into the copyright symbol. To add something to the AutoCorrect dictionary, you follow these steps:

1. **Type the complete word or phrase that you want Word to finish for you (such as** Dear Sir**) and then select it.**

2. **Select Tools⇨AutoCorrect.**

   The AutoCorrect Property sheet appears with Dear Sir already in the With line.

3. **Type an abbreviation, such as DS, in the Replace line, and then click OK.**

   Figure 2-17 shows the AutoCorrect dialog box.

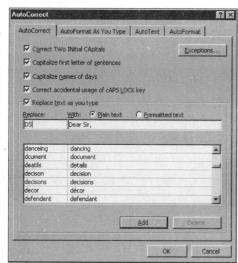

Figure 2-17:
The
AutoCorrect
properties
sheet is the
control
center
where you
tell Word to
fix your
mistakes, or
perform
shorthand
automatically.

Use AutoCorrect to fix words you always misspell. If you consistently type **sich** instead of **such**, let Word fix it for you! Then you never have to learn to actually type correctly!

Be careful with what abbreviations you use in AutCorrect. If you use *US* for *Yours Sincerely,* then you may have an odd looking document the next time you write a treatise on the *Yours Sincerely Constitution* and the *Yours Sincerely Senate.* If you really want *US* to mean *Yours Sincerely*, make it AutoText. AutoText makes you press F3 to convert abbreviations into the full text (see the next section for details).

AutoCorrect tries to change ordinary quotes to special curved quotes, and double dashes to a long em dash. If you're feeding your Word document to a page layout program, that application may not understand these fancier characters. To get around this, you invoke the name of James T. Kirk and shut it down. You can selectively disable AutoFormat features by choosing Tools⇨AutoCorrect and clicking the AutoFormat As You Type tab.

Type less with AutoText

AutoText works a little differently. It is what you use to invoke long but somewhat common phrases with shorthand entries, sort of like AutoFormat. The difference here is that you need to type a part of the AutoText phrase and then press F3. For example, you can type **Atte** and press F3. Word recognizes that as *attention* from the AutoText dictionary, and completes the word for you. Add your own phrases (including formatted text blocks, such as a signature) by choosing Tools⇨AutoCorrect and then clicking the AutoText tab.

If you want to type **Attention** and have it converted to *To the Attention of:,* use AutoText. That way you need to press F3 before it changes. Otherwise, all your *Attentions* change every time you type them.

Let Word format your document

You may not be a graphic artist or page layout expert. Yet, you often need to create printed documents that not only have engaging content, but also look great. Doing this can be hard, so you can let Word format your document. Try this:

1. **With the document open, choose Format⇨AutoFormat.**

   The AutoFormat dialog box appears.

2. **Select the AutoFormat Now radio button.**

3. **Select the kind of document you are creating from the drop-down list: General document, Letter, or E-mail.**

4. **Click OK.**

   Word automatically formats your document for you.

Specifically, Word converts asterisks to bullets, creates clickable Internet links, and makes other formatting changes. If you prefer, you can choose Format⇨Style Gallery. The Style Gallery dialog box appears, as shown in Figure 2-18. Here you can experiment with applying various templates to the document you created.

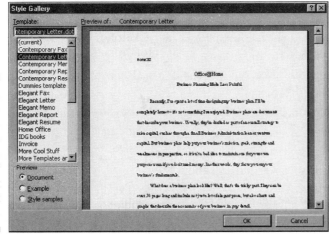

Figure 2-18:
Use the Style Gallery to try out the effect of different document templates.

Check spelling and grammar

Wondering what those little squiggles under certain words are? Microsoft Word constantly checks the spelling and grammar of your document as you write it. Misspell a word, for example, and Word places a squiggly red line under the word. A green squiggle represents bad grammar. You should see this chapter in Word. Ugh. Looks like spinach.

To correct spelling, just right-click a misspelled word. A drop-down menu provides the following options:

✔ **Suggested corrections:** If you see the word you meant to type, select it from the menu.

✔ **Ignore All:** If you know better than the computer, and you want to spell *duck* with a silent *h* everywhere in the document, choose Ignore All. Word won't correct anything spelled that way.

✔ **Add:** A new word. By golly, Word should add MDARC to its dictionary, because that's the name of a new product at your company, and you plan to use it a lot from now on.

✔ **AutoCorrect:** Gosh darn it, you always spell Microsoft as *BillyLand.* Use this option to train Word to automatically correct this word for you, without your help. See the section on AutoCorrect earlier in this chapter for details.

✔ **Spelling:** You want the whole Check Spelling dialog box. This dialog box provides a suite of controls for adding and ignoring words, plus controlling spelling options.

Grammar checking is very similar. Just right-click a green squiggle and choose from one of your options.

✔ **Suggested corrections:** If you seen what you meant to write, go ahead and pick it.

✔ **Ignore sentence:** You choose this option when that's what you meant to be writed.

✔ **Grammar:** Choose this when you want to see the Check Grammar dialog box.

Grammar checking is less reliable than spell checking, so never accept its suggestions without thinking about them.

Is your whole document spell checked? Sometimes you may not be sure, particularly if you have a long file. Just look at the AutoCheck icon in the status bar (see Figure 2-19). If you see a check mark, all is well, but if the book is flipping pages and an X appears, some potential problems still exist. Double-click the icon, and the document scrolls to the next spelling problem.

Figure 2-19:
The status bar keeps track of your document's spelling.

Spelling Status

| Page 1 | Sec 1 | 1/1 | At 1" | Ln 1 | Col 4 |

You may elect to turn this AutoCheck off entirely so that the squiggly lines don't bother you. To toggle the spell and grammar checking on or off, do this:

1. **Choose Tools⇨Options.**

   The Options dialog sheet appears.

2. **Click on the Spelling & Grammar tab.**

3. **Select the Hide spelling errors in this document, or Hide grammar errors in this document check boxes, as shown in Figure 2-20.**

4. **Click OK. If you checked the Hide button, it'll go off. If you un-checked it, it'll go on.**

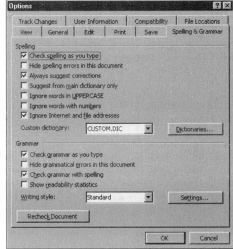

Figure 2-20:
The Spelling
and
Grammar
Options.

Even if the Check spelling as you type and Check grammar as you type check boxes are selected, you won't see any squiggly lines if the Hide spelling errors in this document and Hide grammatical errors in this document options are selected.

Through the Looking Glass: Viewing Options

You can view a document in Word several ways. You may tend to find a view mode that you like and stick with it, or you may bounce from one view to another, depending on what you're doing. All the view modes are available from the View menu (logical, yes — but with computer software you just never know). Here's what the different options do for you:

✔ **Normal:** This mode isn't What You See Is What You Get (WYSIWYG); instead, we call it What You Get Is Anybody's Guess (WYGIAG). Normal view provides a clean, draft-like view that doesn't accurately represent what the printed document looks like. Some people like this mode because it is so unencumbered, and on some aging computers, it allows the page to scroll much faster. This is Todd's favorite mode.

✔ **Online Layout:** This is a good choice for viewing and editing documents on-screen. It is a full WYSIWYG display, except that it doesn't show page breaks for a more seamless view of the action. This view works well with the Document Map enabled (see the upcoming "Document Map" bullet).

✔ **Page Layout:** Similar to the Online Layout view, this view also shows page breaks and is the most realistic representation of what the printed document looks like. It's Dave's favorite.

✔ **Outline:** The outline is what you use to create an old-fashioned outline of your document, just like your 7th Grade teacher, Ms. Wilcox, made you do (we're guessing some of the details, but we think we captured the essence). The outline mode displays an ordered view of your major headings and subheadings, so you can organize your thoughts, lay out the document, and procrastinate actually writing it.

✔ **Master Document:** This one takes a little explaining. You can create a master document in Word that is a collection of multiple Word documents all glued together. This mode enables a view of this Master Document.

All these view modes, except Master Document view, are available from small buttons at the bottom left of the screen, just to the side of the horizontal scroll bar, as shown in Figure 2-21.

Also on the View menu are a few other display modes that come in handy:

✔ **Document Map:** You can use the Document Map in conjunction with any other view. This mode divides the Word screen into two frames, is convenient for keeping track of the flow of your document, and ensures that you have an adequate number of subheadings in each section. The left side is a map of the major headings in your document. Click any heading, and the document loaded in the right window immediately scrolls to the correct location. Figure 2-22 shows the Document Map in use from the Page Layout view.

You can't type in the Document Map — it is only used for navigation.

✔ **Full Screen:** Do you feel claustrophobic with all the menus, toolbars, and other doohickeys that Word crams into the displays? You'll love the Full Screen view mode, which wipes the slate clean and displays nothing but your document on-screen. Return to the Normal view by clicking the Close Full Screen button, which "floats" over your document in Full Screen mode.

Normal View

Page Layout View

Outline View

Online Layout View

You can enable toolbars, even in Full Screen mode. Right-click the Close Full Screen button, and you have access to all the toolbars. Also, the menus are still there — they're just hidden. Move the mouse to the top of the screen, and the menus appear.

✔ **Zoom:** Change the magnification of the document using this control. You probably won't use View⇨Zoom much because you can reach a Zoom control from the Standard toolbar. Common settings include 100 percent, Full Page, and Full Width, but you can type any magnification that suits your monitor and your eyesight.

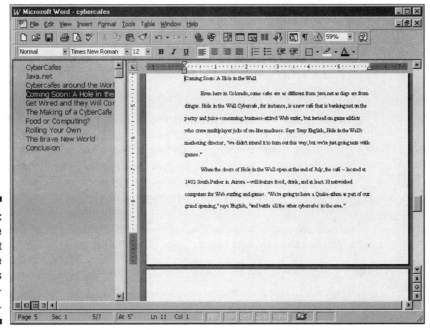

Printing and Saving Documents

Printing and saving are moments of truth. If your word processor can't print, it's barely more useful than all that exercise gear you bought last April. You'll find printing a Word document to be quite simple.

Previewing with Print Preview

Before you print your document, you may want to see how it looks on-screen. To check your preview:

1. **Choose File⇨Print Preview.**

   The Print Preview window opens and displays your document the way it will look as it rolls out of the printer.

2. **Look at the pages in any view mode you choose (see Figure 2-23).**

   You have several options on the Print Preview screen:

   - Click the page and the view toggles between the default size and an enlarged Zoom view.

   - Use the Multiple Pages button in the toolbar to see several thumbnail pages on-screen at once.

   - Click One Page to return to the default Page view.

   - Use the Zoom drop-down menu to change the page magnification.

   - Use the Full Screen button to eliminate the toolbars.

3. **When you're ready to print, press the Print button. The Print Preview window closes, and your printer will make a little more noise than usual. Don't worry — it's not broken. Your document is printing.**

Printing your document

In most cases, you won't need to use the print preview tool; you can just print. Here are two ways to print your Word document:

- Click the Print button in the toolbar. This prints the entire document.

- Choose File⇨Print. The resulting dialog box, shown in Figure 2-24 is where you customize the way the document prints.

  You can specify which printer to use, if more than one is connected to your computer or network, how many copies you want to print, and which pages to print.

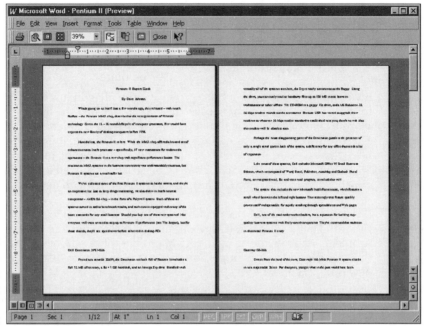

Figure 2-23:
A document
in Print
Preview.

Figure 2-24:
The Print
dialog box.

Saving Your Document

We saved this for last, but we can't emphasize enough how important saving your work is. Save it early and often. To save a file:

1. Choose File⇨Save As.

The Save As dialog box appears.

2. Select a folder in which to save your document.

3. Type a filename, and press Enter. The file is saved.

You can do subsequent saves of this document by clicking the Save button in the toolbar.

If you follow these instructions, you save the file you just made in Word 97 format. That's fine, but make sure that anyone using the file can read a Word 97 file because this is a different file format than earlier Word formats. Microsoft Word 95 users can read your Word 97 file just fine as long as they have the appropriate patch installed. This patch can be found on the Microsoft Web site (`www.microsoft.com/office/`), and it is worth the effort for people who often share data with other Word users.

Did you ever get a flat tire on a bike and patch it up with a makeshift slab of rubber? That's what a software patch is — a small fix that repairs a bigger problem. Many vendors, including Microsoft, offer patches for their software that add features or fix bugs. You can install the patch instead of a whole new program update.

To save your document in another format, choose the format from the drop-down Save As Type menu in the Save As dialog box, as shown in Figure 2-25.

Figure 2-25:
Choose
what file
format to
save your
document,
or use the
Word 97
default.

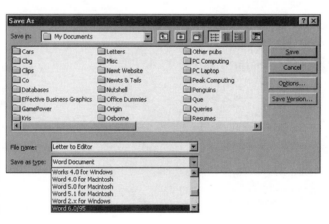

Chapter 3
Crunching Numbers with Excel

• •

In This Chapter

▶ Getting around in Excel

▶ Adding numbers, even if you have a history degree

▶ Making rows of numbers look pretty

▶ Wowing them with charts

• •

*A*lmost by definition, writers aren't spreadsheet people. We begged, cajoled, and even caroled *(Oh, the weather outside is frightful!)* outside the shiny headquarters of IDG Books to get out of writing a chapter about Microsoft Excel, but we're stuck. Not only that, but we had to go back and think about things we thought we'd left behind, like Net Present Value, What-If scenarios, and so-called "dollars."

Excel is incredibly complicated and kind of scary looking, so we sincerely recommend that you hire a bookkeeper and an accountant. Okay? If you've done so, go to Chapter 4. Still here? Darn.

Finding Your Way around Excel

Actually, the first killer application for personal computers (one of those applications that makes everyone want to buy a new computer and talk about it at dinner parties) was a spreadsheet program called VisiCalc. This was designed for that old standard, the Apple II. Suddenly, people were flocking to home electronics stores, appliance stores, and other places of business that had the daunting responsibility of selling personal computers.

VisiCalc would now be considered silly, especially compared to its progeny, Microsoft Excel. After all, our computers are much more powerful these days (well, at least everything looks sort of 3D). But what VisiCalc did do is present to the world the idea that you could enter numbers into your computer, arrange them in rows and columns, and perform some amazing feats of analysis. In fact, VisiCalc made the idea of a computerized ledger book a reality and proved to many business-minded people that personal computers could really be useful in the business world.

Also at that time, a new definition of the word *cell* entered our lexicon, with apologies to Gregor Mendel. The cell became not only the basic building block of an electronic spreadsheet but also the basic building block of go-getter middle management careers throughout the corporate world.

Grab yourself a copy of *The New York Public Library Desk Reference*. It's an unbelievable reference for figuring out questions like "What was the name of that guy who messed around with plant genetics in the mid-1880s?" (Gregor Mendel, father of our understanding of cellular genetics) For example, did you know that aspirin and quantum theory were discovered within one year of each other (1899 and 1900, respectively)?

So, what's a *cell?* In computing, it's the junction of a row and a column in a table of data, like one you may create in Excel (see Figure 3-1). Within the confines of a cell you type all information for your spreadsheet.

Maybe we're spending too much time running in front of the two-ton papier-mâché ball, and not enough time pulling out our trusty whip and swinging to safety. That is to say, what's a spreadsheet?

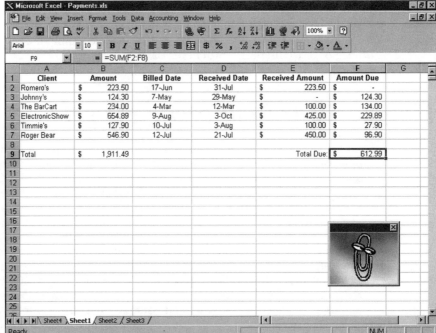

Figure 3-1:
A cell is the most basic part of a spreadsheet. Within a cell you add data and text to your spreadsheet.

At its essence, a *spreadsheet* is the electronic equivalent of a ledger book page. It allows you to place data in rows and columns, then add, subtract, or otherwise mutilate the data beyond recognition. (Spreadsheets, as you may guess, are a big favorite with politicians.) The advantage of a computer-based spreadsheet is that any errors can be blamed on bugs in the Pentium math instruction set.

Starting Excel

It seems the cart is dragging the horse down a steep hill. Before you can get started with a spreadsheet, you need to open Excel.

Here are two basic ways to open Microsoft Excel:

- Choose Start⇨Programs⇨Microsoft Excel (or Start⇨Programs⇨ Microsoft Office⇨Microsoft Excel in Office Professional).
- If you're using the Office Professional Edition, click the Excel button in the Microsoft Office Manager.

This opens a blank spreadsheet, ready to accept your input, your art, and a piece of your soul.

If you want to open an existing document, you can do this several ways:

- Even without starting Excel, choose Start⇨Documents⇨*myfile*, where *myfile* is the name of a document you created recently in Excel. Excel automatically starts and loads the document.
- After starting Excel, click the File menu and choose a recently opened document from the list at the bottom of the menu.
- After starting Excel, click the Open button in the toolbar. Choose the file you want from the Open File dialog box that appears.

The Pentium what?

Sorry, this math instruction set business is sort of an insider computing joke. When the Intel Pentium chip first came out, a highly-publicized error (or"bug") in the Pentium's math instruction set causes it to make errors when calculating extremely big numbers. Intel assured everyone not to worry about it because the error only affected very large calculations like, presumably, calculations of the U.S. national debt, missle guidance launch codes, and aspects of the global air traffic control system. (We're only kidding. All three of these systems use much older computers built in the 1960s. Feel better?)

As in Word, you can easily configure Excel to display more recently opened files. Choose Tools⇨Options and select the General tab in the Options properties sheet. You can set the Recently Used Files List to store up to nine documents.

You may need to get to certain kinds of spreadsheets, like expense logs or sales and use tax sheets, almost every day. Create a shortcut on the desktop for documents you use all the time, and then you won't need to go hunting for them.

Pretending that you plan to use toolbars

Remember the first time you saw a beach boardwalk carnival, or the first time you were allowed to run out to the ice cream truck by yourself? Well, if you're like us, you get a similar feeling when you first open a blank Excel spreadsheet. This is the stuff of legends.

The key to your Excel-based existence may very well be those toolbars at the top of the screen that give you quick access to a number of important commands and formatting options. By default, you'll see the Standard toolbar and the Formatting toolbar (refer to Figure 3-2).

Figure 3-2:
Microsoft
Excel
toolbars.

Standard Toolbar

Formatting Toolbar

In Excel, the Standard toolbar adds a gaggle of numbers-oriented options, like AutoSum and Paste Function, for easy access (we talk about these later). The Formatting toolbar includes not only font size and family commands but also buttons that help you format the appearance and alignment of data within cells.

As with most Microsoft toolbars, you can see what any particular button does by pointing at the button with the mouse pointer. Wait a second, and a little description pops up. Also, right-clicking the toolbars allows you to pick and choose which toolbars appear.

Maneuvering in Excel by keystroke

Obviously, one of the big parts of getting something done in Excel is entering data. You may find that the process is somewhat different for a spreadsheet than it is in a more familiar program, like a word processor, however. Moving from cell to cell requires some fancy finger work, and the process can only be more efficient after you learn the ropes.

You can use two different methods to move around in Excel:

✔ Using the Enter key and the Tab key, you can move down one cell and right one cell, respectively. Use Shift+Enter to move up one cell and Shift+Tab to move left one cell.

✔ Using the arrow keys, you can move one cell in any direction.

Do you want to move farther and faster? Hold down the Ctrl key and press an arrow key (Ctrl+Right Arrow key, for example), and you move to the end of a row of data. Do it again, and you move to the end of the current row or column in your spreadsheet. As always, you can use the mouse to move to a particular cell.

Selecting cells

You can select more than one cell at a time. As you dig deeper into the features and shortcuts in Excel, you discover that you may often want to have an entire row or column of figures selected at once. You can do all this with the mouse, but the keyboard may prove more efficient.

To select more than one cell at a time:

1. **Move to the first cell that you want to select in a particular row or column.**

2. **Hold down the Shift key and use the arrow keys to select additional cells (Shift+Arrow key).**

   You see the highlighted area grow as you press the arrow key (see Figure 3-3).

3. **Release the Shift key after you select all the cells that interest you.**

While you're experimenting with this, notice that you can select both rows and columns using this method. Just hold down the Shift key while you press the arrow keys. The highlighted area grows accordingly.

If you consider yourself a power user, a combination of our last tip, using the Ctrl key, and this process for selecting cells allows you to quickly select a range of cells. Press Ctrl+Shift, and then press an arrow key in the direction that you want to highlight. A row or column is selected until you press a cell that is different. If you selected cells with data, for example, the *range* stops when you reach an empty cell. This is great for setting global formatting, like making an entire row of numbers look like United States dollars.

Are there other ways to select cells? You betcha. You can easily select entire rows or columns using the mouse. Just place the mouse pointer on a cell *heading* (the letters and numbers provided by Excel) and click once. Doing so selects the entire row or column (that is, the entire row or column is highlighted instantly). To deselect the row or column, click directly in a particular cell. Now that particular cell is selected, but any previously highlighted cells are deselected.

Click to select all cells in the row

Highlighted Cells

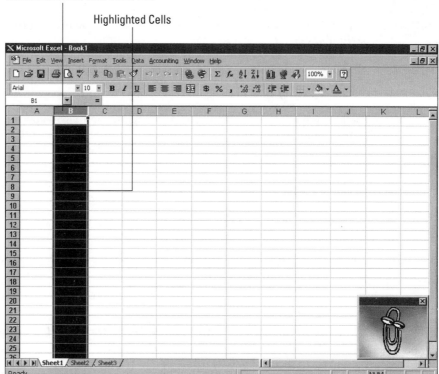

Figure 3-3:
Excel offers
many ways
to select
cells.

Naming cells

Here's one basic, vital piece of information that we decided to withhold from you until now: Every cell has a name! Unfortunately, the original plan was that every single cell would be named Dwight. Eventually, that proved too confusing.

Thus, another plan was hatched to easily identify cells. Even without forcing you to type any sort of headings or special codes, any cell can be referenced by a combination of the letter for its column, and the number for its row. You can see those letters and numbers in Figure 3-4.

Figure 3-4:
Every cell has its own unique name for use in formulas. (In this example, the selected cell is C5.)

Row Numbers   Column Letters

	A	B	C	D	E	F	G
1	Client	Amount	Billed Date	Received Date	Received Amount	Amount Due	
2	Romero's	$ 223.50	17-Jun	31-Jul	$ 223.50	$ -	
3	Johnny's	$ 124.30	7-May	29-May	$ -	$ 124.30	
4	The BarCart	$ 234.00	4-Mar	12-Mar	$ 100.00	$ 134.00	
5	ElectronicShow	$ 654.89	9-Aug	3-Oct	$ 425.00	$ 229.89	
6	Timmie's	$ 127.90	10-Jul	3-Aug	$ 100.00	$ 27.90	
7	Roger Bear	$ 546.90	12-Jul	21-Jul	$ 450.00	$ 96.90	
8							
9	Total	$ 1,911.49			Total Due:	$ 612.99	
10							

These cell names exist so that you can create formulas that add together or otherwise mathematically alter the values in those cells. To add two cells together, you can create a formula that looks like this:

```
=SUM(B2:B5)
```

This means, "Sum together B2, B5, and all the cells between them. Then tell me the result." Type that formula into a spreadsheet cell, and the sum of all those cells' values appears in that cell.

The equal sign (=) is the universal sign for *the formula starts here* in Excel. Whenever Excel sees the equal sign at the beginning of cell data, it knows that it's supposed to think about something. (If only a similar sign existed for romantic relationships.)

Entering Cell Data

Now that you're a maneuvering fool, those folks on the Blue Angels F-16 flying stunt team have nothin' on you. While you're flipping around cells on your spreadsheet like there's no tomorrow, you may actually want to type some cell data, if only to keep things interesting.

So what is *cell data?* Three types of cell data exist that you may want to type in your spreadsheet:

- **Text:** You type text in your spreadsheet for headings, descriptions, titles, and other elements. You just choose a cell and type.

- **Numbers:** Perhaps the most likely candidates, all your calculations are performed on rows and columns of numbers.

- **Formulas:** Every once in a while, you'll type a formula in a cell. If all goes well, the result of that formula (which may do something like add a column of cells that contain numeric data) appears in the cell.

So you have all that stuff you can type. How do you do it? With a particular cell selected you can

- **Just begin typing.** Changes appear in the cell, but you're actually editing the data in the Formula bar, which appears above the spreadsheet at the bottom of Excel's toolbars (see Figure 3-5).

- **Double-click the cell and begin typing.** Now you're editing directly in the cell. The advantage is that you can use the arrow keys to edit cell data. The disadvantage is that you can't use arrow keys to move to other cells. After you're done editing inside the cell, press Enter. Now you can maneuver as usual.

If you don't edit directly in the cell, notice that any typing you do overwrites the contents of the cell (if anything was in it to begin with). Whenever you want to change data that already exists in the cell, double-click the cell to keep from retyping.

Adding Up Cell Data

So far, Excel has only made easier typing data into a tabular form. Well, that's nice, but that sure doesn't help us bring home the bacon. The key to really having fun with spreadsheets is to get under the hood and add numbers to one another. This is called *building what-if scenarios* by people who think knowing how to work a spreadsheet qualifies them for the corner office.

Figure 3-5:
Unless you
like double-
clicking
cells, you
do most of
your editing
in the
Formula
toolbar.

The bottom line to adding things up is something called a *formula* — those silly little mathematical phrases you swore off in college algebra. Excel requires that you build a formula for it to automatically calculate the result of numerical data you typed in your spreadsheet. A simple formula in Excel would be something like =A1+B1 which would simply add the contents of cell A1 to the contents of cell B1. If you typed that formula in cell C1, then you'd see the value of A1 plus B1 appear in cell C1 after you hit Enter or used an arrow key to move to the next cell (see Figure 3-6).

Fortunately, most of the formulas are already written and hidden deep within Excel. Your mission: Find the formulas and put them to good use.

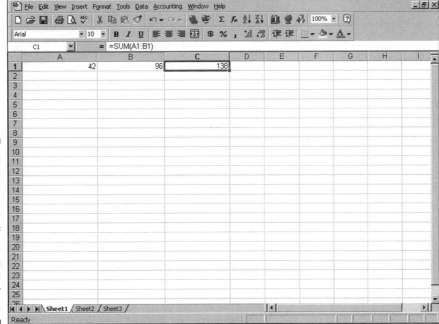

Figure 3-6:
Type a
simple
formula into
a cell and
the result of
that formula
appears
when you
hit the Enter
key.

Avoiding scary formulas with AutoSum

An example of a built-in formula is a simple sum of a row or column of numerical data, like a row of all the clients who sent in big, fat checks this month to thank you for a job well done. In fact, Excel has built this basic sum formula right into the toolbar. The feature is called AutoSum, following Microsoft's tradition of naming features to make them sound like mistakes made in Detroit in the 1950s.

Did you know that both *formulas* and *formulae* are acceptable ways of making the word formula plural? In general, though, only science teachers and Todd use *formulae*.

To add together a row or column of numbers:

1. **Highlight the series of numbers that you want to add together.**

   The series can be an entire row or column, but it doesn't have to be.

2. **In Excel's Standard toolbar (the top one), press the AutoSum button.**

   Excel places a result in the next cell in the row or column (see Figure 3-7). Move to that cell and you see the SUM formula that Excel created in the Formula toolbar.

Figure 3-7:
The AutoSum feature creates a SUM formula in the next available cell of the row or column being summed.

Cells to Be Summed

	A	B	C	D	E	F	G
1	**Client**	**Amount**	**Billed Date**	**Received Date**	**Received Amount**	**Amount Due**	
2	Romero's	$ 223.50	17-Jun	31-Jul	$ 223.50	$ -	
3	Johnny's	$ 124.30	7-May	29-May	$ -	$ 124.30	
4	The BarCart	$ 234.00	4-Mar	12-Mar	$ 100.00	$ 134.00	
5	ElectronicShow	$ 654.89	9-Aug	3-Oct	$ 425.00	$ 229.89	
6	Timmie's	$ 127.90	10-Jul	3-Aug	$ 100.00	$ 27.90	
7	Roger Bear	$ 546.90	12-Jul	21-Jul	$ 450.00	$ 96.90	
8					*Total Due:*	$ 612.99	
9	Total	$ 1,911.49					
10							
11							

Result

If you're in a real hurry, you can use AutoSum without first highlighting the range. Instead, click to select a cell for the result (the cell should be at the end of the same row or column as the data). Then click AutoSum. Excel creates a formula that sums the entire row or column. If you like what you see, press Enter, and the result replaces the formula definition in your results cell. If Excel didn't pick the right range, select the cells you want to add before pressing Enter. Remember, the AutoSum result doesn't have to be anywhere near the cells you're adding together!

Using other formulas

Excel also makes short work of adding a number of other formulae to your spreadsheet by placing a number of common commands right on the toolbar for your clicking pleasure. The possibilities include

- ✔ Average
- ✔ If statements
- ✔ Count cells
- ✔ Max value
- ✔ Sine of an angle
- ✔ Loan Payment calculation

Not that these are the extent of Excel's abilities, but you can see what we're getting at. You can do a lot with Excel. At times, things can get a bit hairy and can make you feel like you are back in that algebra class, but Excel has strong Office Assistant support (see Chapter 1), and most of the built-in formulas make walking through the process easy.

Take, for example, a what-if scenario where you want two quarterly revenue sales totals compared. Using an If formula, you can not only determine whether sales are up or down, you can also have the spreadsheet respond with text that tells you what happened at a glance (see Figure 3-8):

1. **Choose a cell for the result (Click the cell once to select it).**

2. **Click the equal sign in the Formula bar to begin creating a formula.**

   You're building the cell in the Formula toolbar, right next to the equal sign.

3. **In the drop-down menu in the Formula bar, choose IF.**

   The Formula Palette appears to walk you through the formula (see Figure 3-8).

4. **In the Logical_Test text box, type the test to be performed.**

   In the example, the test is B2>B3, which asks Excel, "Is the value of cell B2 greater than the value of cell B3?"

5. **Type the value that the cell should take on if the Logical_Test is true.**

   In the example, Excel puts the words "Gone Down!" in the cell.

6. **Type the value for the cell to take on if the Logical_Test is false.**

   In the example, Excel places the words "Gone Up!" in the cell.

7. **Press the OK button.**

   The formula is now added to your spreadsheet. Now, go get yourself something cold to drink. Come to think of it, could you get us something while you're up?

For most of the text box entries, you'll also see a little spreadsheet button. Click this button to return to the spreadsheet, and choose cells for the values. To return to the Formula Palette, click the button at the right edge of the now "rolled-up" palette.

Obviously, Excel can do a good deal more, even through its quick list of formula possibilities in the drop-down Formula bar menu. Play with them a bit to see if any of that math starts coming back to you.

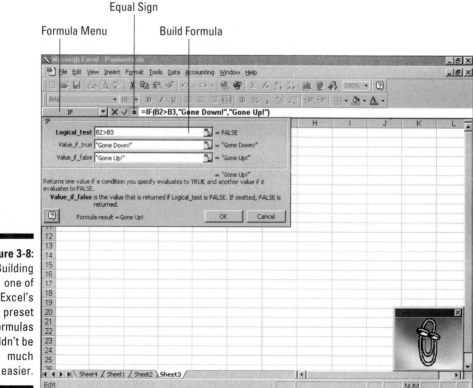

Figure 3-8:
Building
one of
Excel's
preset
formulas
couldn't be
much
easier.

Using the Paste function

In case you thought those menu items were the only functions available to you, wait. We've got hundreds more, but they're hidden. Fortunately, they're only a menu item or two away, so there's no need to go sprinting off on some sort of cyberspace scavenger hunt. (If you really want a cyberspace scavenger hunt, try www.sandbox.net/.)

To gain access to all these Excel functions, you use the Paste function command:

1. **Select a cell for your function.**

2. **Choose Insert⇨Function from the menu.**

   The Paste Function dialog box appears, as shown in Figure 3-9.

3. **On the left side of the dialog box, choose the category of function you want to see.**

4. **On the right side of the dialog box, choose the function that you want to use.**

5. **Click OK.**

   The Formula palette appears as described in the previous section.

After you choose a function, the Function Palette opens, if necessary, allowing you to set values. When you're done, click OK to add the formula to your spreadsheet.

Figure 3-9:
The Paste Function dialog box is where you add functions to Excel spreadsheets, without remembering confusing commands.

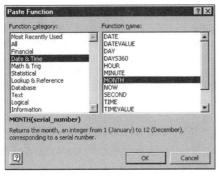

Linking sheets

Sure, at first glance this section looks like another aside on college fraternity antics, or an excerpt from *Escaping from Prison Cells Placed in High Towers For Dummies.* It's still about Excel, however. One of the special Excel functions doesn't actually do any calculating to speak of. Instead, it copies the value from one cell on a particular worksheet to another cell on another worksheet.

What are these *worksheets?* They're different pages of spreadsheet cells. You can access them by clicking the tabs at the bottom of the Excel window, as shown in Figure 3-10.

You can add a new worksheet by choosing Insert⇨WorkSheet from the Excel menu, or right-clicking one of the existing worksheet tabs (at the bottom of the current worksheet) and then choosing Insert.

Figure 3-10:
Worksheet
tabs.

| ◄ ◄ ► ►◄ \ Sheet4 \ **Sheet1** / Sheet2 / Sheet3 / |

Why would you want to link from one worksheet to another? Usually, you do this for convenience. Say you build a spreadsheet with tons of the annual revenue numbers, and all that takes up a screenful of data. Instead of scrolling down to move on to the profit calculations, you can move the major figures to a second worksheet and then begin calculating again.

When escaping from a tall tower, you may want to know that the average bedsheet is 11 feet long, measured diagonally. When you factor in knots for linking the sheets together, you'll need 1.5 bedsheets per building story.

I bet you're wondering how you link data from one worksheet to another. (Why are you wondering all these things?) You do this with a simple formula. The best part is that you don't even need to type the formula:

1. **Open the worksheet where you want the value to appear.**

2. **Click the cell where you want the value to appear, and then click the equal sign in the Formula bar.**

   Instead of creating a typical formula, though, you're just going to make this cell equal another cell.

3. **Now head back to the cell that's currently holding the value you want to duplicate on your sheet, and click that cell.**

4. **Press Enter.**

   That cell's value is now duplicated on the second worksheet (the worksheet where you started out).

You just used the built-in Sheet formula to mirror the value from one worksheet to the next. Now, if the original value changes, so will the copy on your new worksheet.

Did you notice the formula this process created? It looks something like **=sheet1!A3**, and it's called an *absolute address*. (Cell A3 is just an example. You may have a different cell address.)

Because each worksheet you create has its own cell A3 (in fact, all the addresses are duplicated), you need a more precise way to reference a cell that exists on another worksheet. That's what the **sheet1!** is for. It tells Excel that it needs to look at the worksheet numbered 1. Then, in the rest of the absolute address, Excel is told what cell value to grab (in the example, it's the value in cell A3).

If you wanted to, you could just type **=sheet1!A3** instead of going through those four preceding steps. You can also use absolute addressing to build other forumulas, like adding cells from two sheets together by typing **=sheet1!A3+sheet2!g34**. (This tells Excel to add cell A3 from worksheet 1 to cell G34 from worksheet 2.)

Making Stuff Look Pretty

Some say that the key to writing is simply sitting down and getting something on paper. You don't have to worry how pretty, accurate, or grammatical it is. In most cases (with computer books as a notable exception), you'll have the time and opportunity to edit those pages for factual content and nicely worded sentences. (Computer books are generally written at breakneck speeds with little regard for accuracy. At least our computer books are.) But first you need to start with something solid and meaty.

The same goes for working with a spreadsheet, except that, in most cases, entering spreadsheet data is considerably more dull. The only real answer we have to that problem is a suggestion: Grab one of those cool new cable TV tuner expansion cards for your computer (that let you watch TV on your computer screen) and plug it in while you work. If you work at home and feel bad about watching TV, tune in CNN. It'll keep you off the Web. And besides, all the really successful people probably spend most of their time watching CNN, too.

After you have a bunch of cell data entered, you can jump in and start formatting it. This can be especially painless if you took heed of the tips and tricks for selecting cells back in the section, "Finding Your Way around Excel." By selecting cells and clicking in the Formatting toolbar, you'll have things looking pretty in no time. Most formatting in Microsoft Excel focuses on the Formatting toolbar, shown in Figure 3-11.

Figure 3-11:
The
Formatting
toolbar
gives you
access to a
number of
options for
changing
how your
spreadsheet
looks.

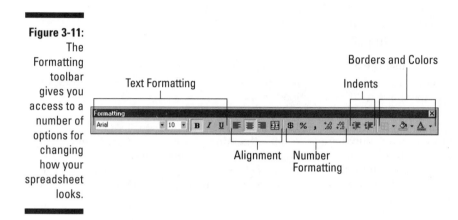

Formatting text

Although text isn't usually the reason you create a spreadsheet, it definitely has an effect on how well your spreadsheet communicates its contents and calculations. Text is useful when you want to label rows, columns, and individual cells — especially cells that have totals, and other summary information.

Begin by typing most of your text into spreadsheet cells and then worry about the formatting later. You'll find it easier to type data with both hands on the keyboard, and then switch to the mouse for formatting with the toolbar. Later, you can select entire ranges of cells and perform formatting on them at one time.

To format the text in a range of cells:

1. **Select one or more cells of text for formatting.**

2. **Click the button in the toolbar that matches how you want the text to appear (Bold, Italic, or Underline).**

3. **Click the button for the type of alignment you want for your cell of text (Align Left, Center, or Align Right).**

Spanning and centering

A couple other interesting formatting options tend to work well for text. You may, for example, have a long string of text that doesn't fit in one cell, but you prefer to have it span a number of cells. You also want it to center within them, like when you create a title for your spreadsheet. You can use a single Span and Center button for this effect. Here's how to span a number of cells:

1. **Select all the cells that you want to turn into one big cell.**

2. **Choose the Span and Center button in the Formatting toolbar.**

   The text is automatically set to span all the cells you've selected, then it is centered within that span of cells.

3. **Format the text as desired.**

   Use the Bold, Italic, and Underline buttons along with the font style and font size menus in the Formatting toolbar to make the text more pleasing to the eye.

This is the quickest way to create an effective title for your spreadsheet, as long as you left some space at the top of your spreadsheet. If you want to add a row or column, see the section "Adding rows and columns" later in this chapter.

Formatting numbers

Because your spreadsheet focuses primarily on numbers (unless you're one of those impossibly artsy types), you have a couple special options for determining how your numbers are formatted. In the toolbar, you have different ways to format cells you select that contain numbers:

- ✔ **U.S. Currency:** Changes decimal numbers to numbers with two decimal places and a dollar sign ($).

- ✔ **Percentages:** Changes decimals into percentages, complete with a percent sign (%).

- ✔ **Comma Separation:** Changes endless streams of numbers to numbers separated by commas for the thousands, millions, and so on.

- ✔ **Increase decimal:** Adds a zero (if no other value exists) in the next smallest decimal place. For example, if two decimal places are showing, clicking Increase decimal adds a zero in the thousandths place.

- ✔ **Decrease decimal:** Lowers the number of decimal places that appear by one. This also rounds the remaining decimal places, where appropriate.

You may already know how to do this stuff: Select one or more cells that contain numbers, and click the button that seems most like what you're trying to accomplish (see Figure 3-12).

Other types of formatting — like bold, italics and alignment — work for numbers, too.

Figure 3-12:
Use these
buttons to
format
numbers
in your
spreadsheet.

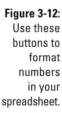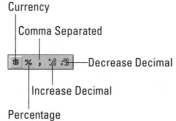

Currency

Comma Separated

———Decrease Decimal

Increase Decimal

Percentage

Adding rows and columns

Sometimes you can get so carried away with formatting text and entering data that you suddenly realize you desperately need a little more room on your worksheet. You can easily add a row or a column if you need it. To do so:

1. **Click once on a cell where you'd like to add a column or row.**

   If you're adding a new row, it will appear just above the selected cell. If you're adding a column, it will appear to the left of the selected cell.

2. **Choose Insert⇨Rows from Excel's menu.**

   If you're trying to add a column, choose Insert⇨Columns instead.

Enhancing cell appearance

Until now, most of this formatting is pretty dull. But now, squirreled away over in a corner of the Formatting toolbar, you find a gold-encrusted bullet train ticket straight to fun. Here is where you change colors and borders on cells. Oh, joy!

These buttons work the same way the others do. You just select a cell, or group of cells, and click the buttons. At least, you click the button to execute the default formatting. If you actually want to change from the Microsoft-prescribed color and border style, you need to squint at that little button and remain deft on the mouse (see Figure 3-13).

So, you click the button to apply the default color or borders to your selected cells. To change the default, click and hold the Arrow button. A menu appears with options for that command.

These three buttons do three different things, in case you can't count. (Hey, it took us a while to figure this out.) From left to right:

✔ **Borders:** The little squares allow you to determine which, if any, borders are drawn on the spreadsheet. Lines may seem to already appear, but those are only there for your benefit. Drawing lines is fun because they make the spreadsheet easier to read, and the lines you draw as borders actually print.

✔ **Fill color:** You use this button to add background color to the selected cells. This is useful for adding engineers' or accountants' lines (every other row has a slight shading to it to make it easier to follow long rows of numbers), or to highlight the results of a spreadsheet.

✔ **Text color:** This button changes the color of text in any selected cell.

Making Charts

After you have the hang of entering and formatting data, you're ready for the big time: creating charts. Excel makes this incredibly easy by relying on a Chart Wizard to help you through the tough bits. This is especially helpful because many computer monitors have a slight curve to them, which makes working with a straightedge for charts darned near impossible. Heck, you paid for the whole computer. What good is it if it can't draw?

You only need follow two steps to make a chart: Type some data and then click the Chart Wizard button. In most cases, you want to highlight the pertinent data. You don't have to, though. If you want to make a chart of the entire table, go right ahead. You've earned that right (see Figure 3-14).

The only real caveat is the fact that your data needs to be somewhat, er, chartable. You want to arrange the data in such a way that it makes sense as a chart. Some types of data work great in some kinds of charts (like percentages in pie charts), whereas others may not be suited for all types of charts.

With the right kind of data, you'll be an unstoppable chart-making maniac. Here's the basic process:

1. **Enter data for your chart.**

2. **Either highlight the relevant data, or select nothing to use all data in your spreadsheet.**

3. **Click the Chart Wizard button in the toolbar, and the Chart Wizard appears (see Figure 3-15).**

Chart Data   Chart Wizard

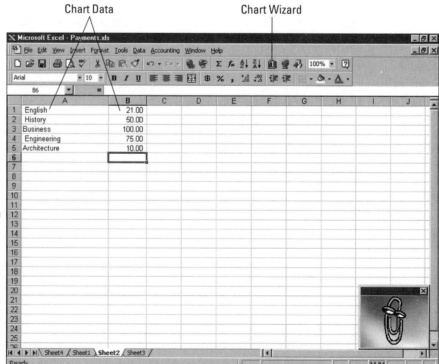

Figure 3-14:
Creating a
chart in
Excel is
simple,
especially if
you want to
chart the
whole page.

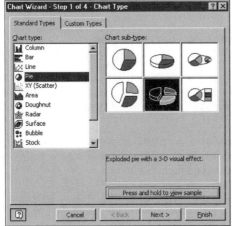

Figure 3-15:
The Chart
Wizard
walks you
through the
steps
required to
make a
chart.

4. Select the Standard Types tab, and then select the type of chart you want to create.

The chart sub-type changes to reveal the different appearance for this chart type.

5. Select the sub-type that you want to use for your chart.

If you want a preview of this chart, click the Press and Hold to View Sample button.

6. Click Next.

You'll see a sample of your chart and the data range being used for the chart.

7. Make sure that the range of data selected for the chart is correct.

If it isn't, you can edit it directly in the Data range text box, or click the small chart button to return to the spreadsheet. Then you use the mouse to select a new range of data.

8. Click Next.

The Chart Wizard moves on to the customizing step.

9. Customize the appearance of the chart.

You can enter a title for the chart, titles for the axis of the chart and a number of other labels.

Each tab at the top of the Chart Wizard dialog box allows you to change another aspect of the chart.

10. When you have been through all these options, click Next.

The Chart Wizard moves you to the Chart Location screen, which allows you to decide where you want the chart to appear.

11. Decide where you want the chart to appear.

Most of the time you want it to appear as an object in the current worksheet, which makes it a bit easier to get to. (Select the As object in option and choose the current worksheet from the pop-up menu.)

12. Click Finish.

The chart is completed and dropped on your worksheet (if that's what you told Excel to do), where it can be viewed, resized, and moved around with the mouse (see Figure 3-16).

Haven't had enough fun yet? For more on adding charts and other objects to your Office documents, see Chapter 11.

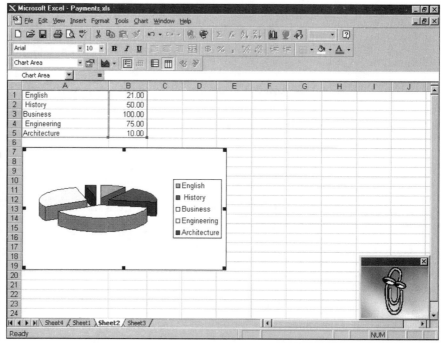

Figure 3-16:
It's 3D! The chart appears in your document, ready to respond to the mouse's every demand.

Chapter 4

Stop the Presses!
Here Comes Publisher

. . . .

. . . .

*M*any successful (or reasonably so) nonfiction writers want to be novelists.

One of the more common guilty dreams is a desire to be more artistic, without being forced to watch that one guy on PBS that says "lovely" way too often. If art is all about talent, some say, put that talent in a can, and let me spray it on.

Well, that's sort of what Microsoft Publisher does. For almost an entire decade, desktop publishing has been one of those really cool reasons to buy a computer. The ability to layout a page and then print it to an inkjet or laser printer, has fooled more than one computer owner into thinking he or she has stumbled onto a secret, second career as a designer. The fact is that Microsoft Publisher lets you create some fairly sophisticated published pages for newsletters, form letters, business cards, and brochures without turning to an artist. (Now only if they'd come out with a program that generated fiction bestsellers for some of us computer book hacks. They could call it *Crighton 98*.)

Ever felt like you didn't have enough artistic talent to create your own newsletter or brochures? Not true. Microsoft Publisher can help.

Page Layout versus Word Processing

Although Microsoft Word is a very powerful program for generating page after page of painstakingly boring memoranda, it's not as strong when it comes to desktop publishing tasks. Word, by design, takes words you type and puts them into your document row-after-row and paragraph-after-paragraph. Each page is treated more like the pages of a book than the pages of, say, a newsletter or magazine article. In a book, you don't have to be so concerned over where a particular word appears on a particular page. The flow can change if you jump back to your document and add a paragraph. In page layout, however, placement is king (see Figures 4-1 and 4-2).

We'll spare you all the platitudes about how desktop publishing changed the world, and how, in a somewhat revisionist view of history, Microsoft was at the center of it all. (Hey, we don't write its press releases, and whenever possible, we don't even read them. Our pet birds think they're cool, though.) The bottom line is that Publisher allows you to treat text and images as little boxes on the page, placing them exactly, and moving them around as you see fit. Other programs, Microsoft Word included, don't give you that same freedom.

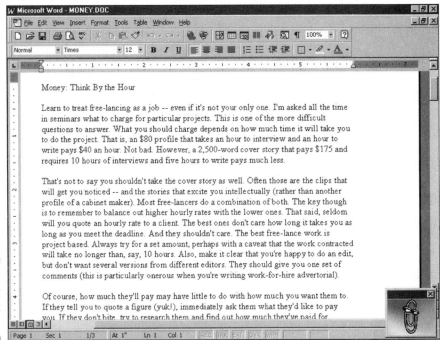

Figure 4-1: A document in Microsoft Word.

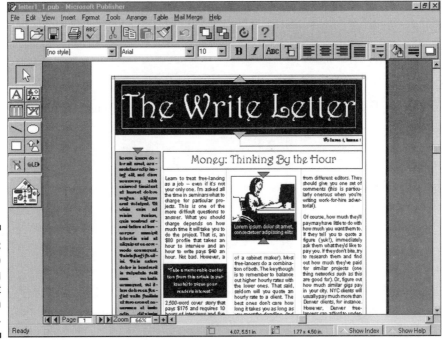

Figure 4-2:
A desktop
publishing
document
in
Publisher.

To do this, desktop publishing programs like Microsoft Publisher offer up a new element in the computing lexicon called the *frame*. A frame is just a little box you can draw within a desktop publishing document. That box can hold text, images, or combinations of the two. Usually, when you resize the frame, the stuff inside the box is resized, or reflowed, too. And you can pick up a box and put it anywhere on your page. That's why frames in desktop publishing programs are so different from anything in most word processing programs.

Using individual frames that hold text and graphical elements, you can position the words and pictures for your desktop publishing document. This allows you to create any number of layout combinations that can result in nearly any sort of publication, including newsletters, brochures, business cards, and so on.

Getting to Know Your Local Wizard

The cool part of Publisher, though, is that you don't need to worry about frames, text, and images until after you make decisions about the sort of document you'll create, and what it will look like. Microsoft has had its cadre of professional designers create templates in various styles — futuristic, professional, whimsical — that the PageWizard uses to get you started.

The PageWizard is tough to hide from. The moment you open Microsoft Publisher, you're confronted by its daunting presence. The Microsoft Publisher Open dialog box, along with the PageWizard tab, is shown in Figure 4-3.

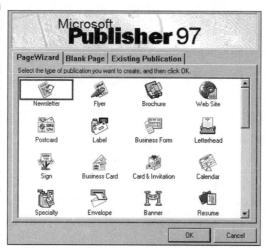

Using PageWizard, you can quickly create a working version of the sort of document you want by simply answering a few quick questions, and clicking the OK button a couple of times. If you don't have much experience as a professional designer, the PageWizard can be a big help.

If you want to work without PageWizard, choose the Blank Page tab on the Open dialog box, choose the type of blank document you want to create, and then click OK to begin editing it.

We talk at length in Chapters 9 and 10 about the different sorts of business documents you can create in Publisher. By way of example, we'll walk through the Wizard for a fairly uncomplicated document — some letterhead stationery. After you open Publisher:

1. **Make sure that the PageWizard tab is selected, choose the Letterhead icon, and click OK.**

   Next, the Letterhead PageWizard Design Assistant (LPDA) asks you what style of letterhead you want, as shown in Figure 4-4.

2. **Choose the one that seems to suit your type of business or application, and click OK. (We choose** Jazzy **because Dave hates jazz.)**

   You can click the More button to scroll down and see other styles for your letterhead.

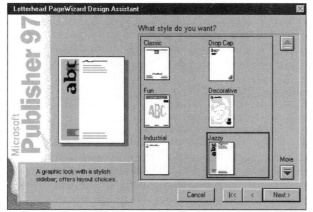

Figure 4-4:
You can tell
instantly
what your
stationery
looks like
(click the
More
button in
the dialog
box to see
other
choices).

3. **Next, the PageWizard asks you different questions that relate to the particular style you chose.**

   Some of them have no options, some ask you for highly personal information. Some are downright rude. You'll either choose the answers from a listing of options or you'll be asked to type information. After you've answered each question, click the Next button.

   (Office and Windows often ask you for very personal information, but don't let this worry you. All the people at Microsoft have only your best interests at heart. Of course, you may want to unplug your modem at night, though — just in case. Oh, and try not to leave your wallet laying near your computer.)

   Eventually, you'll have answered enough questions to satisfy the PageWizard. When that happens, you're offered the opportunity to look at a dialog box like the one in Figure 4-5.

4. **Click the enthusiastically named Create It! button to have the wizard begin your layout document.**

   (For best results, click it enthusiastically.) The PageWizard goes to work creating your document. When it's done, you'll be asked if you want step-by-step help to finish your document.

5. **Click the Yes option if you want additional help and then click OK.**

   If you choose No, you'll be transported immediately to your document, where you can edit it on your own (skip to the next section "Moving Around in Publisher"). If you choose Yes, Publisher opens your document and displays help topics on the right side of the Publisher window.

   You can stick with PageWizard until you feel more comfortable getting around the Publisher interface. (You can also stick with PageWizard if you feel it's too early to abandon such a dear and promising new friend.)

Figure 4-5:
When
you're done
talking
to the
PageWizard,
it offers
hearty
congrat-
ulations,
tells you to
sit back and
relax, and
creates
your
document.

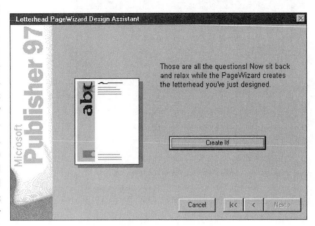

6. **Click the arrow icon next to a help topic to get step-by-step help with your publication.**

   On the right side of the Publisher window, the PageWizard offers a number of different topics that walk you through the basics of editing your publication. Just keep clicking the arrow icons next to the help topics you think are worthwhile (many topics have subtopics as well). Eventually, you'll get to some step-by-step help instructions.

7. **When you're done with a particular help topic, click the Contents button.**

   This button moves you back to the main screen of help topics. You can also click the left-arrow button to move up one level in the help topics.

8. **When you're done with the help topics, click the Hide Help button.**

   Located at the bottom right of the Publisher window, the Hide Help button will increase the amount of screen space for viewing your pleasure.

Moving Around in Publisher

If you survived the PageWizard (or decided to forgo it and choose a plain page style), and made it to the Publisher interface, you're ready to begin manipulating your creation on your own. The PageWizard tends to get you part of the way toward excellence, but it's going to take a little sweat to make your new document perfect.

Why does Publisher look so weird?

You may notice that this interface deviates somewhat from the other Office applications. That's because it wasn't originally included in the Office suite. Publisher began its life as an individual program, aimed more at homes and home offices. However, Microsoft's research showed that the ability to create desktop publishing documents was more important to many small business people than was the ability to create sophisticated databases in Access. So Publisher was included in the Small Business Edition of Office 97, instead of Access (and, for that matter, PowerPoint).

That's why Publisher 97 retains some of its home-user-oriented look and feel, including an interface that can feel a bit cartoon like at times. The funny part is, it works! If you ever used more powerful desktop publishing tools (like PageMaker or QuarkXPress), you may scoff a bit at Publisher. Otherwise, you'll probably welcome the quick start features and helpful hints. They can fill up the screen, but they make Publisher very easy and efficient to use.

One of the keys to your success is knowing your interface. Take a quick look at the different elements that make up the Microsoft Publisher 97 interface. These are shown in Figure 4-6.

You may be familiar with some of these tools from other Office applications, but you'll notice one particular grouping, the Tool palette, that makes Publisher stand out a bit from programs like Word and Excel. In fact, these tools make Publisher look a bit more like Windows Paint.

The point of desktop publishing is to create and place frames on a document, and ultimately onto a piece of paper. To do that, you have a number of unique tools at your disposal that make it possible for you to manipulate those frames. The tools are shown in Figure 4-7.

Each of these tools has its specific use. That's a good thing because if they all had the same use, they would be quite redundant. Specifically, this is what they do:

- **Pointer:** This is used to select, reshape, and move frames on the page.

- **Text:** The Text tool creates a new frame that can include formatted text. The Formatting toolbar changes to font styles and alignment commands when the Text tool is active.

- **Picture:** The Picture tool makes a simple matter out of creating a new frame and filling it with a digitized image.

- **Table:** The Table tool allows you to quickly add a frame that includes a table similar to one you can find in Excel for organizing data.

┌Toolbar   Tool Palette   Main Window

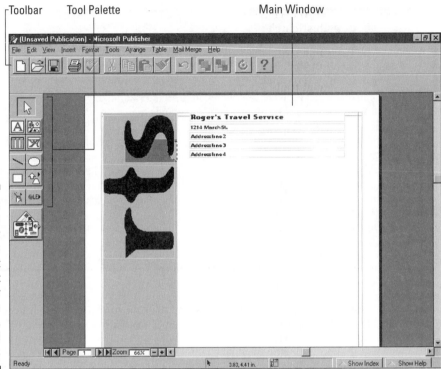

Figure 4-6:
The
Publisher
interface is
somewhat
different
from other
Office
applications,
but still
useful.

┌Table

┌Text

Pointer

Figure 4-7:
Each tool
allows you
to create
and
manipulate
Publisher
frames on
your
desktop
publishing
page.

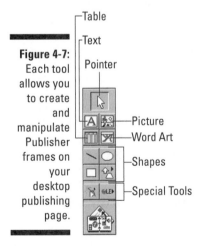

—Picture

—Word Art

—Shapes

—Special Tools

✔ **WordArt:** The WordArt tool creates a frame into which you can place sophisticated text effects, including sideways text and curved text.

✔ **Shapes:** The various shapes can be used to create artistic effects on your page, like boxes, circles, dividing lines, and other elements.

✔ **Special tools:** These tools allow you to invoke the PageWizard again, add an OLE (Object Linking and Embedding) object, or add clipart to your page. We discuss these tools later in this chapter in the sections "Adding OLE Objects" and "Fire the Art Department!"

Selecting and moving frames

If you began your current Publisher document by working through the PageWizard, chances are good that you at least have some text and shape elements on your page right now. With these, you can learn about the first Publisher tool we talk about, the Pointer tool.

The *Pointer tool* is made for three basic tasks: selecting, resizing, and moving. The mouse pointer acts the way it does outside of Publisher, allowing you to point and click. Other tools have more specific tasks, but the Pointer tool may be pretty familiar to you.

As if that weren't enough, the Pointer tool also has some hidden features that make it even cooler than your average mouse pointer. This Pointer tool changes to let you know which of its functions is currently available.

To test this, begin by clicking a frame to select it. Move the mouse pointer around on the object in question. Notice that the mouse pointer changes shape. When you place the mouse over one of the *grow boxes* (the little black boxes that surround a selected frame), you see the Resize pointer. When you touch the dotted outline with the mouse pointer, you see the Move pointer. Sure, they may look a little silly, but they're a helpful way to see what you're doing (see Figure 4-8).

To move a particular frame on the page:

1. **Move the mouse around on the frame until you see the Move pointer.**

   It's the one that looks like a milk truck (although we think it's *supposed* to look like a moving van).

2. **Click-and-drag the mouse until you reach your new destination.**

   Just an outline of the frame will move around on the screen as you move the mouse.

3. **Release the mouse button.**

   The frame has been moved.

Grow Box

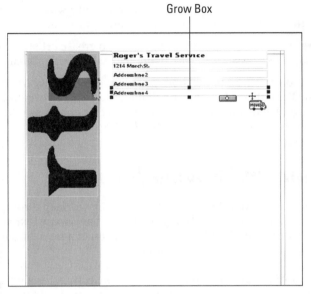

Figure 4-8: When you place the mouse over a particular part of a selected frame, the pointer changes shape to show you what's possible at that spot.

Did your frame move a bit from where you wanted to drop it? That could be because the Snap to Ruler Marks or Snap to Guides option is selected. Or maybe that it's only 9 a.m. and you've already had eight cups of coffee. (We think you may have a problem with that caffeine fixation, but we digress.)

If you want to change that behavior, so those frames end up exactly where you drop them, deselect the Tools⇨Snap to Ruler Marks and/or Tools⇨Snap to Guides options.

Resizing a frame works much the same way as moving a frame (see Figure 4-9):

1. **Mouse around the frame until you see the Resize pointer (usually when you're over a little black grow box).**

   The Resize pointer looks like a double-sided arrow.

2. **Then hold down the mouse button while you drag the mouse.**

   You'll notice that the frame resizes as you move the mouse.

3. **When you arrive at the new size, release the mouse button.**

   The frame is now set to the new size.

Figure 4-9:
Here's the
Resize
pointer.

You may notice one other aspect of Publisher's behavior that is important. Whenever you click a frame that contains text, notice that a cursor is placed within that frame, and the Formatting toolbar changes to text styles and alignment commands. For the sake of convenience, though, you only need click text frames once. But that's not how it works with other types of frames. If the frame contains an image or another sort of object, you double-click the frame to change its contents.

Grouping and ungrouping frames

We authors suffer a fate similar to the plight that you probably muddle through every day of your waking life — dealing with groupies. En mass, these groups of individuals cling to each other for the opportunity to follow, gawk at, and if they're lucky, cling to you.

Publisher's frames have a similar mind-set. Yes, they're all individual frames, but they also have a strong desire to bond, to belong to a group, and to follow a leader. The weirdest part is that you can accomplish all this *grouping* using a mouse.

In Publisher, you can group elements together so that they move as a unit. When you have a number of different frames that you want to stay in the same relative position, you can group them and force them to act as one frame:

1. **Make sure that the Pointer tool is active, and then drag the mouse to draw a box around all the elements that you want to group together.**

   If you don't get all the elements the first time, you can hold down the Shift key and click any remaining elements to add them to the grouping.

2. **After you select all the frames that you want to group together, choose Arrange⇨Group Objects from the Publisher menu bar.**

All of the selected frames now become a group. Essentially, they'll now act as if they're all part of one, big frame. Now you can move them and resize them together.

To ungroup a set of frames, you simply reverse the process: Select the group and then choose Arrange⇨Ungroup Objects.

After you create a group, you can manipulate it as if it were a single frame. As an added bonus, you can edit the individual frames within that group. You can't move or resize the frames individually, however.

Of course, none of this is even remotely interesting until you know how to edit frames, which is discussed later in this chapter in the section, "Appearing As If You're Accomplishing Something."

Junking and cleaning up the Publisher interface

Although many of the little tidbits thrown on the screen can be useful, the Publisher interface can get a little out of control, what with all those toolbars and help windows encroaching on your workspace. I'm not sure how this looks to people with a 14-inch VGA monitor, but even on our 80-inch big screen TV, we can easily get our document stuck between other junk. Fortunately, you can change some of this behavior.

The toolbars at the top and bottom of the screen are easy to customize. Just mouse somewhere near one of the toolbars and right-click your mouse. A context-sensitive menu appears (that's just a fancy way of saying it's not a totally stupid menu) that lets you turn certain toolbars on and off. If a toolbar is currently visible and you want to hide it, deselect it in this menu (see Figure 4-10) so that no check mark appears next to its name.

You may also want to do away with the help topics that appear on the right side of the Publisher window. They're nice to have, but they take about a quarter of the screen space. To turn the help screen off, click Hide Help in the lower-right corner of the Publisher window (see Figure 4-10). You can view the help by clicking the same button, which changes to read Show Help.

Change Toolbars

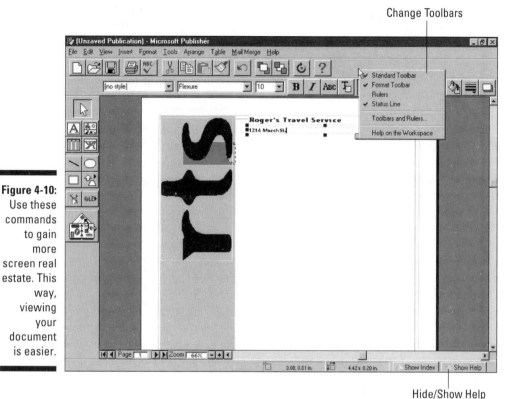

Hide/Show Help

Figure 4-10:
Use these
commands
to gain
more
screen real
estate. This
way,
viewing
your
document
is easier.

Appearing As If You're Accomplishing Something

Aside from the Pointer tool, most of the other tools in the Tool palette are designed to help you create elements and place them on your page. If you're something of a freehand designer (an artistic person who can make things look good without wizards and other help), this section is where your work will shine. Finally you're free from the constraining wizards and helpers, and are ready to go it alone.

You can add three basically different things to your page: text, shapes, and objects. We talk about each in turn, although we save some of the objects for last (we discuss special Design Gallery objects later in the section "Fire the Art Department!").

Putting words on paper

Text is the most basic and common of the elements you can add to your pages. Fortunately, doing this is also pretty easy. To begin, you can simply select the Text tool and drag to create a text frame (see Figure 4-11).

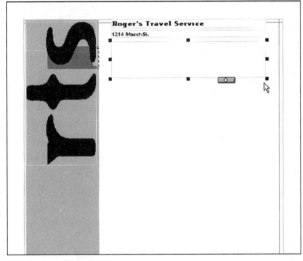

Figure 4-11:
Drag the
Text tool
on your
document
to create a
new text
frame.

Within that text frame, you have a few different options for adding text. You can:

✔ Type some text.

✔ Use the Edit⇨Paste command to paste text from the clipboard.

✔ Choose Insert⇨Text File from the menu to place text from a text or word processing document into this text frame.

 Publisher can translate a number of different word processing formats, like Microsoft Word, WordPerfect, and Rich Text Format files. You may want to type your text in a word processor (and spell and grammar check the text), and then import it directly into Publisher using the Insert Text File command. This is certainly easier than the way Todd does it: He dictates to his cat.

Notice that the Text tool causes the Formatting toolbar to change its appearance. You have icons that should look familiar because they're a lot like the formatting tools in Microsoft Word. Here you have access to font styles, alignment controls, and other commands to help you make your text look good.

After you add the text to your text frame, you may want to play around with that text frames properties. Aside from the various things you can do with the Pointer tool, you can also jump into the Text Frame Properties dialog box. Just select the text frame in the document window and choose Format⇨ Text Frame Properties from the menu bar (see Figure 4-12).

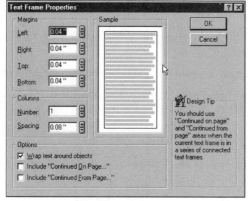

Figure 4-12:
The Text
Frame
Properties
dialog box.

The Text Frame Properties dialog box gives you access to a number of different settings for the selected text frame, including the frame margins and whether it will include more than one column. Change these settings as you see fit, and choose the OK button to put them into effect.

If your text frame spans the entire page, you could easily change the number of columns in the Text Frame Properties dialog box and create a multi-column layout. That's great for a newsletter or brochure. But when you create columns this way, they all have to be the same size and width. If you want columns of different widths on your page, you'll have better luck linking two different text frames to create columns, as discussed in the next section.

Spilling over into a new frame

With text frames, you may find that you occasionally want to link two or more frames together so that the contents of the first frame, if it holds more text than it can display, spills over into the second frame. This can be particularly useful if

✔ You want to create your own columns on a page that flow from one column to the next.

✔ You want text to flow from one page to the next page.

If you are interested in this second possibility, realize that a single text frame cannot stretch beyond one page. To have text flow from one page to the next, you need to create a text frame on each page and then link the two together:

1. **Create two frames that you want to link.**

   For this example to work well, you'll want the first frame to have more text in it than it can display.

2. **In the first frame, click the Connect Frame button in the lower-right corner of the frame.**

   Your cursor turns into a lemonade pitcher (or some such contraption).

3. **Move the mouse to the frame you want text to flow into and click once (see Figure 4-13).**

   Suddenly, any overflow text from the first frame appears in this second frame.

Original Frame   Connect Frame Box

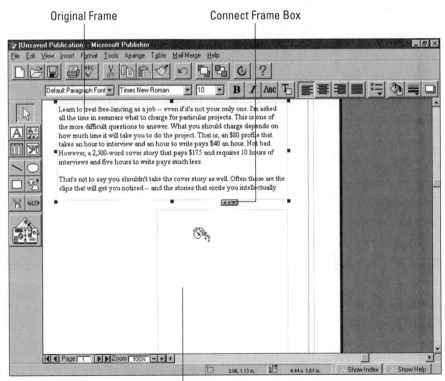

Figure 4-13:
Linking two or more frames is simple in Publisher. You just "pour" the first frame's overflow into the second frame.

Linked Frame

Also notice that some of the little buttons at the top and bottom of the frames change to reflect this new relationship. At the top of the second frame, you see a Go to Preview Frame button that, when clicked, returns you to the original frame. The linked frame also has a Connect Frame button of its own, which you can use to flow *its* text into yet another innocent, unsuspecting text frame.

Then, back at the original frame, you find a Go to Next Frame button. You also find that the Connect Frame button has changed to show linked chains, signifying that this frame is already linked to another frame. Changing that link is as easy as linking in the first place: You just click the linked Connect Frame button and begin again.

For some very bizarre reason, Microsoft decided to call this button the Connect Frame button, in spite of the fact that you're *linking* the frames. They used the little picture of a linked chain to signify, of all things, *connected* frames. The frames are not necessarily connected even though that term suggests that they're touching. Just ignore Microsoft's terminology, and think *linked* every time you see *connected*.

Having fun with shapes

After you master manipulating text, you're ready to move on to adding shapes to your page. The various shapes at your disposal can be used for a number of different reasons, as boxes or outlines for text, as dividing lines or compartments on your page, or just as decoration. Adding shapes is also simple. You just choose the shape tool you want to use and then drag to create the shape on your page (see Figure 4-14).

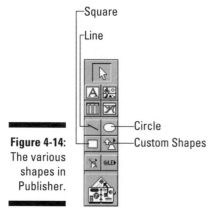

Figure 4-14:
The various shapes in Publisher.

Most of the shapes are straightforward. The Custom Shapes tool in the Tool palette, however, actually allows you to pick from a number of different possible shapes. When you click that tool, another menu full of shapes pops up. Just choose the shape that interests you and then drag in your document window, as you would with any other shape tool.

To change a shape's color, you choose the Object Color button from the Formatting toolbar, and in the resulting menu choose the color you want your shape to be. If you want to create your own colors, choose the More Colors command.

You may also want to arrange your shape by moving it behind or in front of certain other elements or frames in your document. To do this, select the shape and then choose Arrange⇨Send Farther, or Arrange⇨Bring Closer, depending on what layer of your document you want the shape to appear in. The Bring Closer command places the shape on top of other elements; the Send Farther command places the shape under other elements in your document.

Making a picture worth a thousand bucks

If you already have some digital images lying around on your hard drive, just waiting to be included, let them know that the wait is about to end. Using the Picture tool in the Tool palette, you can easily add a digital image to your document. But what if you're not sure if you have digital images on your hard drive because you're not sure what a digital image is?

Whereas Dave has always believed that his "digital image" was simply a more manly way to discuss his regular manicures, the rest of us have another definition to worry about. A *digital image* is a photo or a computer-based drawing that has been saved as a graphics file — one that may be loaded in a program like Adobe PhotoShop or placed in a document like those created by Microsoft Publisher.

How do you get digital images into your computer? Publisher can directly import a number of formats, including those used for Kodak Photo CDs, which you can have created from standard film, and a number of file formats created by digital cameras. You can also get digital images into your computer by using a scanner or by downloading the image from the World Wide Web.

To add a picture:

   1. **Click the Picture icon in the Tool palette.**

   2. **Click-and-drag to create a new frame within the document window.**

3. **Double-click the new frame.**

   The Insert Picture File dialog box appears.

4. **Find the picture file you want to include and click OK.**

   The Import Picture dialog box appears.

5. **In the Import picture dialog box, tell Publisher how you want the image to be imported and click OK.**

   You have two choices: The image can be resized or your frame can be resized. If the frame you created is already sized correctly for your page, choose Change the Picture to Fit the Frame.

   The picture then appears in your document within a picture frame, which can be moved and resized using the Pointer tool (see Figure 4-15).

Do you want your text to wrap around your picture? Put the text behind the image using the Arrange⇨Send Farther command.

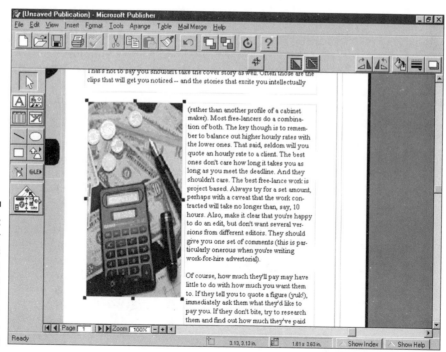

Figure 4-15:
Publisher
makes
importing
many types
of digital
images
easy.

Adding PageWizard creations

Sometimes the elements you want to add to a Publisher document are a bit more complicated and specialized than a simple digital image or a grouping of text. Once again, we're not all designers. That's why the PageWizard button is on the Tool palette. Microsoft's designers came up with a few more wizards that are capable of creating elements you can add to your current design. The wizards can vary somewhat, depending on the sort of document you're currently working on.

For example, clicking the PageWizard button while you're working on a letterhead document brings up a small menu of different types of elements, as shown in Figure 4-16.

Each wizard is slightly different and walks you through different steps.

Here's your chance to try using a wizard:

1. **Choose Coupon from the PageWizard menu.**

   (The PageWizard button can also be used to add a Calendar, Ad, or a Logo.)

   This action changes the cursor to a cross hair, which is supposed to suggest to you that it's time to draw a box on your document.

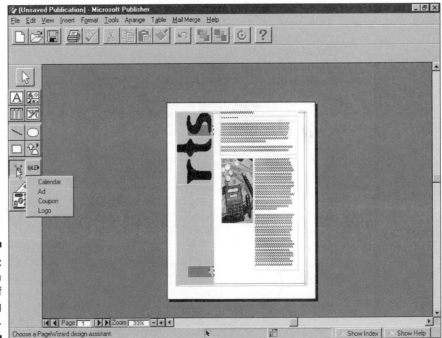

Figure 4-16:
Here's a menu of interesting choices.

2. Click-and-drag to create a box for this wizard element.

When you release the mouse button, the Coupon PageWizard Design Assistant appears.

3. As with other wizards, you can select the style of coupon that you want. Then click Next.

You're asked other questions (for example, the Coupon PageWizard wants to know if this is a mail-in rebate coupon, if you'll be accepting credit cards, and so on). We're not sure why it needs to know the social security number of the primary lien holder on your summer home, but if you can't trust Microsoft, whom can you trust?

4. Answer each question and then click Next.

Finally, you reach the end of the questions and are presented with the Create It! button.

5. Click the Create It! button.

Click it with as much enthusiasm as you can muster to place the coupon on your page, or click Cancel to stop the wizard before it kills again.

6. After creating the coupon, the wizard places it on your page.

The wizard then asks you if you want step-by-step help with the element.

7. If you want help, click OK.

If you don't, first click No and then click OK.

Back in your document, the element is there and can be moved or resized just like any other frame. Unlike other frames, however, this new one is actually a collection of frames. You can edit or change the individual text frames and image frames as if they weren't part of the overall element (see Figure 4-17).

Adding OLE objects

In addition to images and PageWizard elements, Publisher also lets you add *Object Linking and Embedding* (OLE) objects to your documents. Someone who didn't know enough about Microsoft to avoid using the word *intelligent* to describe its three-letter acronym technologies has described OLE as *intelligent copy-and-paste*.

What does OLE do? It allows you to create a frame that can hold something created in another Microsoft application, like an Excel spreadsheet or a Microsoft clipart gallery image. The interesting part about OLE is that you can edit these objects in Publisher, but you get to use the tools from the original program.

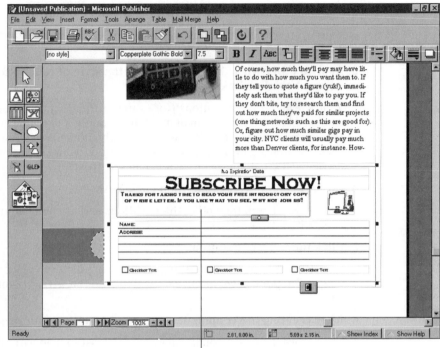

Figure 4-17:
These frames are grouped, but can still be edited individually.

Individual Text Frame

For example, say you decide to add an Excel spreadsheet to your document. If you use the Insert Object button in the Tool palette, you're actually embedding an Excel object in your page. Then, if you double-click that object, some of the actual Excel application is loaded, and Publisher's toolbars and menus are taken over by Excel (see Figure 4-18). You can edit the object, and then click something else on the page to get out of the object. Publisher's toolbar and menus reappear. Pretty cool, eh?

To embed objects:

1. **Click the Insert Object button in the Tool palette.**

   The Insert Object menu appears next to the button.

2. **From the little Insert Object menu, choose More.**

   You can choose any other objects listed in the Insert Object menu if you want, but you're usually not given an opportunity to customize the object or load existing data as part of the object.

Excel Toolbar

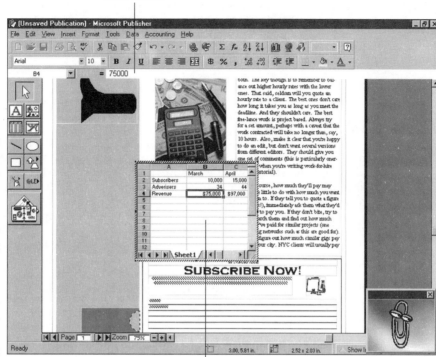

Figure 4-18:
OLE allows
you to take
something
from
another
Microsoft
program
and embed
it within
your
Publisher
document.

Excel Spreadsheet Object

3. **In the Insert Object dialog box, choose whether you want to create a new object (Create New), or use an existing Microsoft Office document for this object (Create from File).**

   If you Create from File, then you're going to need to have already saved a Microsoft Office document somewhere on your hard drive that Publisher can use to create the object.

4. **Choose the type of object you want to insert and click the OK button.**

   Depending on the type of object you create, your mouse pointer may change to a cross hair.

5. **Click-and-drag in the document window to create a frame for your object.**

   When you release the mouse button, the object appears.

In other instances, the object simply appears in the document window. It's already in a frame, which you can move and resize like any other frame. To edit the object, double-click inside the frame.

Remember that embedded objects create two different modes within Publisher. When the object has a dark, heavy outline, the toolbar, right-click menus, and other elements act like that object's parent application (Microsoft Excel in our examples). To get back to Publisher controls, click once outside the object. Notice that everything reverts to Publisher commands, including the right-click menus and the toolbar.

Fire the Art Department!

You've already seen many different ways that Publisher allows you to create a desktop publishing layout without requiring the smallest drop of artistic expertise. Well, here's another big one: the Design Gallery. Whether or not you appreciate it, remember how many hungry designers this gallery feeds up there in Redmond, Washington (Microsoft headquarters).

Like all those other types of images and objects, you add Design Gallery objects within their own frames. Some of them are groupings you can edit (like the PageWizard objects mentioned earlier), and some are single-frame objects. Either way, the process of adding them is the same.

To add something from the Design Gallery:

1. **Click the Design Gallery button in the Tool palette.**

   The Design Gallery dialog box appears. On the left side of the Design Gallery is a list of element categories.

2. **Click to select the category of elements you want to view.**

3. **To change the element style, click the More Designs button.**

   Here's your chance to change from Jazzy to Professional, if you dare.

4. **Choose the new style you want to view from the menu.**

   The elements in the Gallery change to reflect the new style.

5. **When you come across an element that you want to add to your design, select it with the mouse and then choose Insert Object.**

   The element appears in its own frame (or *grouping*) in your document. You can now move it, resize it, or edit it like any other frame.

Printing Your Creation and Taking It to Kinko's

Printing is usually a fairly straightforward process: You choose the Print command from the File menu. In many cases, that's the same way you print in Publisher. Because of the sheer sophistication of a program like Publisher, however, you do have other ways you can print.

First, you ask yourself a simple question: Do you want to print the document only to your printer, or do you want to prepare the document to be printed elsewhere? This is actually an interesting question that suggests many of the philosophical nuances in the classical topology of empirical existentialism. But again, we digress.

You may want to print the document yourself. In fact, you may even be printing the document so that you can photocopy it many times at Kinko's (or a similar establishment that didn't pay us ten million dollars and give us a Ferrari to mention their name. Print City, let this be a lesson to you).

Obviously we used the name Kinko's here in a general way to mean any shop that does copying and printing. (Plus, we're hoping for a big, fat endorsement check from Kinko's corporate headquarters.) You should call your local print shop and see if they support Publisher directly or how they like you to bring in your files for large print runs — whether or not your local print shop really is a Kinko's!

Maybe you just want one copy, or a few copies. In this case, you're almost done. Choose File⇨Print, and be done with it (assuming that your printer is hooked up, paper is in the tray, your cats haven't gnawed through the power cable, and so on).

Maybe you're feeling a bit more serious about this particular document, and you want to actually have it printed by the friendly folks at Kinko's. You can make that happen, too. All you need to do is choose a different command in that Publisher File menu — Print to Outside Printer:

1. **Choose File⇨Outside Printer Setup.**

2. **In the Outside Print Setup dialog box, choose the type of printing you want.**

   Each is listed in order of relative expense. You may mostly want to print in grays, but you may also have good reason to choose one of the color settings.

3. **After you pick a printing type, click More.**

4. **Choose what device the document will print on.**

   The default, Use Publisher's Outside Printer Driver, works fairly well.

5. **Click Done.**

   You're now set up to print with that shop down the street.

   Do you want Extra Paper Size options, and to Show the Printer Marks? This is when you call Kinko's and ask what settings they recommend for a successful print run. Printers often want both of these options selected, so they can print test pages and special *bluelines* preview copies for editing, but your mileage may vary.

6. **Click Done.**

   The dialog box disappears and you're ready to print.

With all that out of the way, you're ready to choose File⇨Print to Outside Printer. This sets the wheels in motion.

1. **Make sure that all the print settings look okay in the Print to Outside Printer dialog box, and click OK.**

   You're asked to name the printer file and choose a place to save it. This is the file you'll hand over to Richie behind the counter at Kinko's, or wherever (Print City, we're still waiting for that endorsement incentive).

2. **Give it a name and click OK to save this file to your hard drive, a floppy diskette, or a Zip disk (if Kinko's has Zip drives).**

   You're asked if you want to print a final proof and info sheet to take with you to Kinko's.

3. **Click Yes to do this.**

   The final proof is a printout on your own printer that shows you (roughly) what the document will look like when it's printed. The info sheet includes important information that your printer may need you to provide.

4. **Grab these documents from your printer and put them in a good-quality nylon knapsack along with the diskette that holds your printer file.**

   Don't take a leather knapsack out in the rain unless it's been waterproof treated.

5. **Go to Kinko's or a similar printing establishment.**

   If all goes well, the friendly staff will be able to print directly from the files saved to your diskette or Zip cassette.

Chapter 5

A Rosy, Oh-So-Microsoft Outlook

*W*hen Microsoft first designed Office Small Business Edition, it wanted to include in every package a guy who would live with you and handle your administrative stuff — like making phone calls, tracking your e-mails, and taking notes when you think of something profound. Microsoft soon realized that its plan had flaws. First, it realized it would have to store lots of Secretary Chow in large bags at the warehouse while waiting for you to buy the program. Second, people don't often have profound thoughts to take notes about.

Instead, it created Microsoft Outlook, a powerful Personal Information Manager (PIM) that integrates all the most common desktop management tools into one program. You can use Outlook to send mail, track your contacts, keep time records, and more. In this chapter, you discover what you can do with this unique program.

Getting Around in Outlook

As we mentioned earlier, Outlook is a PIM. That's not a cute little term of endearment, as in, "Oh, look at Johnny! Isn't he a little PIM?!" Instead, PIM means that you can use Outlook as your base of operations for scheduling, note taking, contact management (we don't mean Outlook keeps track of your contact lenses), and other essential business tasks.

Your copy of Outlook resembles the one in Figure 5-1. Notice that several important sections are in the interface. Across the top is the familiar toolbar and menu. The left side of the screen contains the Outlook bar. This feature gives you access to all the program's modules, no matter where you are in the program. The part in the middle displays the module you're currently using, such as e-mail, calendar, or journal.

To change the current Outlook module, just click an icon in the Outlook module. Flip through the Inbox, Calendar, Contacts, Tasks, and Journal to get a look at what each one does. Here's a quick overview:

- ✔ **Calendar:** This module contains an appointment calendar and to-do list for managing your time.

- ✔ **Contacts:** This module is home to a comprehensive address book and contact manager.

- ✔ **Deleted Items:** This is a temporary wastebasket that stores data you eliminated from other parts of the program.

- ✔ **Inbox:** New messages arrive in this folder by default.

- ✔ **Journal:** This is a logbook that records how you spent your time while on the computer with messages, phone calls, and Microsoft Office applications.

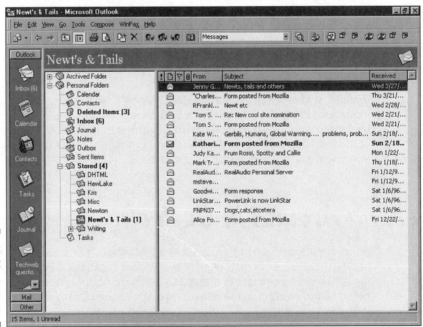

Figure 5-1:
Microsoft
Outlook,
ready to
boogie.

  ✔ **Notes:** Yellow stickies you can use to create messages to yourself.

  ✔ **Tasks:** A list of all the to-do items. This is essentially another view of the same information stored in the Calendar.

Microsoft has added a few new capabilities to Outlook and posted them on the Microsoft Web site. Download the Internet Mail Enhancement Pack from `www.microsoft.com/OfficeFreeStuff/Outlook/` before you go even one step further. We mean it! What? You want us to convince you to download the upgrade? Among other things, Outlook lets you check mail from more than one Internet mail account at the same time. Oh, and the current version is a ticking time bomb, preparing itself to destroy your computer and everything in your office that starts with the letter *M,* unless you upgrade.

Making the Outlook bar work for you

If you're going out to a movie, you'll probably wear something different from what you'd wear to wash your car. At least, you'd put on your cleanest *Where Do You Want to Go Today?* T-shirt, right? Well, in a similar way, you can change the look of the Outlook bar depending on what you're doing with Outlook. While you'll probably want to stick with the Outlook applications, you can display mail folders, and folders on your hard disk in the Outlook bar.

If you're thinking of opening a pub and calling it the Outlook Bar, just remember: Dave thought of it first.

Why the heck would you want to add things to the Outlook bar? Aside from the fact that you can, which is good enough for us, doing so is convenient, particularly if you find that you keep Outlook running all the time. Try this:

1. **Click the Inbox in the Outlook bar to make sure that you're in the e-mail module.**

2. **Find the Outbox in the list of mail folders, drag it to the Outlook bar, and drop it in an available space.**

3. **Click the new Outbox in the Outlook bar.**

    Notice that you switch immediately to that folder in the e-mail module.

You can also add folders from your hard disk to the Outlook bar. Just right-click the bar and choose Add to Outlook bar (see Figure 5-2). Then find the folder you want to add and click OK. When you click the folder icon, Outlook works like Windows Explorer, allowing you to copy and move files, start programs, and use the Quick View file viewer.

Figure 5-2:
Customize
the Outlook
bar by
adding
groups and
folders.

You can organize your Outlook bar into different categories. Three categories come with Outlook by default: Outlook, Mail, and Other, but you can add more by clicking the right mouse button and choosing Add New Group from the menu.

You can also rearrange the icons in the Outlook bar. That lets you put the ones you use the most often right up on top. Just drag the icon to another place in the bar. A line appears between other icons that show when you can drop it in a new location.

Changing Outlook's options

Outlook has a zillion (okay, not a zillion, but, um, considerably more than four) options you can configure to fine-tune the way the program works. They're all accessed from the Tools⇨Options menu. Most of them are self-explanatory, but we wanted to bring Archiving to your attention.

Because old e-mail, journal entries, notes, and so on, tend to add up faster than the national debt, Outlook *archives* (copies, and then hides) everything except contacts in a separate, compressed file after a period of time.

You don't want your contacts to be archived because people's names and phone numbers don't expire the same way that e-mail and appointments do. You therefore won't find an AutoArchive tool in the Contacts module.

That way your hard disk doesn't fill up with Outlook data that you no longer use. Here's how to configure the AutoArchive tool:

1. Right-click the Inbox icon in the Outlook bar and choose Properties.

2. Click the AutoArchive tab (see Figure 5-3).

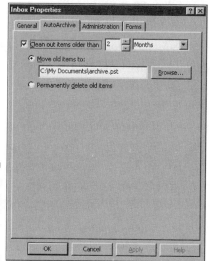

Figure 5-3:
Let Outlook
haul your
trash away
automatically.

3. Choose a time period that sounds reasonable for getting rid of your old mail.

Three or six months are probably about right for most people.

4. Make sure that the check box is selected to enable AutoArchive.

5. Click OK.

6. Repeat Steps 1-5 for every module in Outlook: Calendar, Journal, Notes, and so on.

Each module can have a different AutoArchive schedule.

Not only is each of the modules archived at a different rate, but also are each and every folder in the e-mail module. Set the AutoArchive time for each module.

When Outlook performs its regular AutoArchive session, the data isn't thrown away; it's stored in a compressed data file on your hard disk. You can always go back and find something that has been archived if you decide you need it.

Delete items from your archives periodically to keep the size of the archive file to a managable size.

Before you can read that old archived stuff, though, you first have to enable some other options (no one said it was going to be easy, but after this little hiccup, trust us, the process gets better):

1. **Choose Tools➪Services and click the Add button.**

2. **Choose the Personal Folders service from the list.**

3. **Select the archive file (usually C:\My Documents\archive.pst).**

4. **Close all the dialog boxes, and you're done.**

Now you'll have a new category in the Outlook bar called Personal folders. Open this folder, and you'll see entries for Inbox, Journal, Notes, and so on. This stuff allows you to see archived data from each of those modules.

If you have more than one item in Outlook named Personal Folders, you may get confused, but you can't change the name from within Outlook. Instead, Choose Start➪Settings➪Control Panel➪Mail and Fax, and select the Personal Folders that holds your archived data. Choose Properties and rename it there.

Throw Away That Teletype — Now You Have E-Mail

Outlook is, first and foremost, an e-mail program. Unlike many e-mail programs, however, you can use Outlook to read and send messages not just via the Internet but also via the Microsoft Network, Microsoft Mail, CompuServe, AOL, and fax. In fact, the only kinds of communication it doesn't handle are voice calls and that English-to-Klingon translation thing that they use on Star Trek.

This reminds of the Klingon courtroom scene in *Star Trek VI,* where the prosecuting, Shakespeare-quoting Klingon yells at Kirk, "Don't wait for the translation — just answer the question!" We've had bosses like that.

Setting up e-mail

How do you configure Outlook to handle all those message types? You add a message service to Outlook for each kind of mail that you want to get. Most of them come with Outlook, but as new ones are created, like that Klingon thing, you'll need to download them from the Microsoft Web site first.

To add a message service to Outlook:

1. Choose Tools➪Services.

You'll see the services dialog box, with a list of all the message services currently installed, as in Figure 5-4.

2. Click the Add button.

3. Choose a service, such as Fax or Internet Mail.

4. Fill in all the requested information.

In some cases, like Internet Mail, you may need to get additional information from your Internet Service Provider (ISP) before you start. In particular, you'll need to know the SMTP (outgoing) and POP (incoming) mail server names, and the record labels that own the rights to appearances by certain popular recording artists.

5. When you're done, close Outlook and reopen it so that the new service is initialized.

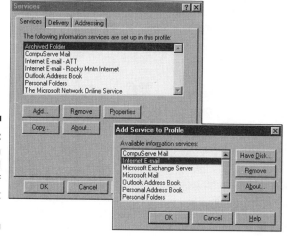

Figure 5-4:
Outlook can check mail from a lot of different sources.

You can find services for AOL and CompuServe at Microsoft's Web site.

Sending and receiving e-mail

Ready to enter the communications superhighway? Well, for goodness sake, don't forget to use your turn signal judiciously.

To send e-mail:

1. Click the Inbox icon so that you're in mail.

2. Click the New Mail Message button in the toolbar.

A blank message appears. The one in Figure 5-5 has the AutoSignature tool enabled.

3. Type an address in the To line.

If you already have names in the address book, you can type a few letters of the recipient's name and then click the Check Names button to finish the address. If you type more than one recipient, separate them with semicolons.

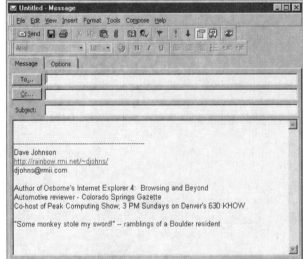

Figure 5-5:
A blank
e-mail
message,
ready to be
filled in.

4. Type a subject and some information in the body.

5. Click the Send button in the toolbar.

In addition to the To line, you can insert names on the Cc line as well. That's shorthand for *carbon copy,* meaning that you're sending this message for informational purposes. You might send To your boss, but Cc your co-workers, for example. If you want to send a message to several people, but want to hide the recipients' names from one another, put them on the Bcc, or *blind carbon copy* line. You may need to enable the Bcc line in a message using the View➪Bcc Field menu item.

When mail arrives in your Inbox, you have several options:

✔ **Throw it away and take an early retirement.** Who needs this kind of aggravation, anyway? Just click the message and press Delete.

✔ **Read the preview.** If Outlook is set to display messages with AutoPreview, then you can get the gist of the message by reading the first few lines in the Inbox, and then throw it away. Who needs this kind of aggravation, anyway?

✔ **Reply to the message.** Click the message so that it is selected, and then click the Reply button in the toolbar.

You can respond to everyone in the message at once using the Reply to All button. Be careful that you don't use Reply to All by mistake, however. You may accidentally send a potentially private reply to everyone who received the original.

✔ **Forward the message.** Select the message and then click the Forward button. You can then send the message to someone else.

If a message contains an attachment (like a Word file, spreadsheet, or a digital picture of Sandra Bullock), replies don't include the attachment. Forwarded messages, however, take the original attachment along for the ride.

✔ **Print the message.** Select it and click the Print icon. Then give the hard copy to your assistant and take off early. After all, who needs this kind of aggravation, anyway?

Add a distinctive signature tag to each e-mail you send by using the Tools⇨AutoSignature command (see Figure 5-6).

Figure 5-6:
Give your
messages a
distinctive
closure
with Auto-
Signature.

Organizing your e-mail so that you can find a message later

If you're anything like the average American, you drink three cups of coffee each morning and lose your car keys twice each week. (Apologies to our international readers.) Your e-mail doesn't stand a chance unless you organize it. The easiest way to get your e-mail cleaned up is to create additional folders in which to store it — one Inbox doesn't quite cut the mustard in terms of raw sorting power. To create new folders:

1. **Right-click a folder, like the Inbox or the top-level Personal Folders.**

   A drop-down menu appears.

2. **Select Create Subfolder from the menu.**

3. **Name the new folder something descriptive, like** Invoices, Personal, **or** Weird Rambling Hate Mail.

Don't keep your Weird Rambling Hate Mail. It will only turn you into a bitter, paranoid journalist.

Now you can drag mail from the Inbox into your new folders, making the mail easier to find. You can even configure the Rule Wizard to move certain mail (such as mail from a specific person, or with certain words in the subject line) to those folders automatically. Just imagine how you can discard junk mail before you even have to see it. Check out Chapter 17 for instructions on how to use the Rules Wizard.

Your Rules Wizard menu item (in the Tools menu) is not available? You need to download the Rules Wizard program from Microsoft's site at www.microsoft.com/OfficeFreeStuff/Outlook/. Once installed, the Rules Wizard lets you automatically perform actions on mail based on rules, like File all mail from Todd and Dave in the Deleted Items folder.

In addition to folders, you can sort and arrange mail, as well as everything else in Outlook, with Categories. Categories provide tremendous control over how you view and store information in Outlook. Using a master list of categories like Work, Leisure, and Responses to Weird Rambling Hate Mail, for instance, you can file messages and look at just the ones you need at any given time.

Creating a categories list

The master categories list is found at Edit⇨Categories. You can add new categories or delete ones you don't need by clicking the button marked Master Categories List (see Figure 5-7). To add a new category, simply type the name of the new category in the New Category box at the top and press Enter. Delete a category by clicking on the desired name, and then click Delete.

Reset returns the list to the default entries supplied by Microsoft. This is useful if you accidentally delete important categories and want to get back to where you started. When you're done, click OK until you're back to Outlook.

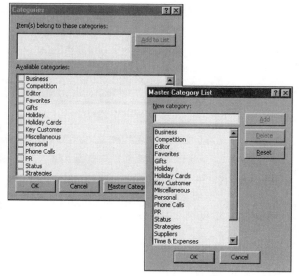

Figure 5-7:
Create
categories
to more
easily sort
your
Outlook
data.

If you reset your categories, you delete any new ones you added. Make sure that's what you want to do!

Assigning categories

After you establish categories, you'll want to use them. Right-click a message, contact, journal entry, or any kind of Outlook object, and select Categories. The category list appears and allows you to assign the object to one or more categories. Click OK when you're done.

Viewing e-mail by category

Now that you've gone to all the trouble to set up categories, here comes the payoff. You can configure your Inbox to display messages by category (see Figure 5-8) by following these steps:

1. **Choose View⇨Group By.**

   A Group By dialog box appears.

2. **Choose Categories from the drop-down Group Items By menu.**

3. **Click OK.**

After you set up this category system, you can assign new mail to categories without opening the category list. Simply drag your new mail into the desired category. You can use the Plus and Minus buttons on each category separator to expand and collapse the categories.

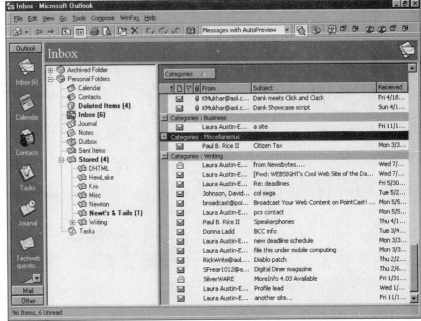

Getting Organized with the Calendar

So you want to start a rock and roll band? Oops — sorry, wrong book.

So you want to throw away that stupid paper day planner and get rid of all those yellow stickies with cryptic messages like *3 p.m. meeting, invite jhddjakd.* Well, you're in luck because Outlook has a Calendar module that lets you track tasks, appointments, and events, complete with desktop reminders. You can even print them, punch holes in the paper, fish the day planner out of the trash, and snap the pages in.

When you're in the Calendar module, you'll find the left side of the screen unchanged. It still displays the Outlook bar. As you can see in Figure 5-9, the right side is divided into three zones: a daily schedule down the middle, with a monthly calendar atop a list of to-dos. While the display looks simple, you can do a lot of things here, and do them many ways.

Creating appointments, meetings, and events

You can use Outlook to schedule major events throughout your day and get timely reminders before they occur. To schedule an appointment:

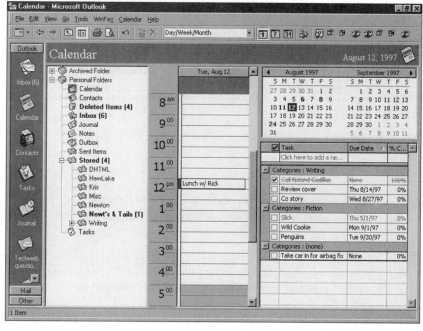

Figure 5-9:
Outlook's
Calendar
displays
appointments,
tasks, and
daily
events.

1. **Position the pointer over the time of day that you want to schedule an appointment, and drag the mouse through the length of meeting you want.**

   The slot turns blue to indicate it is selected.

2. **Right-click the slot and choose New Appointment.**

   A dialog box appears, as shown in Figure 5-10.

3. **Type a descriptive title in the Subject line.**

   This is how the appointment appears on-screen.

   Optionally, you can type a location for the appointment, or add extra notes in the large text area at the bottom of the dialog box.

4. **If you want to be reminded of this appointment, select the Reminder check box in the middle of the dialog box.**

   You can click the drop-down box to the right of the Reminder check box to set how early the reminder occurs. The default is 15 minutes.

5. **If you want to change the start or end time of the appointment, do so in the drop-down menus that are provided to adjust either the date or time.**

6. **When you have finished setting up the appointment, click the Save and Close button at the upper-left part of the dialog box.**

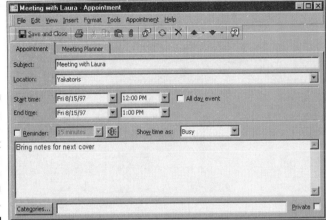

Figure 5-10:
The
Appointment
dialog
boxes give
you room
for notes.

The procedure for creating meetings and events is essentially the same. Meetings are just like appointments, except that you can invite others. Open a new meeting request the same way that you did an appointment. Notice that an additional line labeled To: appears above the dialog box. Click the To: button, and you can add e-mail recipients to the meeting. Recipients receive an invitation to the meeting you set up via e-mail.

Events are a bit different from appointments or meetings in that they are associated with a day, not a time. Open a new event dialog box with the right mouse button as explained in the preceding steps. Notice that the dialog box is similar to the one for appointments, except that it has no start and stop time.

If you open a new appointment by accident, you can turn it into an event by selecting the check box marked All Day Event.

Creating tasks

Not everything you need to do can be scheduled into a specific time of day. Events are useful for marking the entire day, such as a training day, or the annual Sheepherder's Convention. The bread and butter of a PIM, however, is its ability to list, sort, and track the myriad tasks that we all have to do every day. Going to the post office, getting some cat food, and firing Ed are all examples of tasks you may choose to track in Outlook. To create a task, follow these steps:

1. **Move the mouse over the task list region of the screen and click with the right mouse button.**

2. **Choose New Task.**

   A dialog box appears, as shown in Figure 5-11.

3. Name the task in the Subject line and assign a due date, if appropriate.

You can add extra details in the large text box, if you want.

4. Click the Save and Close button to exit.

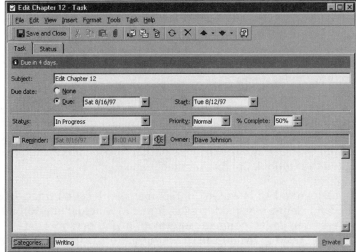

Figure 5-11:
You can
track the
status of
tasks within
Outlook.

Displaying tasks

Outlook gives you a lot of power to track your tasks. You can enter priority
and percent complete, for instance, to keep tabs on which tasks are most
important and how close to completion they are.

You can modify the way the tasks display on-screen to help you track your
progress. Choose View⇨Taskpad Settings⇨Show Fields. A dialog box lets
you customize the displayed fields. Move the fields you want to see, like
Percent Complete, from the left side of the dialog box to the right and click
OK. The Calendar view will update to the requested fields.

Want to see more than two months at a time on the Calendar module? Grab
the bottom of the monthly calendar pane, and drag it down. You'll sacrifice
some taskpad space (the part of the screen that shows your tasks), but you
can see four or more months at once.

Keeping in Contact with Clients and Suppliers

In the Middle Ages, knights exchanged greetings with a sword, staff, or axe raised above their head, and a business card extended with their other hand. When the opposing knight reached out in friendship to take the business card, the first knight would invariably lower the weapon, killing the enemy instantly. It was a good trick that avoided a lot of dangerous jousts and saved on expensive business card paper (and hand printing services offered by monks).

For whatever reason, we continue to use archaic business cards, despite the ever-present danger that the bearer will lower a deadly weapon in the act of exchanging them. At least we've mostly moved past the ancient Rolodex (let's not even get into the dangers of that horrific Inquisition device) and adopted the Outlook Contact module instead.

This full-featured and flexible Contact manager lets you track details that go far beyond simple e-mail addresses. It includes fields for addresses, phone numbers, Web pages, company information, and personal data. You certainly don't need to include all that information; just type what you have or need. You can always go back and add more information later.

To create a Contact entry:

1. **Click the Contact icon in the Outlook bar.**

2. **Find an empty space in the Contact display area and double-click.**

   A blank Contact entry opens, as shown in Figure 5-12.

3. **Type the individual's name.**

   By default, the name is rearranged into Last, First format in the File As line. The latter is the way it appears on the Contacts screen.

   When creating a new contact, the first name you type into the dialog box, whether it is the company name or individual's name, is the default name that Outlooks uses to file the contact.

4. **Type an e-mail address and press Enter.**

   Outlook verifies that the address is formatted properly and underlines it. If it is formatted wrong (perhaps it is missing a .com extension, for example), a dialog box appears to help you correct it.

5. **Type a phone number.**

6. **Click the <u>S</u>ave and Close button to leave the dialog box.**

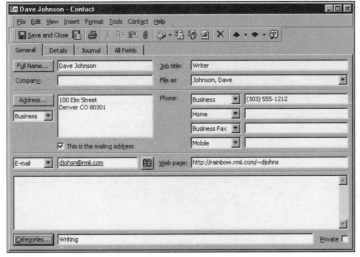

Figure 5-12:
Outlook's
Contact
manager
allows you
to type
tons of
information
on every
individual.

When you get new e-mail, you can add the sender to your Contacts list. Just right-click their name in the From box and choose Add to Contacts. A new Contact dialog box opens, with the name and e-mail address already filled in.

You can reopen the contact at any time, and type more data or edit information that you already provided. Simply find the entry and double-click the name.

You can customize the information that you input many ways. The Details tab, for instance, has additional data you can type. And if you have different phone numbers than the ones displayed on the General tab (such as two business lines, for example), just choose the phone number descriptions you want from the drop-down menus. You can create your own user-defined fields by going to the All Fields tab and choosing New at the bottom of the dialog box.

You can easily add additional contacts for the same company. Choose a contact and right-click on it. Then choose New Contact from Same Company on the menu.

Finding contacts

Need to find a contact fast? Just switch to the Contacts module and click the Find Items button in the toolbar. Type a search phrase, like **IDG** or **Pizza Hut**, and select Frequently-Used Text Fields in the In text field. Then click Find Now. Use Frequently-Used text to ensure that your search text is found, no matter where you typed it in the Contact (see Figure 5-13).

Figure 5-13:
The Find
tool in
Contacts
lets you find
individuals,
based on
text you
entered
anywhere
in their
sheet.

Don't forget that you can categorize contacts just like e-mail, and if you have
several hundred contacts, sorting them according to categories is a real
lifesaver for finding names quickly. But then again, if you have several
hundred contacts, what are you doing sitting in front of your computer?

What good are contacts, anyway?

You can use the Contacts list many practical ways, and a few impractical
ways as well. We won't dwell on the impractical ones (they involve goldfish,
a pickup truck, and phonograph needles), but you can certainly use Contacts as a launching point for all the ordinary messaging you do each day.

Placing calls with the AutoDialer

You can use your computer as an autodialer for names in your Contact list.
Choose this option, and Outlook dials the contact's phone number. To use
AutoDialer, follow these steps:

1. **Select the desired contact and choose AutoDialer from the right
   mouse button's context menu (see Figure 5-14).**

   The New Call dialog box opens.

2. **If the contact has more than one phone number, choose the appropriate number from the drop-down menu.**

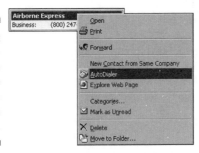

Figure 5-14:
Use the
right mouse
button to
perform
actions on
contacts.

3. **If you want to keep a record of the phone call, be sure to select the check box for Create New Journal Entry when Starting New call.**

4. **When you're ready to place the call, click the Start Call button.**

   When the number begins to dial, the Call Status dialog box opens.

5. **Click the Talk button, pick up your phone, and wait to begin to talk.**

6. **If you chose to record the call in the Journal, type any notes you want in the large text box and click the Save and Close button when you are done with the call.**

   The record of the call is stored on your computer forever.

Outlook has a speed dial! Add a number to the speed dial list from the New Call dialog box — just click the Dialing Options button and type the name and number. Then dial from the AutoDialer button in the toolbar.

Explore your contact's Web page

Another way you can use Contacts is to automatically surf to someone's corporate or personal Web page. Simply choose Explore Web Page from the right mouse button menu. Outlook launches your Web browser and sends it directly to the site you typed in the Contact file.

Send e-mail to your contacts

You can use Outlook as a personal address book when sending and receiving e-mail. Here are two ways to send e-mail to someone in your Contact module:

✔ Type a part of the recipient's name in the To box and click Check Names. The address is automatically corrected.

✔ Select an individual in the Contact module and choose New Message to Contact from the toolbar.

Record Your Every Move with the Journal

A generally accepted scientific conclusion is that, had he used a Journal, Gilligan wouldn't have gotten stranded. Likewise, those people from the TV show *Lost in Space* would have found their way home without having to stop on that planet with the giant iguana.

Do you need to account for your time? Do you want to log all your phone calls, or at least the important ones and keep track of who said what? Do you want to know how long you worked on particular documents for precise invoicing? Outlook's Journal lets you do all this without much effort on your part.

Configuring the Journal

Before you can start tracking all these things in Outlook, you have to turn it on first. To enable the Journal feature in Outlook, follow these steps:

1. **Choose Tools⇨Options and click the Journal tab.**

2. **Select the types of activities you want to appear in the journal.**

   Four main areas need to be configured in this dialog box, as shown in Figure 5-15:

   - **Automatically record these items.** This list in the upper-left determines which kinds of tasks you want to record in the Journal. You'll probably want to select just E-mail Message, but you can also mark items like Meeting and Task Requests. If you check these items, every time you invite someone to a meeting or give them a task to do, it shows up in the Journal.

   - **For these contacts.** The upper-right section lists all the names in your Contacts database. Journal entries are established just for e-mail you send to, or receive from, these people. If you later add names to Contacts, you'll need to revisit this Options dialog box and select their check boxes. All names are not selected by default.

   - **Also record files from.** This is where you let the Journal track when and how long you use each of the applications from Microsoft Office.

   - **Double-clicking a journal entry.** When you double click a journal entry, do you want to open the journal's dialog box that has additional information about the activity or just open the document that you were working on?

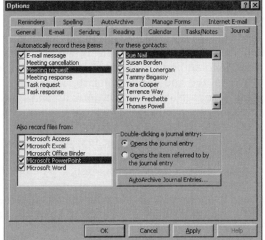

Figure 5-15:
Configure
the Journal
Options
before
using the
Journal.

Viewing the Journal

Now that the Journal is configured, close the Options box and investigate the Journal itself. You can view it by clicking the Journal button in the Outlook bar. You see a timeline that is divided into a series of horizontal segments. Each segment contains a timeline for a specific activity, such as e-mail, Word documents edited, and meetings requested. You can modify the view to suit your taste. Try these options:

- **Expand and collapse timelines.** Use the Plus or Minus sign to the left of the Entry Type on each horizontal segment to expand and collapse the display.

- **Change the scale.** By default, the Journal shows a week at a time on the screen. If you spend a lot of time in the hot tub, this may be okay, but a large number of events will crowd this view so that it is nearly illegible. The toolbar has day, week, and month views to see more or less on-screen at once.

- **Change the view settings.** You'll find a drop-down menu to the left of the day, week, and month buttons in the toolbar. The default is By Type, though you may prefer the more tabular views like Entry List or Last Seven Days, which show all your combined activities in strictly chrono-logical order. You can switch between any of these views on the fly, so don't worry about experimenting.

Using the Journal

Now you're finally ready to use the Journal. Anything in the Journal can be referenced later, to check on notes you've made, how long you worked on the activity, and even to load and edit documents, for example. Scroll to a Word document that you edited and double-click the icon in the Journal. An e-mail type of dialog box opens. Notice that Outlook displays the person who edited the document (you, probably) as well as how long the document was open. If you double-click the document's icon, the document is loaded into Word. Finally, you can add notes in the large text box for future reference.

Because each of Outlook's tools is tightly integrated, they can share information with each other. Switch back to Contacts, for example, and open a name from the database. Click the Journal tab, and you find a complete history of the messages you exchanged. This makes it a snap to keep an audit trail of the calls, e-mails, and documents you exchanged.

If you delete a document from the hard disk, the associated Journal entry still shows you information about when you worked on it. You won't be able to view or edit the document from the Journal, however.

Those Little Yellow Sticky Things

How many times have you wanted to jot down a note to yourself but you didn't have a place to write it? If you keep Outlook open all the time, you can take advantage of its Notes function to jot down messages on little yellow stickies:

1. **Click the Notes icon in the Outlook bar.**

2. **Double-click anywhere on the right side of the screen.**

    A note pad appears.

3. **Type your message.**

4. **Click the note's close box in the upper-right corner to close it.**

Want to rename a note? Notes take the first line of text as their title, so simply open the note and change the first line to any text you want. You can change the color just as easily. Just click the Control button in the upper-left corner of the note and select Color. Then pick the color you prefer.

Chapter 6
Truckin' with Automap

- -

In This Chapter

▶ Finding your way around

▶ Finding your way home (Steve Winwood would be proud)

▶ Customizing maps for clients

- -

*W*hen we first heard that Microsoft decided to feature a route-planning program with Office Small Business Edition, we were taken aback. We asked ourselves why Microsoft was going to do this. Did it need to sell copies of Automap, and bundling it with Office was the best way to do that? Or perhaps Microsoft has the perception that entrepreneurs tend to get lost on the way to office supply stores. Or maybe — maybe — they used the same focus group that sold IBM on the PCjr back in the '80s.

Eventually, we came to our senses. This is a pretty smart bundle when you consider how much time we all spend on the road. You can use Automap to find distant locations, plan routes, learn about other cities, and create customized maps for clients. What more could you ask for?

Finding Your Way Around

Automap is one of the more intuitive programs that have graced the Microsoft Office suites. It includes a limited number of options and really cool ToolTips that clearly explain most of the program's controls. They're better than the traditional ToolTips because they actually explain what the feature does instead of providing a one-word description.

Automap begins on its main screen (see Figure 6-1). This screen provides a one-click jump to all the major activities you can perform within Automap.

Figure 6-1:
The Automap main screen has buttons for all the program's major features.

Driving around the map

Time to get your feet wet with Automap by going to the Map view. From the main screen, click View the Map. The initial view is one of the entire continental United States (if you're in the know, you call it CONUS) with a toolbar at the top, which is shown in Figure 6-2. Don't worry, Alaska and Hawaii are fully represented; you need to pan over to them. Without further ado, we now talk about moving around this rock that we call Earth.

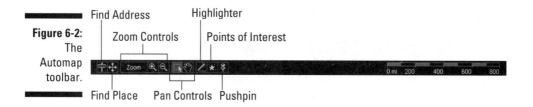

Figure 6-2:
The Automap toolbar.

Find Address
Zoom Controls
Highlighter
Points of Interest
Find Place
Pan Controls
Pushpin

Panning

You can move the map around two ways to see things that don't fit on your monitor. Pick the method you like best:

- ✔ **Move the mouse pointer to any edge of the screen.** Notice that the pointer becomes an arrow. Hold down the mouse button, and the map scrolls, or make one click at a time to move the map in small increments.

- ✔ **Choose the Hand button from the toolbar at the bottom of the screen.** The pointer becomes a hand, and you can *grab* the map and drag it around to your heart's content.

Adjusting the detail

Pretty map, eh? It may not display what you need to know, however. You can adjust the map to emphasize roads or geographic details. Choose View⇨Map Display. The Map Display dialog box appears, as shown in Figure 6-3. Click the Map Styles tab, and choose the format you prefer.

While you're in the Map Display dialog box, you can also adjust things that you want the map to display, using the other two tabs:

- ✔ **Points of Interest.** Select the kinds of places you want to display. You can still search for these items, even if you choose to hide them on the map display to reduce clutter.

- ✔ **Pushpins.** We talk about pushpins later in the chapter in "Adding pushpins to identify locations," but this is the tab where you decide which pushpins to display on the screen.

Figure 6-3:
Change the display options to customize the map.

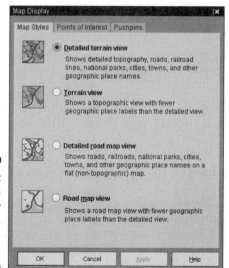

Zooming

At this altitude, you may not see much of anything, unless you're a secret spy satellite that can read the label off a bottle of aspirin from 250 miles in space. The first thing you want to do is zoom in to see cool stuff.

You have a few ways to zoom around the map, and which one you choose depends on your personal preference. Keep in mind that you can better use certain tools at different times.

✔ **Use the Zoom button in the toolbar for course adjustments.** This is a cool toy, but it isn't useful for precise zooming. When you click the button, you can drag a slider that positions you a certain altitude above the Earth's surface (see Figure 6-4). Zoom all the way to 8,700 miles, or down to a mile above ground level.

✔ **Use the Box tool to define a zoom region.** This is generally the best way to zoom. Draw a box around the area you want to include, and then click inside the box. The pointer is shaped like a magnifying glass, as shown in Figure 6-5.

✔ **Use the Zoom in and Zoom out buttons.** Each time you click the button, you zoom in or out one increment. This is handy for adjusting the map's magnification when you have the target in view.

✔ **Go all the way back to the CONUS map.** Choose View⇨Zoom⇨U.S. to return to the main map.

Figure 6-4:
Choose
your
altitude
to view
the U.S.

If you use the Box tool to define a zoom region and choose the wrong square, click the map anywhere outside your box to start over.

Getting a little help from your tools

Automap includes a few tools to help you tool around. Try these out:

✔ **Locator Map.** If you zoomed in and feel like you're getting lost in the woods, try the Locator. Choose Tools⇨Locator Map. A small window appears that shows the big picture of what your surroundings look like.

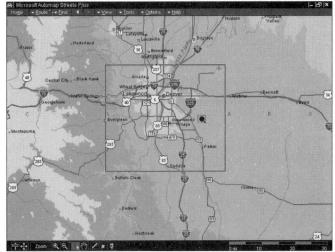

Figure 6-5:
The zoom
box is the
easiest way
to zoom in
Automap.

You can use the Locator Map to pan around the main map. Put the mouse in the Locator, and drag it around to your heart's content.

✔ **Location Sensor.** Another nifty tool is the Location Sensor. This tool senses if you're looking at somewhere like New Jersey and, if so, automatically shuts down. (Please, no Weird Rambling Hate Mail — Dave's originally from New Jersey and loves it there. Really — have a sense of humor about our lovely Garden State, okay?)

Seriously, the Location Sensor is found at Tools⇨Location Sensor, and it displays nifty information like the latitude, longitude, and time zone of the current location (see Figure 6-6).

✔ **Measuring Tool.** Do you need to measure the distance between points on the map? Choose Tools⇨Measuring Tool. Every time you click the mouse, the dialog box displays the cumulative distance measured from the very first click. This is great for finding the total length of a non-linear route.

If you're starting a new rock band, let me suggest that *Total Length of a Non-Linear Route* isn't a good name. Instead, go with *Isolinear Feedback* or *Hard Core Llama.*

If you want to permanently or semipermanently capture the path you're measuring on the map, use the Highlighter mode instead. It's discussed later in "Highlighting a route so that your clients can find you."

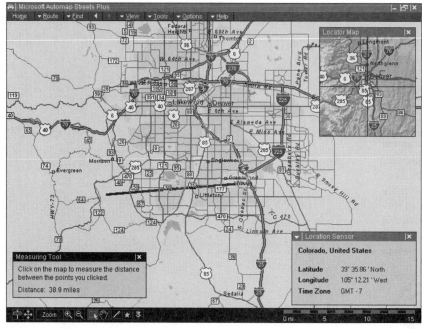

Figure 6-6:
The Locator Map, Location Sensor, and Measuring Tool are all enabled for your viewing pleasure.

Finding Your Way Home (Steve Winwood Would Be Proud)

Now that you know how to navigate the map, you can do something useful with your new skills. What do you do with a map program? If you're like Dave's wife, you'll spend hours looking up your old high school, finding out if that pizzeria is still at 5th and Main (in a town you haven't visited in 15 years), and exploring the digital domain.

Find an address, anywhere

The rest of us have things to do, like hiding in the shadows for hours, spying on our wives' computing habits so that we can later taunt them. For example, you have to make a trip across town, or even across the country, but you don't know where the office that you'll visit is. If you have an address, Automap can probably locate it precisely for you:

1. Click the Find an Address button in the toolbar.

The Find dialog box appears, as shown in Figure 6-7.

2. Type the address in as much detail as possible.

All of the addresses that come close to what you want appear in the dialog box.

3. If there is more than one match, scroll through the list until you find the entry you want and select it.

4. Click the OK button.

Automap immediately repositions you at the location you searched for.

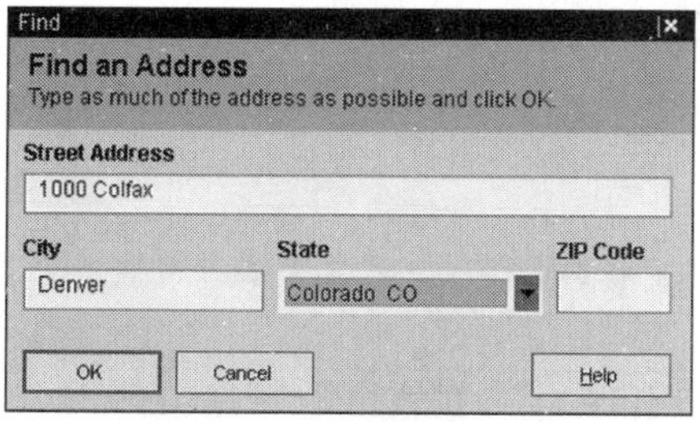

Figure 6-7:
Type the
address
that you
want to
pinpoint
with the
Find an
Address
tool.

Automap displays the location for you, complete with a pushpin that identifies the address it found. You can close the balloon that displays the address, and the pushpin won't be lost. In fact, you can later click the pushpin and choose the address from the list. The balloon reappears.

Find an Automap location

Automap keeps track of nearly every street address in the United States, but it also tracks a lot of other information: restaurants, points of interest, motels and hotels, airports, and city names. You can search for any of these items as easily as you do when you want to find a street address. Say you want to find the Denver Museum of Natural History, but you aren't even sure what state it is in:

1. Click the Find a Place button in the toolbar.

The Find a Place dialog box appear.

2. Type Denver Museum of Natural History **in the dialog box and click Locate.**

3. **Automap gives you a list of all the likely matches, as shown in Figure 6-8.**

    Didn't know there were so many things to do in Denver when you're alive, did you?

4. **Choose one and click OK.**

    The map again transports you to the appropriate location.

If you pick the wrong location, go back to the Find a Place button and try again. Or click the Undo button to go back to your previous location.

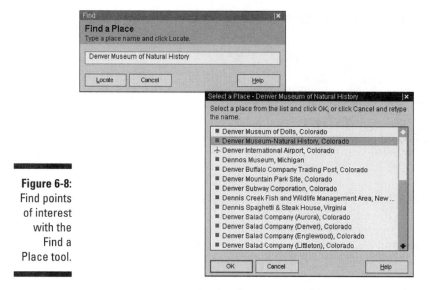

Figure 6-8:
Find points
of interest
with the
Find a
Place tool.

Customizing Maps for Clients

We recently overheard this conversation at a computer store's customer service desk:

(phone rings)

"Hello, this is Pinewood Computers. May I help you?"

"Hi, yes, is this Pinewood Computers?"

"Yeah."

"Cool."

"Hey."

"What?"

"Nothing."

"Oh."

"Sir, did you want something?"

"Oh, yeah. Who is this again?"

I don't know about you, but I don't want to be the guy giving directions to that customer over the phone. That's why you can create customized maps and print them out. That's right — Automap lets you generate maps for people who may benefit from a map with the route to a particular address, outlined for easy navigation.

Adding pushpins to identify locations

That caller who wants to know directions to the store is on the line. Wouldn't it be great if you could send a map that marked the spot? You know, like the way pirates used to mark their treasures (except that they used odd terms like *port, starboard, blow me down,* and *Har har*). Plus, they tended to bury their treasures in the exact spot where a minimall was due for construction a mere 100 years later.

If you ignore the most egregious of their crimes (and you're not big into parrots), you can borrow pirate mannerisms, and use Automap to create a custom map that marks the spot:

1. **Find a spot on the map that you want to mark with a pushpin.**

2. **Click the Pushpin button in the toolbar.**

3. **Click the map where you want to plant it.**

   A dialog box like the one in Figure 6-9 appears.

4. **Fill out the dialog box.**

   First, give the pushpin a title. Next, choose the kind of symbol you want the pushpin to appear as on the map. Then decide what kind of information you want to display:

   • **Name only:** No balloon is associated with this type of pushpin. Instead, the title appears in the drop-down menu when you click the symbol.

Figure 6-9:
Define the
way you
want the
pushpin
to look.

• **Balloon for short note:** If you want to add text, it appears in a balloon. You can close the balloon at any time and reopen it from the drop-down menu.

• **Window for long note with optional picture and Internet link:** This is the most flexible display option for lots of information. You can type and format text, insert graphics, and associate a Web site with the pushpin (see Figure 6-10).

4. Select a Pushpin Set from the drop-down list.

By default, new pushpins go in the My Pushpins category, but you can create new sets. A set is just a category — like a folder — that you store pushpins in to keep them organized.

If you choose to use the Window for Long Note option, you don't exactly get a word processor to work with. You right-click in the window to format the text and paste graphics into the window. Specifically for graphics, you open images in another program, select the Copy command, and then return to Automap and paste the image into the window.

You can also add pushpins for specific addresses, much like we describe in the section, "Find an address, anywhere." We kept a secret from you, though: You can add information to the balloon. When you find a new address and Automap first displays the new pushpin, click the pushpin and then type additional text.

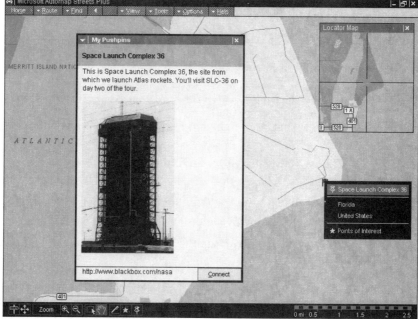

Figure 6-10:
You can make elaborate windows for your pushpins that include formatted text and images.

If you decide to change a pushpin display style after it's created, don't fret. Click the drop-down menu control on the pushpin's display and choose Properties. Change it to whatever style you like.

Dave's one and only pirate joke

An old pirate planned to retire and turn over his successful plundering and pillaging operation to his first mate. On that fateful morning, he welcomed the first mate into his cabin, explained his plan, and wished him well. The new captain stopped the old pirate as he started to leave the ship.

"Wait," said the new captain. "You haven't told me everything."

"Certainly I have," said the old pirate.

"Look here." the new captain said. "Every morning for the past twenty years, I've watched you rise and get dressed. Then before giving the crew your orders of the day, you unlock your top desk drawer, take out a piece of paper, read it carefully, return the paper, and then lock up the drawer. What's so important on that paper?"

"Oh, that," said the old pirate. "Here, see for yourself." He tossed the first mate a key, and left the ship.

The new captain rushed to the cabin, eagerly unlocked the drawer, and withdrew the secret paper. He unfurled it and read the weighty words: *Port is left. Starboard is right.*

Highlighting a route so that your clients can find you

To highlight a route, do this:

If you've already drawn a route, you need to erase it before creating this new one. Start (call it *Step Zero,* in honor of that famous Japanese monster that tried to beat up Godzilla) by choosing Route⇨Clear Route. Then proceed with Step 1.

1. **Choose Route⇨Highlight a Route.**

   The pointer changes to a pen, and a dialog box appears that tracks the total distance that you highlight.

2. **Mark the route with the pointer (see Figure 6-11).**

3. **When you're done, close the dialog box to end the highlighting session.**

You can easily adjust the view while highlighting. The entire route that you're drawing may not be visible on the screen, so you can use these tools to get the map to look just the way you want:

- Use the Arrow keys on the keyboard to move around.
- Use the Zoom tools with reckless abandon.
- Draw a box and zoom in. The highlighter is temporarily suspended while you draw the square.

After you create a route that you want to keep for future reference, you can save it. In fact, you can build an entire library of routes and load them whenever you need to. To save a route, choose Route⇨Save As and give it a descriptive name. Automap saves the filename with a .ASR extension.

Printing the map (because driving with a computer in your lap is hard to do)

After you create a map with custom pushpins and route highlights, you can print it for use away from the computer:

1. **Display the map the way you want it to print.**

   You can use the zoom and pan tools that we discussed earlier in "Finding Your Way Around" to change the map's appearance.

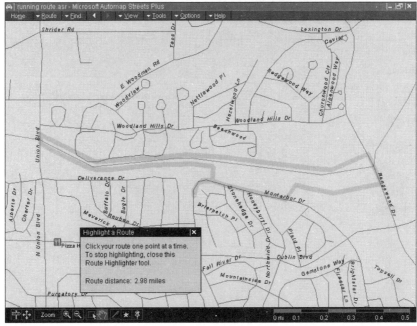

Figure 6-11:
Draw a
route on the
map and
save it for
future
reference.

2. **Choose Options⇨Print.**

   You see the Print dialog box, shown in Figure 6-12.

3. **Type an optional title for your map, which will appear on the printout.**

4. **Click the Optimize button.**

   The Print Optimization dialog box opens. This allows you to change the way Automap prints depending upon how much memory your computer has.

5. **Select a mode that reflects the memory your computer is equipped with.**

   You may need to do some test prints to see what works best for your system.

6. **Click Print and then start driving. Wait — first get in your car.**

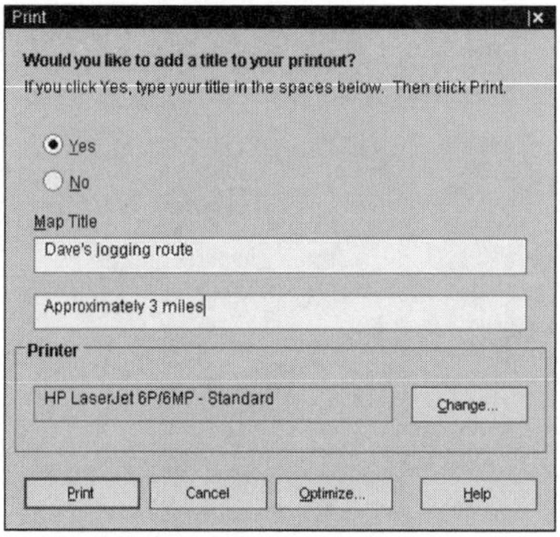

Figure 6-12:
They're not
trapped in
your
computer.
You can
print these
maps.

Print	|x|

Would you like to add a title to your printout?
If you click Yes, type your title in the spaces below. Then click Print.

- ● Yes
- ○ No

Map Title
Dave's jogging route

Approximately 3 miles

Printer

HP LaserJet 6P/6MP - Standard   Change...

Print   Cancel   Optimize...   Help

Chapter 7

Persuading with PowerPoint

. . . .

In This Chapter

▶ Finding your way around

▶ Creating your first slide show

▶ Importing graphics done by accountants in, like, WordPerfect 1.3

▶ Dressing up your presentation

▶ Actually delivering the presentation in front of, you know, other people

. . . .

*N*ot long ago, Dave worked as an instructor for satellite operators. At the start of Dave's career working for one of the most technological organizations on the face of the earth, the company used transparencies on overhead projectors to deliver training lessons. There was a TV the size of a drive-in theater to play movie clips from *Aliens* to inform students of the dangers of space operations ("They mostly come at night, mostly"). The classroom wasn't catapulted into the Space Age, however, until management hauled computers that could handle PowerPoint into the room.

Ah, those were the days. No more Kepler's Law, Trending Analysis, and hypergolic fuel discussions. Now, we have `General Protection Fault`, `Error Reading Drive A`, and `This Application Has Performed An Illegal Operation` messages. That's okay because the students started to get afternoons off while the instructors frantically searched for their old-fashioned overhead slides. The moral of the story is to always have a backup plan when using technology. The best backup plan is to keep the director's cut of *Aliens* handy in case the computer won't start.

But we digress. This chapter is all about PowerPoint. If you're a Small Business Edition owner, like Todd, you've probably noticed a problem: PowerPoint isn't on your hard disk. That's right, PowerPoint and Access (discussed in Chapter 8) are found in the Office 97 Professional Edition. If you need to make presentations (*Aliens* clips are optional), you'll need to purchase a stand-alone copy of PowerPoint or buy Office 97 Professional.

Getting Around in PowerPoint

PowerPoint works a bit differently than many other Office applications. When you first start the program, a start-up dialog box, shown in Figure 7-1, greets you. Here are your choices:

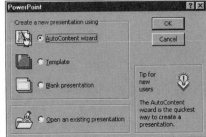

Figure 7-1:
The
PowerPoint
start-up
dialog box.

- ✔ **AutoContent Wizard:** Use this option to quickly build a presentation using a step-by-step wizard.

- ✔ **Template:** Choose from among a number of templates that cover many common presentation styles.

- ✔ **Blank Presentation:** You don't need no stinkin' help! Templates and wizards are for weasels! You know what you want, and by golly, you're going to do it — yourself!

- ✔ **Open an existing presentation:** Continue working on something you started.

You may want to open a recent file from the Recently Used list in the File menu, rather than use the Open an Existing Presentation button and find the file folder. Click the Cancel button on the start-up dialog box and open the presentation directly from the File menu.

The AutoContent Wizard

If you haven't created anything in PowerPoint, here are a few ways that you can start to create a presentation:

- ✔ Run around the office screaming, "Paper cut! Paper cut!" Someone will eventually volunteer to do some work for you.

- ✔ Make the presentation from scratch.

- ✔ Use the AutoContent Wizard to get started, and fine-tune the presentation later.

We recommend the first option, but unfortunately, it only works a few times. Then people start to ignore you. Eventually, you'll need to use the AutoContent Wizard. Here are two ways to start the wizard:

✔ Start the wizard from the start-up dialog box (refer to Figure 7-1).

✔ If you already moved past the startup dialog box, choose File➪New and click the Presentation tab. Select the wizard from the list of presentation files.

When you're in the wizard, you can simply answer its questions to craft a presentation:

1. **Choose a presentation based on choices like Corporate, Projects, or Sales/Marketing (see Figure 7-2).**

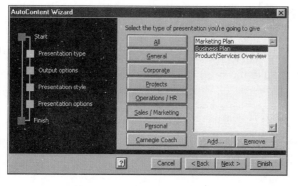

Figure 7-2:
Choose a type of presentation using the AutoContent Wizard.

If you create your own presentation template, you can add it to the appropriate list in the AutoContent Wizard using the Add button.

2. **Select whether you want the presentation to be delivered before a group, or on the Internet.**

Depending on your selection, the document is formatted for live delivery, or in the form of a Web page.

3. **Decide whether the presentation is on 35-mm slide, overhead, or on-screen.**

If you choose the Internet presentation, the wizard skips this step. You can also elect to print handouts.

4. **Tell the wizard what kind of header information you want PowerPoint to place on every page.**

After completing the wizard, PowerPoint launches your presentation.

A room with a view

When you first start PowerPoint with the AutoContent Wizard, you're dropped into the Outline view. You may not like working in Outline view. Dave doesn't. Several views are at your disposal. Choose the View menu and pick the view that best suits you:

- ✓ **Slide:** This is a What You See Is What You Get (WYSIWYG) view of the current slide (see Figure 7-3). You can edit the slide and have a reasonable expectation that it will look the same when you deliver the presentation.

- ✓ **Outline:** This provides a text-based outline view of the entire presentation (see Figure 7-4). A thumbnail representation of the current slide appears on-screen as well, so you can see a preview of what you're doing to it.

- ✓ **Slide Sorter:** View all the slides at once. This view is handiest for rearranging slides in your presentation. Drag-and-drop the slides where you want the slides to appear.

- ✓ **Notes pages:** If you're the kind of person who uses notes when you make a pitch, use the notes page to record your speech. While you design the presentation, the notes appear on the same page as the slide itself, so you can easily keep things in context.

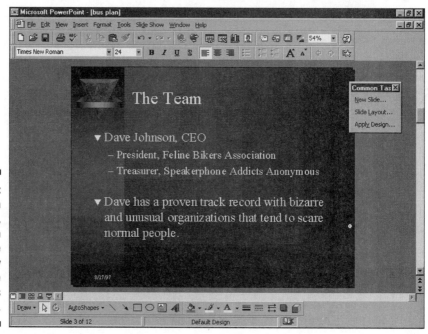

Figure 7-3:
Work in
Slide view,
in which
you can see
exactly
what the
slide looks
like.

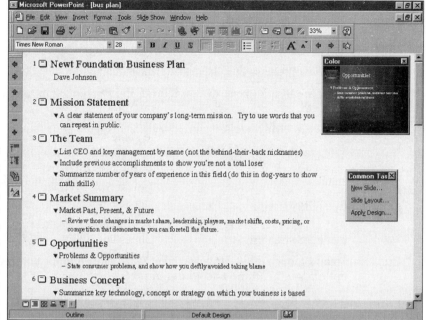

Figure 7-4:
Use the
Preview
window
while
working in
Outline
view to see
the slide's
appearance.

> ✔ **Slide Show:** This is a full-screen presentation of your slide show. Use this option to actually deliver the presentation or preview the show ahead of time.

Creating Your First Slide Show

Your presentation is due to the boss on whether cats are likely to purchase your company's new product. Time to get started. The boss, a cat lover, is waiting.

We know you're about to complain. After all, we showed you how to use the AutoContent Wizard to simplify your life, and now we take a step back and do it completely from scratch. In this process, you discover how you customize a presentation to suit your needs. Like they say, "Give someone a fish, food for a day. Teach him or her to fish, now that's a pointless hobby that will drain hours out of your life." Sounds like the woman in the "Door Opening and Closing" episode of *Star Trek* that could sap your life energy with a touch.

Or something like that. We were never very good with old sayings. Here's what to do:

1. **Choose File➪New.**

   The New Presentation Dialog box appears.

2. **Click the Blank Presentation icon in the Presentation tab, and click OK.**

3. **Choose a slide style for your very first slide.**

   Talk about desolate — you're really on your own now. The best choice is usually the very first one, laid out to display a title, as shown in Figure 7-5.

4. **Add some text.**

   Just click a text box (called a *placeholder*) and type. Be sure to type a name for your presentation.

5. **To add more slides, click the New Slide button and choose the second option — a headline and bulleted text.**

   A new slide — with space for a headline and bulleted text — appears onscreen.

6. **Type information in the placeholders and add slides as needed to complete the presentation.**

7. **When you're done, choose File➪Save As and save the presentation to your hard disk.**

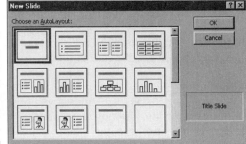

Figure 7-5:
Choose slides from the New Slide dialog box.

You can change the layout of a particular slide, from a headline to a text slide, for example, by clicking on the Slide Layout button. PowerPoint does its best to reformat the text you already typed into the new slide layout.

Changing the color scheme

Before you go any further, you need to change the background of your slides from plain white. Otherwise, your audience will gnaw their arms off to stay awake, and you don't want that, particularly if your company's payroll officer is in the audience.

One way to modify the background is to change the color. This is also helpful for making the slides more readable. To change the color of the slides, choose Format⇨Slide Color Scheme. The Color Scheme dialog box appears, as shown in Figure 7-6. You see a few selections. Choose the one you want and click Apply to All.

Figure 7-6:
Adjust the
color
pattern of
your slides
in the Color
Scheme
dialog box.

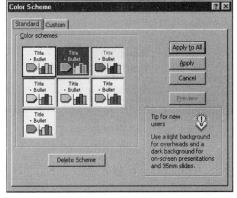

Generally, you want all your slides to have the same color scheme. You can choose to apply the color scheme to the current slide if you really want to, though.

You don't have to stick with plain old solid colors. If you prefer a pattern, choose Format⇨Apply Design. You see a dialog box full of color patterns that are sure to spice up your presentation (see Figure 7-7).

Designs override the color scheme you may have selected for your slides.

Using placeholders for text

You may have figured out that text in PowerPoint can only appear in a placeholder. You can't type anywhere on a blank part of the slide. Though using the Add Slide tool is a great way to format your slide, it has profession-ally formatted placeholders. After all, you can actually release that great artistic *placeholder muse* that you know resides deep in your psyche and add placeholders anywhere on the screen.

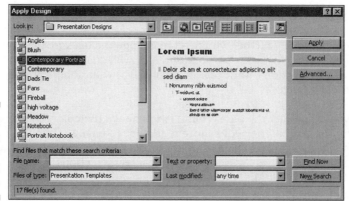

Figure 7-7:
Choose a
design from
this dialog
box.

Creating and editing a text box

To add a test placeholder to your slide, choose Insert⇨Text Box, draw a rectangle on the screen where you want the text box to appear, and then click the text box and begin typing. The box dynamically adjusts its size in response to how much you type (not unlike the way your belly dynamically adjusts in response to doughnuts).

A placeholder isn't permanently affixed on the slide; you can move it around. Grab the placeholder by its border and move it wherever you want. You don't have to size it because it automatically adjusts in size. Doughnuts, remember?

Formatting text

As in Word, you can change the appearance of text in PowerPoint. Unlike Word, though, we don't suggest using 11- or 12-point fonts very often — not unless you intentionally want to blind your audience in some misguided insurance scheme.

To change text formatting, select the text you want to change and make the appropriate choices from the toolbar (see Figure 7-8): Change the font, point size, emphasis (bold, italic, and so on), or the justification.

In general, the default font and format settings in PowerPoint are pretty good. If you insist on using the old adage, "If it ain't broke, you're not hitting it hard enough," never select a font for onscreen use smaller than 20-point, and test your slides from the back of the room to make sure they're legible.

Using bulleted text

One of the best ways to get your point across in a slide show is with bullets. By arranging your thoughts into bulleted points, you convey to the audience the distinct impression that you've given the topic at hand a lot of thought

Figure 7-8:
The
Formatting
toolbar.

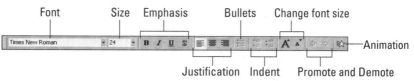

and carefully mapped out your argument. In fact, bullets convincingly mask the fact that you wrote the whole thing ten minutes before you entered the conference room.

To turn on bullets, either choose a layout that has a bulleted placeholder, or click a placeholder and then click the Bullets button on the toolbar. Every time you press Enter, you get a new bullet on the next line. To indent bullets, press the Tab key. Likewise, you can return to the outer level of bullets by pressing Shift+Enter.

Saving your presentation

In the Dim Times, before Microsoft invented the Save feature, everyone who made PowerPoint presentations also had to make an artist's sketch of their slide shows and carry the charcoal rendering into the presentation. Eventually, people stopped using PowerPoint and just used the drawings. So Microsoft added a Save button, and made all our lives a bit easier. You actually have a few ways to save your work:

- ✔ **File⇨Save As:** Save your presentation in the standard PowerPoint format. You can play it back in PowerPoint or the smaller PowerPoint Viewer.

- ✔ **File⇨Save As HTML:** Save the presentation as a set of Web pages that you can post on an Internet or intranet site.

- ✔ **File⇨Pack and Go:** Spend time on the road? Pack and go is the ideal solution if you're not going to deliver the presentation from your own hard disk. Using a step-by-step wizard, Pack and Go lets you bundle the slide show onto a set of floppies or a Zip disk and deliver it elsewhere.

Even though Pack and Go may sound like a bitter memory from a former member of the PowerPoint design team, it's actually a handy tool if your presentation computer isn't the same as your development computer. Create your presentation, and when you're ready to hit the road (or walk down the hallway), do this:

1. Choose File⇨Pack and Go.

Now you step through the wizard using the Next button (see Figure 7-9).

2. **Pick files to pack.**

   You can choose from the active file, which is the presentation currently open, or other presentations. Choose the latter if you want to pack several shows at once.

3. **Choose a destination.**

   Pick a drive to copy the files to. You can also copy them to a folder on your hard disk and move the files to a portable drive later.

4. **Decide if you want to include linked files and embedded fonts. That way, you're sure that the presentation plays properly on the other system.**

5. **Choose whether to include the PowerPoint viewer in the packed file.**

6. **Click Finish to close the Pack and Go dialog box.**

   It will save your presentation to floppy.

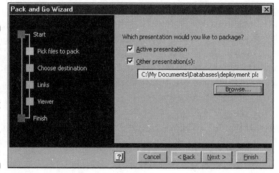

You can save space on the Pack and Go disk by not embedding fonts, linking files, or packing the PowerPoint viewer. The presentation may not play properly (or look the same) at the final destination, however, without those files.

When you reach your destination, insert the Pack and Go disks and run the file called **pngsetup**. This file extracts the PowerPoint files so that you can run your slide show.

Importing Graphics Created by Accountants in WordPerfect 1.3

You can use all kinds of graphics, charts, and tables in a PowerPoint presentation. Some placeholders, for example, are intended to hold images or charts.

Adding art to your presentation

PowerPoint includes a selection of clip art that you can feature in your presentation to liven things up. Double-click a clip art placeholder, for example, to launch the Microsoft Clip Gallery, a veritable cornucopia of stock clip art images.

Dave is pretty sure that *Veritable Cornucopia* opened for Derek and the Dominos in the late '60s.

On the other hand, you can let PowerPoint suggest art for you. Granted, this is a lot like asking Dave to select a jazz artist for this evening's entertainment, but humor us for a moment. When your presentation is more or less complete, you can let PowerPoint scan your slides for certain keywords that let the Pentium chip (an entity known to add 2 and 2 and get 3.9999) suggest appropriate images.

To give it a shot, choose Tools⇨AutoClipArt. Use the AutoClipArt dialog box, shown in Figure 7-10, to view the clip art for each keyword it matched. Select Insert from the AutoClipArt dialog box if you want to use it. The image is automatically inserted on the correct slide.

Figure 7-10:
AutoClipArt
chooses
images
for your
presentation.

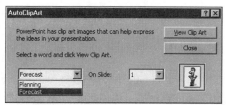

Adding line art to a slide show

Sometimes the easiest way to convey an idea is with simple line art: shapes, lines, and the occasional organizational chart. All these options are available from Insert⇨Picture.

Adding charts and graphs

You can also add fancy looking charts and graphs. We think this is a good thing because Todd's presentations typically need all the external credibility they can get (especially because most of them seem to focus on the relationship between a societal appreciation of jazz and increases in the U.S. Gross National Product). To add a graph:

1. **Double-click a placeholder or choose Insert⇨Chart.**

2. **Type the data you want to display on the datasheet (see Figure 7-11).**

   The *datasheet* is a simple spreadsheet that you can fill in to reflect data to display. Just enter numbers and headings in the columns and rows so that it conveys your intent — like explaining how many cows you milked each day in June. For a knock-your-socks-off explanation of datasheets, look in Chapter 11.

   If you have data, maybe from Excel or Lotus, that you want to import, delete all the data in the sample datasheet. Open your spreadsheet with the existing data and copy it. Then paste it into the datasheet.

3. **Right-click the chart and choose Chart Type from the menu.**

   A dialog box appears that offers you lots of choices for kinds of charts to use.

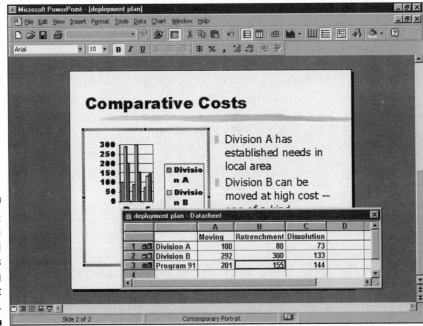

Figure 7-11:
Create charts and graphs using spreadsheet data.

4. Select the kind of chart you want to display (see Figure 7-12).

The chart immediately turns into the type you selected.

5. Right-click on the chart again and choose Chart Options.

Use this menu option to fine-tune the way the chart displays. Notice that the chart updates in real-time as you make changes.

6. When you're satisfied with your chart, click the PowerPoint slide.

The chart is then embedded in the Powerpoint slide.

To change the chart later, right-click the chart area in the slide, and choose Open Chart Object. Change it using the techniques we just discussed in Steps 3, 4, and 5.

Dressing Up Your Presentation

According to our calculations, you now know enough to be dangerous. To become a downright menace, that's what we're shooting for. Now you need to find out about adding some special effects to your slide shows. PowerPoint has a whole arsenal of tricks you can use to grab attention.

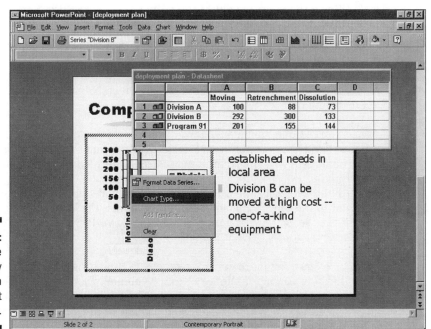

Figure 7-12: Change the chart to any of a dozen different styles.

Add pizzazz with animation

Here's what you'll need to collect before you start: a human brain, three eyes of a newt, a conductive metal lightning rod, and a medical gurney.

Excuse us. We were just reminded that we're animating, not *reanimating*. Sorry.

Okay, here's the deal: You can attach a variety of animation effects to any object on the screen, whether it's text, clip art, charts or graph, to help you make whatever point it is that you want to convey. You can let text dissolve onto the screen or fly in from the edge.

When displaying a bar graph, wouldn't it be, like, totally cool if the individual bars grew out of the x-axis baseline?

Have you noticed that Dave is one of the few people alive who believes that he can successfully pull off using the words *"be, like, totally cool"* and *"x-axis baseline"* in the very same sentence?

On a PowerPoint slide that has a few different elements, like text, clip art, and a bar graph, try this:

1. **Click a text box and choose Slide Show⇨Preset Animation⇨Dissolve.**

2. **Click a piece of clip art in the slide and choose Slide Show⇨Preset Animation⇨Camera.**

3. **Click the bar chart, and choose Slide Show⇨Preset Animation⇨ Wipe Up.**

Experiment with different, cool animation effects. You'll only learn what they do by trying them out.

When you're done, you may want to preview this new, hyperactive slide. Choose Slide Show⇨Animation Preview. A thumbnail of the slide appears, and animations you stored are demonstrated in the order you typed them.

PowerPoint's Preset Animation tool displays those animations that are relevant to the object you select. In other words, the Wipe Up command only makes sense in the context of a graph, so you won't see it when selecting clip art.

You can exert even more control over these animations. You may be happy with the slide you made the way it is, or you may want to fine-tune it. Choose Slide Show⇨Custom Animation. The Custom Animation dialog box appears, as shown in Figure 7-13, which gives you the ability to adjust your slide. The most important options are

✔ **Animation order:** The objects animate in the order in which you added the animation effects. To change the order, use the Up and Down arrows.

✔ **Timing:** What if you want the second effect to wait ten seconds before it does its thing? Or better yet, perhaps each effect should wait for a mouse click. Click the Timing tab and select the appropriate option.

Figure 7-13:
Use the
Custom
Animation
dialog
box to
rearrange
animations
or create
custom
effects that
go beyond
the tools in
the Preset
Animations
dialog box.

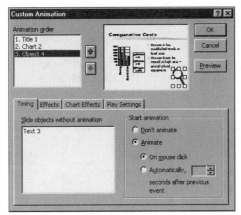

Add transitions to your slides

Do you, like Todd, spend a lot of time watching television for hidden messages from Zoltan, Leader of Planet Klaath? If so, you no doubt have observed that transitions (like fades, dissolves, and wipes) are very popular professional tricks you use to move from one scene to another. The transitions also disguise Zoltan's ongoing dialog with the Chosen. PowerPoint has the same ability to transition from one slide to another with a professional flourish.

To add a transition to your slide, choose Slide Show➪Slide Transition. The Slide Transition dialog box appears, as shown in Figure 7-14. In this dialog box you can select the kind of transition, how fast the transition occurs, and method for advance (such as when you click the mouse) that you want.

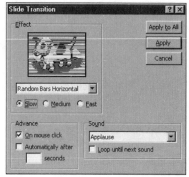

Figure 7-14:
Select transitions to smoothly move from one slide to another.

You can click Apply to apply transitions only to a particular slide, or click Apply to All to apply the transitions to all the slides at once. Slide Shows that use a different effect on every transition, however, have a decidedly unprofessional look to them, like an 8-year-old kid who spent too much time alone with his Dad's slide show before the big presentation. We recommend that you stick with a subdued, single transition approach.

Add interactive tools

Not all your presentations are going to be "Next slide, please," affairs. You may create kiosk or Internet presentations, for example. If that's the case, you need to know how to add interactive buttons to your slides. You can use these buttons to take the viewer to a specific slide, play sounds, visit a Web page, or even launch an application stored on the hard disk. To add a button, try this:

1. **Choose Slide Show⇨Action Buttons.**

   The Action Buttons palette appears with a wide selection of buttons that you can add to your show.

2. **Grab the Action Buttons palette by its title bar and drag it off the menu.**

   It becomes a free-floating dialog box. Cool, huh?

3. **Click a button and then use the mouse to define a square region on the slide where you want the button to appear.**

4. **If you haven't yet saved this slide show on your hard disk, a dialog box appears recommending that you do so now.**

Our experience is that if Microsoft asks you to save your work, you sure as heck ought to take them up on it. Kind of like the way cats can sense an earthquake, if you catch our drift.

5. Choose the action that you want the button to perform (see Figure 7-15).

Two tabs, Mouse Click and Mouse Over, are at your disposal. On each of those actions, you can:

- Visit a Web site.

- Run an application.

- Execute a macro (you first need to create a macro and save it).

- Perform an action with an OLE object that you embedded in your presentation (like an Excel spreadsheet, for example).

You can also play a sound in conjunction with any of these actions. After you close the Action Settings dialog box, notice a yellow diamond that appears next to the button. You can drag that diamond around to control how much 3-D effect the button displays.

Figure 7-15: Use the Action Settings dialog box to hyperlink between slides or perform advanced actions.

We don't suggest using the Mouse Over action setting very often. Mouse over means that whatever action you assign to a button happens as soon as the user moves the mouse pointer over the button. This action is counter-intuitive for folks who have grown up clicking things to suddenly find that a button does wacky stuff because the pointer passed overhead.

Actually Delivering the Presentation in Front of, You Know, Other People

You may be surprised to know that the fear of public speaking is the number one fear among Americans, even more so than the fear of death. You may also be surprised to know that we just made up that statistic.

Actually, the fear of public speaking ranks way up there, as evidenced by lots of surveys we couldn't track down at the moment. (We considered typing a fake Web address here and then pleading no contest when it seemed to be *down* when you visited the site. Fortunately, cooler heads prevailed.) Nonetheless, with PowerPoint, you can make your pitch with fewer jostled nerves.

Running the presentation

If you're running your presentation in PowerPoint, the easiest way to start the presentation is simply to choose Slide Show➪View Show. The slides play in sequence, changing every time you press the left mouse button. To go backwards, right-click the screen and choose Backwards from the menu.

Don't get nervous and click the mouse button several times. Some slides take longer to load. Clicking that mouse button a few times can get you totally lost when your show finally catches up with you.

Creating a custom slide show

Frequently, you may need to give similar presentations to different groups. Change a slide or two, and you can deliver the same presentation to your boss, your boss's boss, the janitor, and finally your client (see Figure 7-16). Instead of making a different PowerPoint presentation for each group, you can create a custom slide show in one:

1. **Choose Slide Show➪Custom Shows.**

2. **You won't already have any custom shows stored, so choose New.**

3. **Move the slides you want to show from the left side of the screen to the right side.**

   You can now rearrange them into any playback order you want using the Up and Down arrows.

4. **Give the custom show a name, like** For the Boss.

5. **Click OK.**

6. **Add as many custom shows as you need — just follow Steps 2 through 5 over again.**

When it's time to run your slide show, choose Slide Show⇨Custom Shows, and select the show you want to use. Then click the Show button — the show starts.

AutoPilot: Running PowerPoint on a timer

You can automate your slide show to run without any assistance from you. Sheesh — a few minutes ago all you had to do was hold the mouse and click. Now, you don't even need to show up.

Actually, automating your slide show comes in particularly handy for automated environments, like a trade show kiosk. You first need to tell PowerPoint how long to loiter on each slide. To do that, load your presentation, and choose Slide Show⇨Rehearse Timings. The presentation goes to full-screen mode, and a small timer appears in the corner. Simply proceed through the show at whatever pace you're trying to achieve. If you need to stop in the middle of the rehearsal — that coffee finally got to you, perhaps — click the Pause button.

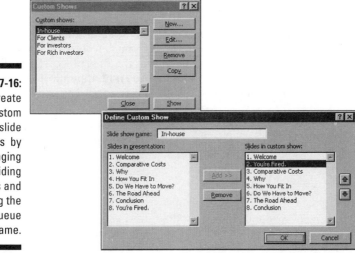

Figure 7-16: Create custom slide shows by rearranging or hiding slides and giving the new queue a name.

When you're done, PowerPoint applies those timings to your slide show. To run the slide show autonomously, simply choose Slide Show⇨Set Up Show and make sure that the button is selected for Use Timings, If Present. Then play the slide show normally.

Marking up slides like a sports commentator

In the course of a presentation, you may get bothered by annoying people who seem to be in the room for the express purpose of confusing and distracting you. They typically have important sounding comments like "observations," "questions," and worst of all, "action items."

You can use PowerPoint to take notes on these interruptions without leaving the slide show. In addition, you can mark up the slides, with the Pen tool, not entirely unlike a sports commentator draws on your television screen.

In fact, you have a lot of controls for customizing the display. When a presentation is running, try these options:

- **Draw with a pen:** Right-click the screen and choose Pen. The pointer is now a highlighter that you can use to draw and write on the screen. To change the pen color, right-click and choose Pointer Options⇨Pen Color. To resume your presentation, right-click and choose Arrow, or press the Spacebar.

- **Blank the screen:** If you need to digress, such as tell the wonderful pirate joke in Chapter 6, you may want to blank the display. Right-click and choose Screen⇨Black screen. Resume the slide show by choosing Screen⇨Unblack screen.

- **Take notes:** If you need to record comments during the slide show, right-click anywhere on the slide and choose Meeting Minutes. You can take freeform notes on the Meeting Minutes tab or add rigorous action items, including the assignee (hopefully you can throw the action items back to the clown that interrupted you in the first place). PowerPoint automatically creates an Action Items slide and appends it to the end of the slide show. You can also export the action items and minutes to Word.

Chapter 8

Be One of the First to Use Access

In This Chapter

▶ Fighting your fear of databases

▶ Getting around in Access

▶ Defining your database with tables

▶ Creating a form for data entry

▶ Using queries to learn stuff

▶ Telling the world about your data with reports

The fact is, people buy Office 97 Professional Edition, but they don't use Access (not that we've taken a survey or anything). When we say *fact,* we use the word in the same way that people often use the word *literally,* when they really mean *figuratively.* For example, they may say, "My dog was so hungry he literally chewed my leg off," when, in fact, nothing of the kind transpired. I guess we're saying that the word *fact* is used not to suggest actual, um, fact, but simply emphasis.

So the fact of the matter is that about three people use Access. All of them are disqualified, though, because they only used Access to write about it in other Office 97 books put out by this and other publishers. Just like we did — literally.

Access is the database program included with Office 97 Professional Edition. If you have any other editions, such as the Small Business Edition, you're off the hook. Skip ahead and read something interesting. If you must, read about databases in this chapter and then run out and buy a copy of Access so that you can very purposefully fail to use it.

But what is a database? Well, if you run a small business, all joking aside, a database may be the lifeblood of your company.

Why Be Scared of Databases?

Around town, and in many of the more exclusive nightclubs, people come up to us and admit that they're afraid of databases. Sheepishly, they look to us for support and guidance. We then have to admit to them that we're just as scared as they are. "There's good reason to be scared of Access," we said recently to a burly fellow, hardened by years spent in the Australian Outback. "But with some planning, you should survive creating a database," we consoled.

Our words proved fatally wrong, however. He didn't survive, but others can learn from his plight. You have two reasons to be very afraid of databases in general and of Access in particular. Of course, these reasons shouldn't keep you from attempting to create a database. These bullets may offer a bit of perspective:

- **Creating and maintaining a database is a lot of work.** Access makes creating basic databases somewhat easy. The databases that work for a small business, especially in point-of-sale situations, can take quite a bit of data entry, programming, and maintenance, however. Your records need to be well kept, mistakes need to be at a minimum, and you'll need a system for regular updating.

- **Databases require forethought.** Before leaping into database design, think very carefully about your needs. Of course, to do that effectively, you also need to know what you can do with Access and databases in general. We talk about getting the knowledge you need and planning for a database.

All about databases

Databases are for storing information. What's interesting about a database is that it stores information in a way that is unique. Consider, for example, that you can probably type and save information in a word processor without many hassles. The only problem may be cross-referencing items, like determining the status of a particular customer's order. You can store the customer information in one Word document, and the order information in another Word document, but how do you link the two bits of info?

Instead of using haphazard documents for storing information, a database uses a method referred to as a *table* for storing its data. Each table is made up of rows and columns, just like a spreadsheet document. To make matters just a bit more frightening, databases use different terminology to refer to the rows and columns. Each row is a *record,* and each column is a *field* (see Figure 8-1).

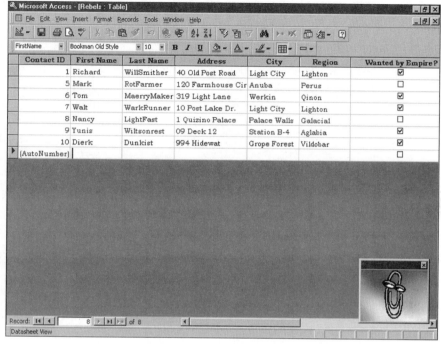

Figure 8-1:
Although
this table
is the
beginning
of a
database in
Access, it
looks quite
a bit like a
spreadsheet
in Excel.

If each row represents a record, what's a record? (Our children will be asking that same question one of these days when we break out some of our old Rolling Stones memorabilia.) A *record* is simply an entry that relates to a particular person, company, product, or idea, for example. A record is a full description of whatever noun you're tracking.

Take, for example, a database that is organized to track people who aren't properly allied with the glorious Empire. For each perpetrator of rebel lies, you create a record (a row in your database table). That record contains a number of fields, including fields for first name, last name, political affiliation, military expertise, and psychological profile codes. You may even have check box fields for recording whether this person is perceived as a charismatic leader, an unfriendly financier, or a grunt in the Rebellion.

This sounds interesting but is not much different than what you can do with a spreadsheet, right? You can create a spreadsheet that has the names of records down the left side, and field names across the top.

Access makes working with these tables even easier, though. By giving you different views of each record, including individual record windows called *forms* (see Figure 8-2), Access gives you the ability to generate sophisticated reports, and the opportunity to query the database for particular answers (like, how many people named *Ralph* are lieutenants in the Rebellion).

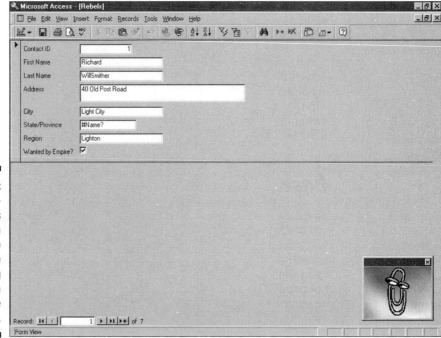

Figure 8-2:
Custom-
made forms
make data
entry a little
more
interesting
than just a
basic table
view.

Table relationships

Here's another reason that Access is so powerful: It can support more than one table. Access does so in a way that's described as *relational*. These tables can all have a relationship to one another. What does that mean?

Use the example of a database of Rebel Alliance personnel. Each individual is assigned to a rebel base somewhere in the quadrant, and each base has its own address, phone, fax, and e-mail domain. You can record a lot of information about each base.

Think of something annoying. Now, think of retyping that information about each rebel base on *every* rebel personnel record. Compare the two thoughts. How many times are you going to type the words *Koyala base, 124 Red Dirt Formation Road, 675-555-3425, Koyala Home World,* and so on? If, instead, you could create one record about the base and then link it to each individual person record, wouldn't that be much cooler and more efficient? You betcha, and you can do so.

Instead of including all the information about a particular base in each record of your Personnel table, you can type a one-line name, like *Koyala base*, and build a relationship between that entry and your base table (see Figure 8-3).

The use of certain proper names and planetary designations is not intended to convey any opinions we may hold regarding allegiance to the Empire. These names are used for the purpose of illustration only.

You now have tables that can hold records that are filled with fields of data. You also have forms for data entry, queries for asking questions, and reports for printing and showing to the Dark Lord. Plus, each table can have a relationship to data in other tables. Taken together, tables and table relationships are what make databases unique — this is why you'd use Access instead of Excel. That's not so scary after all, is it?

Database things to think about

To create a quality database, sit down and think through not only what data you want to track but also what sort of relationships exist between the data.

We recommend that you grab a piece of paper and a pencil and map out the data that you want to track. (In fact, you can save a lot of time and energy if the piece of paper and pencil prove useful for actually tracking that data. Just create some rows and columns, enter the data and head home for the day. Job well done, and you didn't have to learn Access.)

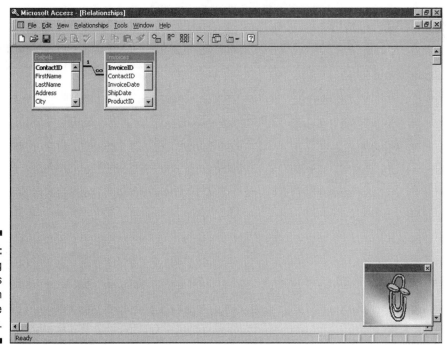

Figure 8-3:
Building relationships between database tables.

To determine how you'll track data in your database:

1. **Start with the types of tables you think you need: one for customers, transactions, inventory, and so on.**

2. **Then decide what fields need to appear in each database (see Figure 8-4).**

   When you have a list of your requirements, take a close look at each set of fields.

3. **Take any fields that are duplicated, and delete them from one of your tables.**

   You should be able to group fields in such a way that obvious divisions between each table exist. For instance, if you have a table of invoices and a table of customers, you only need address fields to appear in the customer table.

4. **Make sure that each table has a unique key field, and if it doesn't, come up with one.**

   A key field is a field in each table that is guaranteed to have a unique value for each record. For example, a last name in our Rebel database is a bad key because more than one SkyRunner may exist in the database (after all, it's a popular name). A better field for a key field is the *Empirical social security number,* which is guaranteed to be unique among the Dark Emperor's subjects.

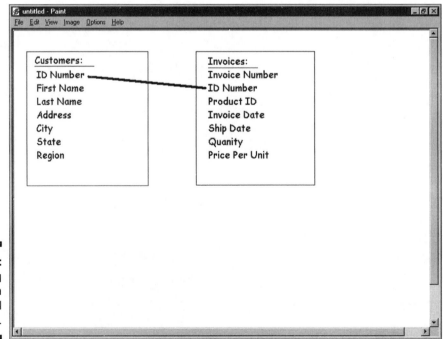

Figure 8-4: Mapping out a relational database.

Getting Around in Access

To Access, the database is king. Every time you open Access, you also need to open or create a database file, which serves as a sort of project coordinator for any tables, reports, and queries you create. All these are accessible when you open your database project document, making everything a little easier to manage.

Starting Access

Access won't even let you touch a menu item before opening a database. After starting Access, you see the Microsoft Access dialog box, as shown in Figure 8-5.

Figure 8-5:
The
Microsoft
Access
dialog box.

In the dialog box you have three choices: You can create a blank database, use the Database Wizard, or Open an Existing Database.

If you performed a full installation of Access, you have at least one additional option when you first start the program. You can load the Northwind sample database. This is a database that Microsoft has created to allow you to check out all the nifty database possibilities. Simply select it and click OK to see a demonstration of Access power.

✔ **To create a new, blank database:** Click the Blank Database option and then click OK.

✔ **To begin using the Database Wizard:** Click the Database Wizard option and then click OK. You're presented with the wizard, which allows you to create a number of preformatted databases.

✔ **To open an existing database:** Choose the Open an Existing Database option, choose the path and filename for the database you want to open, and then click OK. If you don't see the database you want to open, double-click More Files in the text area to move on to the Access Open dialog box.

In this chapter, we talk about the nuts-and-bolts tools of Access, by creating a complete database from scratch.

To start creating your own database:

1. **In the Microsoft Access dialog box, choose the Blank Database option and click OK.**

   The File New Database dialog box appears.

2. **In the File New Database dialog box, give the database a name, save it somewhere on your hard drive, and then click Create.**

   The Database window appears, showing an empty database project.

The Database window is the heart of your operations. Get to know it and love it, soldier — 'cause if you're not careful, you'll be cleanin' it with a toothbrush. Now, down and give me twenty!

Here's lookin' at your database

The Database window is a tabbed interface into the future of your business prosperity. Here, you can see a lot of the elements we already talked about back in the section "All about databases," including tables, queries, forms, and reports. (See Figure 8-6.)

Here are some tips to getting around the Database window:

✔ Click a tab at the top of the Database window to view elements of that type. To create a new element, click the New button. After you actually create elements, you can open and design those elements.

✔ To delete a table, query, or report, simply select it in the Database window and press the Delete key. A dialog box appears and makes sure that you want to delete the stuff. Click Yes to delete the element.

Figure 8-6:
The
Database
window
gives you
tabbed
access to
all the
elements of
your
database.

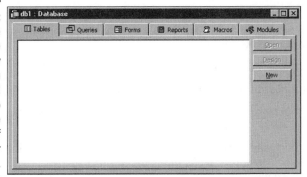

▸ You can also rename elements (tables, queries, and reports) from the Database window. Select the element, and then choose Edit⇨Rename from the Access menu.

▸ The View menu controls many of the options you have in the Database window, including the capability to view the items in the Database window as large icons, small icons, list, or details (List view is the default).

Saving and closing

Database files are saved and closed the same way any other file is, although the individual elements (tables, reports, and so on) are all saved as part of the database file. Choose File⇨Save to save the database, and File⇨Close to close the database file.

Defining Your Database with Tables

To get moving on your database, you need to come up with a few tables to start saving data in. Remember that tables are the heart of your database project. Each table holds individual records, which are a collection of related fields. If you haven't already, define some database tables (using paper and pencil) that make logical sense and have relationships between them.

Though tables are the heart of an Access database, you probably don't want to look at them, just like you don't want to really see someone wearing their heart on their sleeve (now *that's* disgusting). After you set up tables, you may spend most of your time viewing data in Access's other views, using either the Datasheet view or a data entry form.

To create a new table:

1. **Make sure that the Table tab is selected in the Database window, and then click the New button.**

   The New Table dialog box appears.

2. **In the New Table dialog box, choose Table Wizard and click OK.**

   The Table Wizard appears, allowing you to choose fields from the sample tables.

3. **Choose the Sample Tables you'd like to "borrow" field definitions from; then choose the fields that you want to include in your table Sample Field's box.**

   Highlight each field and then click the right-arrow button to move it to your new table. These sample tables and fields allow you to add fields that are similar to those you want for your table. (You can change them later, if necessary.)

4. **Continue choosing fields, until you have most or all the fields you want for your table (see Figure 8-7).**

   You can rename any of the sample fields in your new table by highlighting the field and clicking the Rename Field button. Rename the field in the Rename Field dialog box and click OK.

5. **Click Next when you're done adding fields.**

   You move to the next section of the wizard, where you give the table a name.

6. **Rename the table to something more meaningful.**

7. **Determine whether you want the Table Wizard to choose your key field (the field in your table that has a unique value for each record).**

   If you chose an ID field from the sample, you can select Yes, Set a Primary Key for Me and click Next. The last section of the wizard appears.

8. **Select one of the following check boxes:**

   - **Modify the Table Design:** If you have other fields you want to add to your table.

   - **Enter Data Directly into the Table:** If you're ready to begin adding data.

   - **Enter Data Into the Table Using a Form the Wizard Creates for Me:** If you'd like Access to generate a data entry form (instead of using a spreadsheet-like worksheet for data entry).

Figure 8-7:
In the Table
Wizard, you
can easily
add fields to
your table
by selecting
sample
fields from
sample
tables
created by
the wizard.

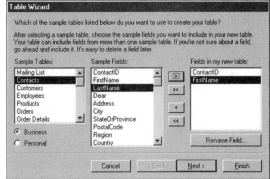

9. Click Finish.

The wizard responds by sending you to the appropriate screen, based on your check box response.

If you want to get ahead a bit, you can choose Enter Data Into the Table Using a Form the Wizard Creates for Me to have the Table Wizard create a form for data entry. You'll create your own form soon enough, but this is an interesting exercise if you want to see how forms work.

Editing the table design

If you choose to edit the table design from within the Table Wizard, you are presented with the Table Design window, where you can make more advanced choices about your table structure. You can also get to this window from the Database window by selecting a table and then clicking the Design button. The Table Design window is shown in Figure 8-8.

You can accomplish a number of different tasks in the Table Design windows:

- ✔ Change Field names
- ✔ Change data types for field names
- ✔ Change the key field
- ✔ Edit the description of the field
- ✔ Change the accepted values of the field

Some of these may seem to be fairly advanced concepts, but don't worry. The following sections walk you through the basics.

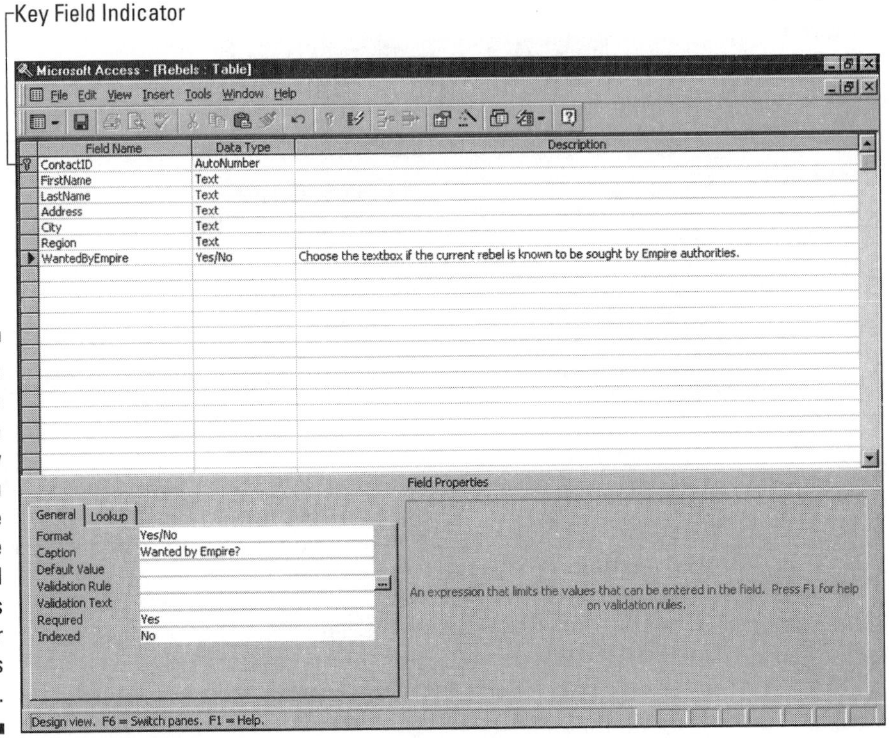

Key Field Indicator

Figure 8-8:
The Table
Design
window
allows you
to make
more
advanced
choices
about your
table's
structure.

Changing the field name and data type

To change the field name in the Table Design window, click the Field Name cell and edit away. Try to keep field names to one word, even if you use capital letters to separate words, like *RebelCustomerID*. Doing so makes the table easier to import into other programs. Field names can be up to 64 characters long.

Notice also that when a field name is selected, the field properties (in the bottom half of the window) change to reflect the field you selected. You can edit other values by clicking the General tab, including the caption for the field. This caption is used by Access to give a name to the field when generating forms for data entry. (Because captions are what your data entry users will see, they should be more user-friendly. *RebelCustomerID* is a suitable field name, but the caption should be a more approachable *Customer ID Number* or something similar.)

To change the data type for a given field, click once in the Data Type cell for that field. An arrow appears to the right of the cell, allowing you to choose data types from a pop-up menu. Click the arrow to view the various data types. Data types include the following:

- ✔ **Text:** Supports up to 255 characters. Text is useful for text, or text and number combinations that don't require computations (like phone numbers).

- ✔ **Memo:** For long text and number entries that don't require calculations. A memo can be up to 64,000 characters.

- ✔ **Number:** Numbers used for calculations, unless the number is supposed to be money. In that case, use Currency.

- ✔ **Date/Time:** For dates and times.

- ✔ **Currency:** For money values to be formatted like currency.

- ✔ **AutoNumber:** For numbers, like ID numbers, that Access is supposed to generate for each new record.

- ✔ **Yes/No:** Fields that contain an on/off style answer. Yes/No can be changed to reflect True/False, Good/Bad, and so on.

- ✔ **OLE Object:** Allows you to link or embed an OLE document within the database record. Great for mug shots.

- ✔ **Hyperlink:** Allows you to add a clickable URL to a Web page or other resource on the hard drive or the Internet. The resource referenced by the URL will automatically load in a Web browser when clicked in an Access form or report.

- ✔ **Lookup Wizard:** Adds a field (a "lookup field") that allows you to search for values in another table. Starts a wizard to help you create the lookup field.

Changing the key field and description

You can remove the primary key designation from a particular field. To do this, choose that field (click once in any of its cells) and click the Primary Key button in the toolbar (it looks like a little key, strangely enough). To set a different field as the primary key, select a cell within that field and click the Primary Key button again.

The primary key is important for creating tables that relate to one another. Somehow, Access needs to be able to make every single record in your table unique from every other record. The best way to do this is with a special ID number. If you choose a last name or similar field as your primary key, you may have duplicate last names in a database, which will wreak havoc on your reports and queries.

To change a field description, click in the description cell and type away. The description is purely optional. When you're using a form for data entry, the description appears in the status bar of that form.

Are you creating a database that others (employees, contractors, family pets) will use for data entry? A good description line can be used for instructions for each field on the data entry form that you'll eventually create.

Adding a specialized field

The Table Wizard is good for adding basic fields like names, addresses, and phone numbers to your database of Alliance sympathizers. What about something more specialized, like a Yes/No field, for example?

Now you get to create a quick Yes/No field in the database, by way of example. Say that you want a check box field that your data entry minions can use to track whether or not a particular rebel contact is currently wanted by Empire authorities. Here's the process:

1. **Click in a blank Field Name cell and type the name for your field.**

   When you're done, you can move to the Data Type cell by hitting tab.

2. **Click the down-arrow that appears in the selected Data Type cell.**

   A pull-down menu appears with data type choices.

3. **In the pull-down menu, choose Yes/No for this example.**

   Once selected, the field properties at the bottom of the screen change to reflect the new data type.

4. **Click once in the Field Description cell and type a text description for this field.**

5. **In the Field Properties box, choose the General tab (see Figure 8-9).**

   These are the appearance and validation options for the selected field.

6. **Type a caption for this field in the Caption text box.**

   The caption will appear in place of the Field Name when you generate for form for data entry.

7. **If you want to require that this field be filled in, click once in the Required text box and choose Yes from the menu.**

   Now the data entry user will not be able to save a record in this table without filling in the required field.

You can also dabble in the Validation Rule and Validation Text entries. Validation Rule brings up a rather complicated dialog box that allows you to create an expression — think algebra — that can be used to evaluate what the data entry user types and decide if it's appropriate for this record, or if the data entry user made a mistake. The Validation Text entry accepts text that pops up in a dialog box when the data entry person types something that doesn't meet the Validation Rule's criteria.

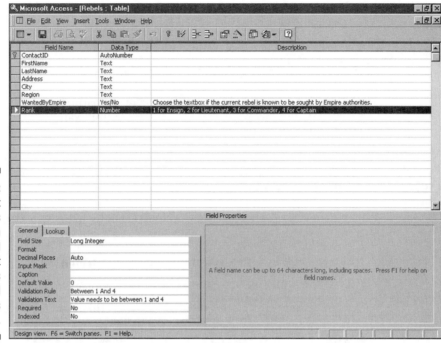

Figure 8-9:
You can set various validation and requirement properties in the Field Properties box.

Deleting a field

Did you create a field that you no longer want to use? You can easily delete the field. Simply click one of that field's cells, and then choose Edit⇨Delete from the Access menu. Confirm your deletion in the dialog box or with the Office Assistant (see Chapter 1), and it's gone.

Closing the Table Design window

When you've designed the table to your satisfaction, you're ready to close it and move on. To do so, click the Close box in the upper-right corner of the window. You're asked if you want to save changes. Choose Yes. If all goes well, your table design properly updates.

If all doesn't go well and you have already typed data in your table, Access asks you if you want the data checked against the new design. Choose Yes. Access then tries to determine if the new table design works with the data that has already been typed. If that fails, Access returns you to the Table Design window to change the design. This is especially likely to happen if you changed the primary key in your database. Try these:

✔ Change the primary key back to the field that it originally was.

✔ Change back any fields in which you changed the data type.

🖝 Close the table design again, but choose No when asked to save the changes. Doing so returns the table to its original design.

Adding data to your table

Most of the time, you want to create a special form for data entry. Maybe in this case, though, you want to get data stored in the table right away. You can do that using the Datasheet view of your table.

You can quickly switch back and forth between the Datasheet view and the Design view (the Table Design window). Choose View⇨Datasheet view or View⇨Design view from the Access menu.

Typing data in the Datasheet view is almost exactly like typing data in Microsoft Excel or any other spreadsheet application (see Figure 8-10):

1. **Select a cell in which you want to type some data.**

2. **Type the data and then press either the Tab key or the Right Arrow key to move to the next cell.**

   You can use the Arrow keys to move in nearly any direction.

3. **When you reach the last cell in a particular record, press the Tab key to move to the next record.**

   If you're finished altogether, you can close the Datasheet view (use its window's close box) to return to the Database window, if desired.

As with spreadsheets, you can widen columns by passing the mouse pointer over the lines between each column heading. The cursor changes to a two-sided arrow, indicating that you can click-and-drag to change the column size.

Deleting records

To delete a record, first open the datasheet where that record exists. Then choose the record by clicking the gray box to the left of the first data entry cell in that record's row. Next, choose Edit⇨Delete Record from the Access menu, or click the Delete Record button on the toolbar. A dialog box appears, asking if you really want to delete the record. Choose Yes.

If you're using an AutoNumber field, you may notice that the next record you create is given the next unique number, even if you deleted records. For example, if you type three records and then delete records number 2 and 3, the next record you type is still number 4.

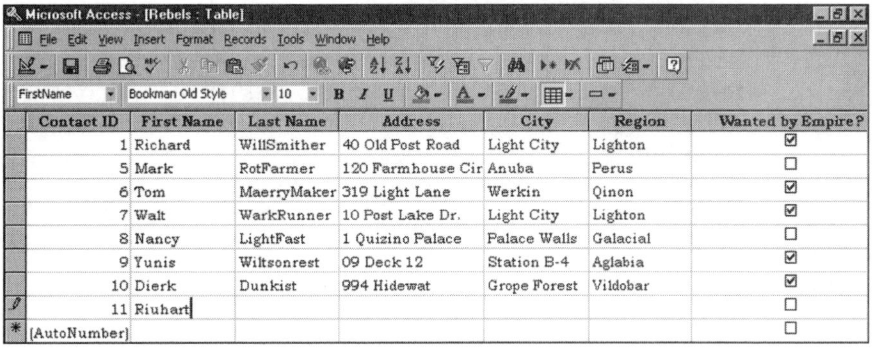

Figure 8-10:
The
Datasheet
view allows
you to
quickly type
data in a
table, like
you do in a
spreadsheet
document.

Contact ID	First Name	Last Name	Address	City	Region	Wanted by Empire?
1	Richard	WillSmither	40 Old Post Road	Light City	Lighton	☑
5	Mark	RotFarmer	120 Farmhouse Cir	Anuba	Perus	☐
6	Tom	MaerryMaker	319 Light Lane	Werkin	Qinon	☑
7	Walt	WarkRunner	10 Post Lake Dr.	Light City	Lighton	☑
8	Nancy	LightFast	1 Quizino Palace	Palace Walls	Galacial	☐
9	Yunis	Wiltsonrest	09 Deck 12	Station B-4	Aglabia	☑
10	Dierk	Dunkist	994 Hidewat	Grope Forest	Vildobar	☑
11	Riuhart					☐
[AutoNumber]						☐

Changing the Datasheet view design

Though the datasheet is primarily for quick data entry, you can also change
the way the table appears in the Datasheet view window:

  ✔ **To change a fielding heading:** Double-click in the heading cell and edit
    the text. (This changes the field caption, not the field name.)

  ✔ **To change the appearance of the data entry cells:** Choose
    Format⇨Cells and then edit changes in the Cells Effects dialog box.

  ✔ **To change the font for your table:** Choose Format⇨Font from the
    Access menu.

  ✔ **To hide columns, freeze columns (make the left column always
    visible), and unfreeze all columns:** Head to the Format menu, where
    you also have other options.

Finding things in your table

If you typed data that you later want to find (without going to the trouble of
creating complicated lookup commands), you can simply use the Find
command. Place the cursor in the field that you want to search and then
choose Edit⇨Find from the menu bar. In the Find dialog box, type the value
you want to find (like a particular customer's last name, for example). Click
the Find First button to search the table for a match.

Closing the Datasheet view

When you're done altering the datasheet design, or finished with your data entry, you can click the close box in the upper-right corner of the Datasheet view window. A dialog box appears and asks if you want to save the changes to the design of the Datasheet window. Choose Yes. The Database window reappears.

Data that you type in the Datasheet view is automatically saved as you type it, so you have no special command for saving the data — just the design of the window.

Sorting and filtering tables

After you have all these mounds of data added to your tables, you'll probably want to manipulate the tables so that you can, well, find things. This is easy to do with two powerful, but different, features that you can access directly from the Datasheet view — just a few menu commands.

Sort the table

You can sort the table in either ascending or descending order based on any field in the table. To do this, place the cursor in any cell of the field you want to use to sort the entire table. (Just place the cursor in one cell, which tells Access which field you want to use for the sort.) Then choose Records➪Sort➪Ascending or Records➪Sort➪Descending. After a few seconds, the table is resorted.

Filter the table

What, exactly, is a filter? In regular life, a filter is something that keeps certain things out while allowing others to come through. For example, sunglasses are supposed to filter ultraviolet light while allowing enough of the visible spectrum to shine through so that you can see comfortably. Unfortunately, that causes your irises to open wider, causing massive long-term damage to your eyes that can't be reliably diagnosed for years. But we digress.

In database parlance, a filter allows certain data to appear in your table, while it hides other values. This is good for two reasons:

- ✔ Filters help you cut through all your data to find the entries that are important at that moment (for example, filtering to find all invoices that are due out today).

- ✔ Filters allow you to act on just the filtered data (for example, creating a report that shows what invoices are due today).

To create a table that's gotta wear shades:

1. **In Datasheet view, place the cursor in the field where you want to filter the data.**

2. **Choose Records⊏⟩Filter⊏⟩Filter By Form from the Access menu.**

   The view changes slightly, so that only one record is visible.

3. **In the field you chose, either type the value that you want to be the basis of your filter or choose that value from the pop-up menu in that field's cell (see Figure 8-11).**

   If you want to choose everything with the first name "Ricky," type that name in the box. Or use, the pop-up menu to choose a value that will be used for the filter.

Figure 8-11:
Choose the value that the database will be filtered to show.

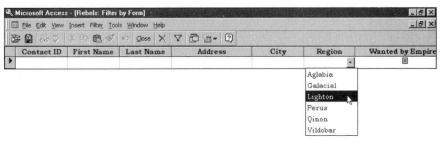

4. **Choose Filter⊏⟩Apply Filter/Sort from the menu.**

   Your table is now filtered to show only the records that match the criteria you set.

Suddenly don't feel like filtering? Click the Close button in the Filter/Sort toolbar. You'll be back in the regular worksheet view.

Other filters in the Record⊏⟩Filters menu work in similar ways:

- ✔ **Filter by Selection:** This one cuts out a step. It filters the database based on the value that appears in the currently selected cell.

- ✔ **Filter Excluding Selection:** Filters the database to show only records that don't include the value in the currently selected cell.

Get rid of filters and sorts

Has a certain filter got you down? Whatever your emotional state, you can easily get rid of filters and sorts and return to a full view of your table. Be warned, however, that doing the following task removes all filters and sorts — not just the last one.

Just choose Records⇨Remove Filter/Sort from the menu and your worksheet will once again hold all of the table's records.

You can't selectively undo any filters or sorts, so think about them twice before implementing and removing them.

Getting tables to talk it out

You found out about relational databases in the section "Building table relationships" early in this chapter. Using table relationships, you can build more than one table and then get the data in each table to talk to one another. Why would you do that? To avoid redundancy, for one thing. In the example in this chapter, you're creating a database of rebel supporters who may or may not be wanted by the Empire. What if you wanted to do more than simply track these traitors? What if you wanted to sell them something?

First, you need to create a table that can track the invoices you're going to generate for the equipment they order (see Figure 8-12).

Figure 8-12:
Here's a database table for tracking invoices.

Invoice ID	Customer ID	Invoice Date	Ship Date	Product ID	Quantity	Price Per Unit
1	5	9/7/97		231453	2	$49.00
2	1	9/6/97	10/7/97	78654	23	$7.00
3	5	9/4/98	9/12/98	123467	12	$97.50
4	7	10/12/98	12/10/98	345672	10	$312.90
5	8	2/1/99	2/28/99	453216	5	$215.00
6	9	12/8/99	12/28/99	123564	2	$1,200.04
7	10	11/4/98	11/30/98	342156	1	$453.23
(AutoNumber)						

Instead of forcing your data entry representative to get full address and personal information every time a rebel wants to order a product, you can create a relationship between the two tables based on the key field in the Rebels table: ContactID. Because every value of ContactID is unique in the Rebels table, this is a perfect field to use as a relationship between the two.

When you have a relationship between the two database tables, you can get them to work together as part of your order entry system. Now, when callers want to order a product, you can look them up in the Rebel database using the Find command or the filters discussed earlier in "Sorting and filtering tables." After you find them in the database, their ContactID numbers can be used for the invoices. If they've ordered before, you already have an address and phone number, which saves redundant data entry. Later, you can create a report that combines both the information from the Contact table and the Invoice table — maybe a report that tells shipping what they need to box up, and where they need to send it.

ID numbers are almost always the best way to key between databases because a computer program can easily generate unique numbers. An ID number generated by Access is not always the best way to refer to a person, because that person isn't terribly likely to remember a number you assign to him or her ("Please, remember your customer number for future reference. It's 34982173."). If you can get that person to give you another unique number (like a social security number), you may want to set your contact table so that it *doesn't* automatically generate new ContactIDs.

If you really are dealing with military rebels, they may be more than willing to memorize a secret ID code that they can use over unsecured phone lines. That's a best case scenario for a small business, however.

Creating the table relationship

After you've created the tables that you're interested in relating to one another, you can create the relationship relatively easy:

1. **From the Database window, choose Tools⇨Relationships.**

   The Relationships window appears, along with the Show Table dialog box. If you've already visited this window, you may need to open the Show Table dialog box by choosing Relationships⇨Show Table from the menu. (That way you can view relationships you've already created.)

2. **In the Show Table dialog box, select a table you'd like to add to the Relationships window and click Add (see Figure 8-13).**

   Repeat for each table you want to add to the Relationships window. You may also find it useful to place the tables on the Relationships window in some sort of order.

Figure 8-13:
You may want to start with the contact database and then add the invoice database.

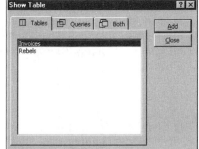

3. **To close the Show Table dialog box when you're finished, click the Close button.**

   Now you should see the two tables you've created in the Relationships window.

4. **To create a relationship between one field in each the table, click-and-drag from the field in the first table and then release the mouse button over the related field in the second table.**

   In this example, you click and hold the mouse while you point at the ContactID field in the Rebels table. You then release the mouse button when the pointer is over the ContactID field in the Invoices table.

   The Relationships dialog box appears, and the fields to be related are shown.

5. **Select the Enforce Referential Integrity option so that a check mark appears, and then click Create.**

   What is referential integrity? Click the Office Assistant while the Relationships dialog box is open. You see a Help topic that explains the term — at least we hope it explains the term. It seems to be saying that Access tests the integrity of data you enter on one table if that data is supposed to be related to a key field in another table. (But frankly, we can't make heads or tails of it. We just know it's a good thing.)

   The relationship is created (see Figure 8-14).

6. **If you want to get away from this window (who can blame you?), use the Window menu to change back to the Database window, or click the Close box to close the Relationships window.**

After you create the relationship, you see a line between the two fields with the type of relationship defined with little numbers for each field. In this example, the relationship is a *one-to-many* relationship (the *one* is associated with the contact database, and the *many* are associated with the invoice database). The relationship defines how often the related value is expected to appear in each database. In the contact database, each ContactID is unique, so each appears only one time. You may have more than one invoice for a particular client (in fact, you hope this happens), so the invoice database has the ability, in the relationship, to deal with many instances of the same ContactID.

Creating Forms So That Uncle Jed Can Use Your Database

Forms can really set your database apart from the mundane entry tables of the Datasheet view, or the Excel spreadsheet. Not only can you inject a bit of creativity into your database, but you can also create data entry screens, so

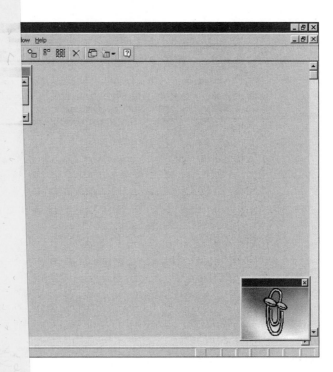

is an easier and user-friendlier process. Using
miliar layout principles, you can create an attrac-
nakes typing database values a pleasure (yeah,

Create a new form with the wizard

From the Database window, you can create a form quickly and fairly painlessly using the built-in Form Wizard. Here's how the wizard works:

1. **Make sure the Forms tab in the Database window is selected and
   then click the New button.**

   The New Form dialog box appears.

2. **In the New Form dialog box, choose Form Wizard from the menu.**

3. **In the pop-up menu, choose the table that you want the wizard to use
   to create your form and then click OK.**

   The table you choose in this dialog box won't completely limit your
   choices. You can mix and match elements from different tables later,
   using the wizard and other tools. After you click OK, you move to the
   next section of the wizard.

4. **In the Form Wizard window, choose each field that you want to add to the form and click the right-facing Arrow button to add it to the form. Repeat for each field you want to add to the form. Click Next to move on.**

   You can also add all the fields at once by clicking the right facing Double-Arrow button. Because you'll use the form for data entry, you'll probably want to add all the fields. After you click next, the next section of the wizard appears.

5. **In this portion of the wizard, choose the type of layout you think is best for your form and then click Next.**

   Columnar style is best for forms that look like Windows applications, while the Justified style makes the form look a bit like older DOS-based database applications. After clicking Next, you move to the really fun part.

6. **Select the style that pleases you from the menu and click Next.**

   To sample the styles first, select each style name to see the pretty little graphical elements you can add to your form (we told you this was fun). After clicking next, you move to the title section of the wizard.

7. **Give your data entry form a title in the text box, and select the radio button option that determines whether you want to open the form for data entry, or modify the design of the form.**

   For the example, choose to open the form for data entry.

8. **Click Finish.**

   The form pops up on the screen, ready for you to do some data entry (see Figure 8-15).

Do you need proof that you're just doing basic data entry? If you choose View⇨Datasheet from the menu, you're right back where you started with the Datasheet view.

Data entry in a form

Getting around the form is fairly straightforward. Just start to type data, and then press the Type key or the Tab key to move to the next entry box. Press Alt+Tab to move backward (or upward) to the previous entry box. You can also use the arrow keys on the keyboard to move around. When you reach the last entry box, pressing the Enter, Tab, or down arrow key moves you to the next record. Data in records is saved automatically as you type it.

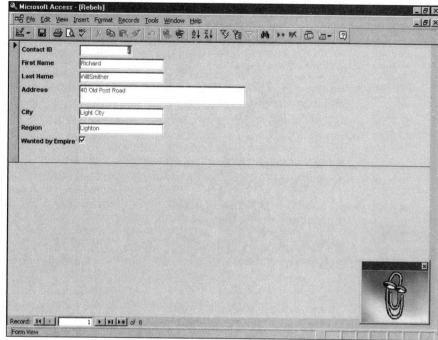

Create a form including related tables

You found out how to create relationships between two tables in the earlier section, "Defining Your Database with Tables," but here's a really cool trick.

Using the example of the Rebels table and the Invoices table, create a form that includes elements of both. Design the form for data entry so that it automatically updates with information already stored in the Rebels table if you type the correct ContactID.

There's a good chance you're wondering how all this Rebel stuff could possibly be applicable to your small business. Well, chances are good that it's not — you probably have very little reason to create a table of rebel alliance members. However, this table is really just a (silly) example of a basic contact or customer table. If you try this hands-on example yourself, you could just call the Rebels table a Customers table and it would work in the exact same way.

Here's how it works:

1. **Make sure the Forms tab in the Database window is selected and then click the New button.**

   The New Form dialog box appears.

2. **In the New Form dialog box, choose Form Wizard from the menu.**

3. **Choose the Invoice table in the pop-up menu, and then click OK.**

   The next section of the wizard appears, where you can add fields to your form.

4. **In the Form Wizard window, choose to add all the fields at once by clicking the right facing Double-Arrow button.**

   Now, all of the field names in the Available Fields menu are duplicated in the Selected fields menu.

5. **In the Tables/Queries menu, choose Tables:Rebels.**

   The Available Fields menu items change.

6. **Add individual fields by highlighting them and then clicking the right-facing Arrow button.**

   Add first name, last name, address, and city.

7. **Click Next.**

   The wizard moves to its page layout section.

8. **Choose the type of layout you'd like from the menu and then click Next.**

   For this example, choose Columnar.

9. **Select the style that you want and then click Next.**

   The style doesn't matter for this example — choose one that you find attractive.

10. **Give your data entry form a title in the text box at the top of this screen, and choose the** Open the form to view or enter information **option.**

11. **Click Finish.**

    A data entry form appears on-screen, and looks something like Figure 8-16.

This example works best if you already typed some records in the Rebels table. If you haven't, do so using the Rebels worksheet, or a form created specifically for that table.

On the data entry screen, begin typing data. When you get to the ContactID entry, type a number that you know has been assigned in the Rebel table (probably a low one, like **1** or **2**). If you have data associated with that ContactID stored in the Rebels table, the information pops up automatically in the name and address boxes. Pretty cool, eh?

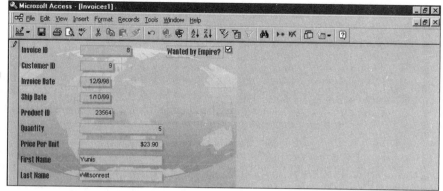

Figure 8-16:
A data
entry form
that uses
fields from
both tables.

We think this is very cool. Because this form includes fields from both the contact and the invoice tables, your data entry folks can easily take orders while they're on the telephone (assuming that they can talk and type at the same time). If the customer already has a ContactID number, your data entry employee can just type the number in the database and double-check the address with the customer. If they edit the address using this form, they're actually editing the address in the Rebels (or contact) table — the original information on their address and name is changed, if necessary.

Using Queries to Get All Kinds of Cool Information

Libraries are computerizing all their card catalog files for good reason — actually, two reasons. The first reason is that one member of the city council is married to a local area network and database specialist, who inevitably gets the contract. The second reason is more applicable to this chapter: Databases allow sophisticated queries that help you quickly find the answer to a particular question. If you're looking for someone in particular, or a book title, author, or publisher, a computer-based database query is a quick and easy way to find that information (assuming that the information is already in the database).

If you were dealing with a card catalog, you'd look a bit silly standing in front of it saying, "Hello? Hello?! I'd like a listing of the books by Edgar Allen Poe that deal with death, please." You would also probably get in trouble with the librarian if you said it too loudly.

If you're going to talk to furniture in a library, do it quietly. Most urban libraries don't really mind if you babble on in endless conversation with shelving, kiosks, or chairs about ethereal topics, as long as you don't disrupt other patrons.

With Access, you can create some powerful queries in your own right. A query is nothing more than a question asked of the database, although it can include a number of different tables, allowing you to pull together answers from different groups of data.

In this chapter's example, you're tracking whether a particular rebel is currently wanted by the Empire. Well, you can build a query that would determine which rebels are wanted and which of them has placed an order with your business. The query can then respond with a table of invoices that involve wanted rebels only. Armed with this information, you can then either get the products out more quickly, or more slowly (more covertly), depending on your loyalties.

Here are a few of the queries you can use:

✔ Which invoices are due out today?

✔ What products have been ordered by a particular region?

✔ What's the dollar amount of product being shipped to a particular city?

✔ How much has one particular individual ordered from us?

Notice that all these queries can be culled from the data that exists in the two example tables you created. After you create different tables with relationships between them, the opportunity to ask the database queries becomes increasingly more useful. This is powerful stuff, which explains why a discernible drop in sales of 3-by-5 note cards to libraries around the world has been reported.

Designing a query

In our experience, the best way to build a query combines both a wizard and the Query Design view. To begin, you set out with the Query wizard to determine which fields to add to the query.

By way of example, you'll work once again with the Rebels and Invoices tables. The following steps show you how to build a query that determines what orders have been taken from rebels that are currently wanted by the Empire:

1. **From the Database window, choose the Query tab.**

   You can use the Window menu to switch to the Database window if you're currently looking at some other part of the database.

2. **Click the New button to begin the query.**

   The New Query dialog box appears.

3. **In the New Query dialog box, choose the Simple Query Wizard from the menu and click OK.**

   The Simple Query wizard appears.

4. **In the Simple Query Wizard dialog box, choose the fields that you want to add to the query.**

   You can change the table in the Tables/Queries menu, which gives you access to fields in other tables.

   To add a particular field, highlight the field in the Available Fields menu and click the right facing Arrow button. To add all fields in a given table to the query, click the right-facing Double-Arrow button.

5. **Click Next when you're done adding fields.**

   You'll actually have another opportunity to change which fields are visible in your query later when you edit the query in Design view. You may want to just add all the fields from each table at this point so that all the fields are accessible in the Design view.

   Next up, you're asked if you want a detail or summary query. A detail query results in a table of records that correspond to your query. A summary query results in a summary answer, like the sum, average, or high of a particular field, among all records that match the query.

6. **In keeping with the example, choose Detail and then click Next.**

7. **Give your query a name (in this example, name it** Orders from Wanted Rebels**) and then choose the** Modify the query design **option.**

   No, you're not done yet.

8. **Click Finish.**

   The Query Design view window appears, showing which tables are being used for the query in the top half of the window, and which fields are being used for the query.

9. **Uncheck the Show check box for any field that you want to hide in this query.**

If you don't want the query to display the CustomerID from the Invoices table for a particular order (especially because this would be redundant if you also displayed the ContactID from the Rebels table), you can deselect the check box to empty it. Doing so hides the field.

10. Choose one or more of the fields on which you want the results of the query to be sorted.

For example, you may want them sorted alphabetically by region, or by the last name of the rebel in question, which would allow you to see at once all invoices for a particular rebel.

Note two important things about queries:

- Queries are sorted by field from left to right first, if you select more than one field for sorting.

- Consider how sorting might later affect the way you'd like to report your data. (For instance, would you like data sorted by the Rebel's last name so that the data can be printed in that order later?) This can be a timesaving step for creating reports, discussed later in the chapter in the section "Tell the World about Your Data with Reports." The better sorted your query results are, the less time you spend sorting for your reports.

  Now, you need to create the query criteria. These will include all the invoices related to a rebel who is wanted by the Empire.

11. To create these criteria, move to the WantedByEmpire field and right-click the Criteria line in that field (see Figure 8-17).

A pop-up contextual menu appears.

12. Choose Build from the contextual menu.

The Expression Builder dialog box appears. In the Expression Builder dialog box, you create the expression for the criteria of the query. In this example, the expression needs to be something like "Add this invoice when WantedByEmpire equals true."

13. Begin in the row of fields and double-click WantedByEmpire.

That field name appears in the Expression text area.

This is more basic algebra: Essentially, you're just building a formula that tries to figure out if A=1. In this case, A is *WantedByEmpire* and 1 is *True*.

14. Click the Equal button in the Expression Builder window to choose the operator.

An operator is a mathematic sign (like "equals" or "greater than") that's used in the expression. You want an equal sign for this example.

Now you need something for the field to equal. For a check box field, the answer can either be True or False (the answer is True if the check box is selected).

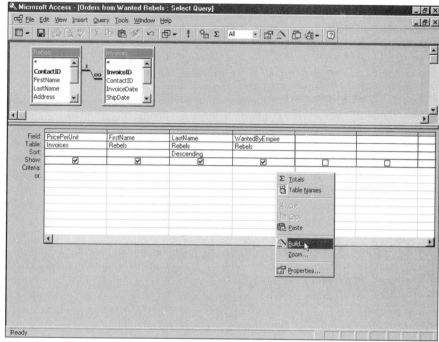

Figure 8-17:
This contextual menu allows you to build a formula to be used to evaluate records.

15. Because you want the answer to be True, double-click the Constants folder in the Express Builder and double-click True.

True appears in the Expression builder text area (see Figure 8-18).

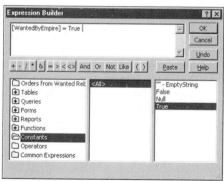

Figure 8-18:
Here's a successfully built expression. Now, if a record's Wanted-ByEmpire field has a value of True, all that rebel's invoices are revealed by this query.

16. Click the OK button to close the Expression Builder.

Back in the Query Design view, you're done designing.

17. Click the close box on the window to move on.

A dialog box appears to ask if you want to save the query.

18. Choose Yes.

The query is saved and you're returned to the Database window.

If you closed the query, you can get back to it by choosing the Query tab in the Database window and selecting the query by name. You can click the Open button to run the query and see the results, or click the Design button to edit the query another time.

Tell the World about Your Data with Reports

At some point — no pressure — you'll want to create reports based on the data you typed in your database tables. Reports are designed so that they can be printed and then handed around to various middle managers at meetings or the partners in your small business. At that time, the reports are reviewed, studied, and — if all goes well — understood and found useful by the recipients.

As you may imagine, reports are best when they work hand-in-hand with a useful query. That is, you often don't want to simply print out the entire database for your report — instead, you want the report to display data that answers a particular question, just like a query does. Forms are used to make table data entry more attractive and convenient; reports are designed to make query results more presentable.

You can create rather complex reports in Access, or you can use some quick shortcuts to create them. If you're interested in a quick report, experiment with AutoReports before moving on to the slightly more complicated Report Wizard. You can also create reports completely from scratch, but because we've never had a reason to design a report from scratch (the wizard is pretty good), you'll need to find another book on the topic (try IDG Books' *Access 97 For Windows For Dummies*). Hey, at least we're honest.

Before beginning your report with the Report Wizard, you need to build a query that generates the results that you want. Using a query to build a report, you can still choose the fields in the query results that interest you.

To begin using the Report Wizard:

1. **From the Database window, choose the Report tab.**

2. **Click the New button.**

   The New Report dialog box appears.

3. **In the New Report dialog box, choose the Report Wizard from the menu.**

4. **Choose the query you want to use in the pop-up menu and then click OK to begin the wizard.**

   The Wizard appears.

5. **In the Wizard, choose each field that you want to add to the report from the Available Fields list.**

   To add a field, select it, and then click the right-facing Arrow button to add it to the report. You can select fields from different tables and queries, but selecting them from a single query is best at this point, because a query is the best way to sort the information in your database.

6. **Click Next after you add all the fields that interest you.**

   Next, you'll choose how your data is grouped. (This can take one or more screens.)

   Do you want to add all but a few fields? Click the right-facing Double-Arrow button to add all the fields to your report. Then select fields you don't want in the report and click the left-facing Arrow button to remove them from the report. Doing this may be faster than adding them one at a time.

7. **Select which table's key field you want to use for grouping the results of your report by clicking it in the menu, and then click Next.**

   The sample page in the wizard window shows you how each choice will affect the layout of the report.

8. **Choose subgroups under which you want the report grouped.**

   For example, if your key field is the customer number, you generate a report that includes a customer's name and address, followed by all the invoices that customer has generated. You can then group those invoices by the invoice date, for example, for a more organized report. To add a grouping level, select the field that you want to use to organize the level, and click the right-facing Arrow button.

   Grouping determines how the report layout looks, not how things are sorted. You find out about sorting next. In the meantime, you don't need to group things if you don't want to. Just ignore grouping if the concept is confusing, or if you feel that it signifies another wizard that hardly manages to help.

9. Click Next after you add your grouping levels.

Next, you can choose the sorting for your report.

10. Next to number 1, choose the field that you want the first sort to focus on from the pull-down menu.

The button next to it indicates ascending order. Click the button to change the sort order to descending order, if desired.

Repeat this step as necessary. You can also sort your query before you run the report, and you won't have to worry about this part of the wizard.

11. From this screen you can click the Summary Options button to automatically generate a summary of certain fields.

The Summary Options dialog box appears, allowing you to select the check boxes next to those options that you want to include in your summary. By default, the Show option is for Detail and Summary, which prints the report, and then prints a quick summary at the end that includes any of these options.

12. When you're done creating your Summary O' Love, click the OK button.

13. Back in the Wizard, click Next.

The wizard changes to the layout section.

14. Find a report layout that you like in the Layout section, select it by clicking its radio button, and check it out in the preview window.

15. Determine whether you want to print in landscape or portrait mode, also select whether fields will be adjusted to fit on the page.

16. Click Next. (Is this wizard long enough for you?)

You move on to the styles section of the wizard.

17. Choose the style of text and labels you want, and click Next.

Now you're ready to name the report.

18. Give your report a name, choose to Preview the Report, and click Finish.

Part II
Making Your Business Look Bigger

The 5th Wave® By Rich Tennant

FIRED

YOU

"NIFTY CHART, FRANK, BUT NOT ENTIRELY NECESSARY."

In this part . . .

All businesses rely on other businesses to take care of common tasks that are often too difficult or too expensive to perform unless one happens to be specifically set up to do such tasks. We're talking about designing and outputting documents, setting up a Web presence, and generating reports. Office can make these tasks easier for you to perform, and the chapters in this part show you how.

Chapter 9

Avoiding Those Expensive Printing Bills

*W*e don't know how often we see the power of a couple hundred bucks worth of Office programs go virtually untapped, because corporate IS (Information Services) departments like the idea of their users doing as little as humanly possible on their computers. Hey, IS keeps the computers running, right? What more do you want from them? Microsoft doesn't help much, either, in our opinion, by making some of these features hard to get at.

That's why small business people need to unite against a common enemy and forge ahead to new levels of productivity. Though you may find the tips and tricks discussed in this chapter (in fact, in all of Part II) without the assistance of this book, you don't have time for that. Why not let a couple of computer dweebs with an IDG contract go ahead and do the work for you, eh?

We want to talk about *power* word processing. In this chapter, we take a look at some of the buried commands in Microsoft Word, including creating your own templates, adding envelopes to the mix, and working your way through the wizards, to create documents like fax cover sheets. These tasks often end up outsourced to a print shop, or copy-and-go storefront, at an extreme profit to the shop. Instead, you can do this stuff yourself, look like a professional, and do so quickly so that you can concentrate on your business at hand.

Creating Letters and Memos

With the quality of today's home office printers (whether you're talking about laser printers or the color inkjet printers you can get for around $200 - $300), you have less of a reason to hand your document creation needs over to a print shop. You probably never planned to send your letters and memos out because you know how to type and print within Microsoft Word (see Chapter 2). But what about your letterhead, memo layouts, and press releases? All these things can also be preformatted in Word, allowing you to quickly create and print them as needed.

If you're the boss around your small or home office, you may want to hand this chapter to your assistant, your intern, or your eldest child's tech-savvy significant other. Read the chapter first, just to get an idea of what's possible, and then pay someone a nice, comfortable contractor's fee to come in and create your company's templates for business correspondence and cards. Seriously, don't forget to value your time highly. If you enjoy the template-building process, fine, but remember that you're playing an important component of a very promising company. Can you afford *you,* instead of someone who comes a bit cheaper?

Although you may think that Microsoft has buried these capabilities deep within Word, these things are easy to do, without those crazy workarounds that most people come up with in an office environment (see Figure 9-1).

How about creating some templates? In the next few sections, we work a template up for memos and one for letters. Then we look at the easy way to print an envelope.

Communicating with the help

Two levels of Office power users exist: People who *use* templates and people who *create* templates. We're not judging either type — both are necessary for a balanced ecology and for decreasing the strain on the global court system. All we ask (to paraphrase Robin Williams' cameo character in one of the best films of recent times, *Dead Again*) is that you decide which you want to be, and be that. You can follow our instructions, as you like.

You begin by creating a business memo from the templates in Microsoft Word. If you are part of a small, family-owned business, you may not have much use for creating memos. (Memos to family members tend to upset them and do not fulfill your psychologist's suggestion for "a forum for open communications." E-mail is out, too.) On the other hand, you may find this not only a useful tool for talking to employees but also a morale booster in some cases. Employees may feel good to know they're working for a company that's serious and successful enough to have professional memos.

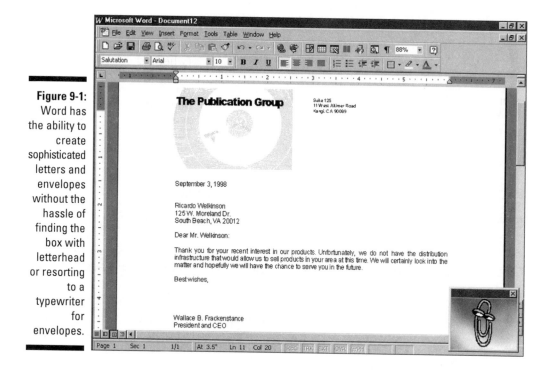

Here's how you create a business memo:

1. **Begin by choosing File⇨New Document from the Microsoft Word menu bar.**

2. **In the New dialog box, click the Memos tab.**

   You're presented with a number of different template choices (see Figure 9-2).

3. **Click one of the template choices.**

   You get a preview of the document that you click in the window to the right.

4. **You can click the other templates if you want to see them previewed.**

5. **After you choose your favorite, click OK.**

   The New dialog box disappears and a new page in the format that you chose for your memo appears in Word.

6. **On that page, you can fill in the To, From, and similar information by clicking once on the** [Click here and type name] **text that appears in the document and then typing the appropriate names and addresses.**

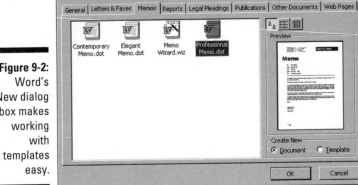

Figure 9-2:
Word's
New dialog
box makes
working
with
templates
easy.

7. To add text to your memo, highlight the text in the body of the memo and press the Delete key on your keyboard (see Figure 9-3).

Now, you can begin typing to create your memo.

This memo template takes advantage of not only Word's template technology but also Word's styles technology, which allows the programmers and designers at Microsoft to prebuild different styles that you can use for different parts of the document.

To create a header within your memo, for example, you can start on a new line and choose one of the headings from the Styles drop-down list in the formatting toolbar. After you type a heading, press Enter. Now the style is back to regular Body Text, and you can type information below the header.

You can also set styles for entire paragraphs after you type them. Just place the cursor somewhere in the paragraph and choose the style that you want to apply from the Style drop-down list in the Formatting toolbar.

From here, you can save and print your memo, just as you would any other document in Word. Choose File⇨Save to save this memo as a document. Choose File⇨Print to print it and fire it through the food chain of your business, customers, or suppliers.

You can edit the graphical elements on your page, too. Some memos, for example, have a gray box with the word Confidential in it. If that word is inappropriate for your circumstances, just click the box and press Delete to remove it from the page (you may have to click and delete the text, and its enclosing box separately).

Delete to Add Text   Type Name

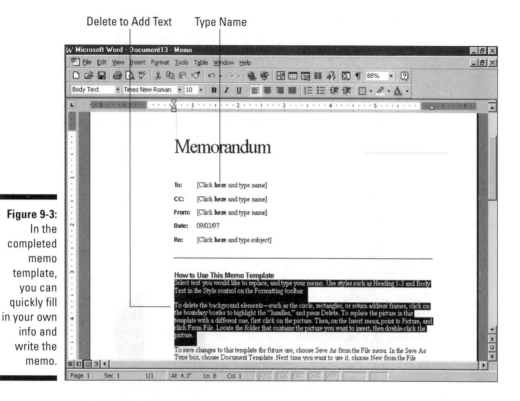

Figure 9-3:
In the completed memo template, you can quickly fill in your own info and write the memo.

Talking to the wizard

We sincerely regret Microsoft's use of the word *wizard* for these little scripted tidbits of programming magic. Unfortunately, as is demonstrated by these first two sentences, you cannot conjure a quippy metaphor that doesn't come directly from the world of sorcery and spells (and we live for quippy metaphors) when you talk about wizards. Fortunately, we gave up that dragons and knights stuff years ago because worrying over those silly fantasy worlds and role-playing games is hopelessly geeky.

Plus, the extra time gave us the window we needed to work on ultra-realistic Vulcan makeup effects for the *Star Trek* conventions.

If you're not a big fan of the prebuilt memo templates, you still have another option that doesn't require much in the way of artistic skills. You can consult the Memo Wizard:

1. Choose File⇨New from the Word menu bar.

The New dialog box appears.

2. In the New dialog box, select the Memos tab.

3. Click the Memo Wizard icon and click OK.

To save time and money, you can double-click the Memo Wizard icon. The Memo Wizard pops on your screen after Word is done, thinking this whole process over.

The intro screen doesn't have a lot to say, although you may notice that this process is outlined in a little flowchart at the very left of the Wizard's dialog box (see Figure 9-4). That's pretty businesslike, ain't it?

Flowchart   Options

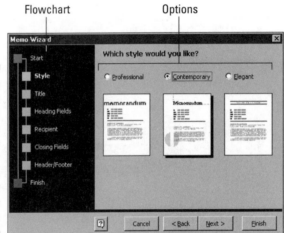

Figure 9-4:
The Memo
Wizard
walks you
through the
steps for
creating
your very
own memo
format.

4. Click Next.

5. Choose the style for your memo by clicking the radio button next to its name.

You can choose from Professional, Contemporary, and Elegant.

6. Click Next when you're happy with the style.

Now you can decide what the title text is.

7. Do one of the following:

- If you don't have pre-printed memo letterhead, edit the title that appears under the Yes radio button.

- If you do have letterhead, click No. Then tell the wizard what your letterhead looks like and how much space to leave for it when printing.

8. Click Next when you're done.

9. **Tell the wizard what header items you want on the page.**

   The typical memo headers are Date, From, and Subject. Select the check box next to each header that interests you and then edit its text box to suit.

10. **Click Next.**

11. **Add your To: and Cc: recipients.**

    You can either type their names or click the Address Book button to add them from an Exchange or Outlook address book, like the one you may have created in Chapter 5.

12. **Click Next.**

When you're addressing your memo, you can choose to have a separate distribution list page (click the Yes radio button), which you staple to the front of the memo — just one of those options for the never-ending quest to justify additional office supply purchases in a multinational corporation. After all, the wheels of commerce must turn.

13. **Select the check boxes next to any item that you want to include, type any initials you want for writer and typist, and then type the number of enclosures your unsuspecting reader is to expect in this termination packet, or similar memo.**

    For example, you can type the initials **TS/dj** if Todd dictates the memo to underling Dave, or, if you awoke from the nightmare, type **DJ/ts**.

14. **Click Next.**

15. **Finally, the header and footer: Select the check boxes next to the items that you want to appear in small text at the top (header) and bottom (footer) of the page.**

16. **When you're finished, Click Next to see a happy little congratulatory message from Microsoft's Happy User Communications division, or click Finish.**

    You're done! The wizard takes a few seconds to generate the completed memo (at least, the wizard takes a few seconds on our ultrapowerful, decked out, often-augmented-by-tech-company-Public Relations-departments PCs) that eventually appears onscreen. Then you can edit away, like you would in any other Microsoft Word document. The only difference is that you probably feel a little better about yourself for having saved so much time.

Coming up next — create your own memo template. If you use the wizard to create a template, you want to leave out all the very specific bits, like the memo's subject, the closing initials, and the date. That way you can use the memo you create with the wizard over and over again, after it begins its life as a template.

Building your own memo template

In the preceding section, "Talking to the wizard," you created a single memo. Pretend that you really, really like the way that memo turned out. Now you're ready to create a customized template of that memo so that you don't have to go through the wizard every time you want to fire off a few additional thoughts (or fire a few additional employees).

You can create that template two ways: You can work from the memo you just created, or you can create a new template for scratch.

Create a template from your original memo

Here's how you save the original memo as a template:

1. **With the memo opened onscreen, choose File⇨Save.**

   If you already saved the memo once, choose File⇨Save As.

2. **In the Save As dialog box, move down to the menu called Save as type, and choose Word Template (*.dot).**

   Notice that the folder that you save in becomes to the Templates folder (see Figure 9-5).

3. **Give your template a name in the File name text box.**

   You have plenty of letters to play with in the name of your file. For the best viewing in the New dialog box, put spaces in the name of your template. Basic Business Memo works better than Basic_Business_Memo, when viewed in the New dialog box.

4. **Click Save.**

   The template is saved in Word's Template directory and is available to you as a template the next time you open a New document.

Create a new template

If you'd like to cut out the middleman and set out to create a template, you can do that, too, using an existing memo template or wizard:

1. **Choose File⇨New and click the Memo tab to see the templates and wizards for memos that Microsoft created.**

2. **In the lower-right corner of the New dialog box, choose the option marked Template in the Create New section.**

3. **Select one of the templates with a single click of the mouse.**

4. **If you like the preview, click OK.**

   You can also choose a wizard and select OK.

File Location

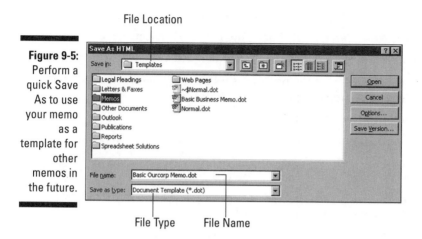

Figure 9-5:
Perform a
quick Save
As to use
your memo
as a
template for
other
memos in
the future.

File Type   File Name

5. **Then follow the procedures in the earlier section, "Talking to the wizard," before returning to Step 6, below.**

   The memo is generated and shown onscreen.

6. **Edit the memo to taste (as described in the earlier section "Communicating with the help").**

7. **Choose Save.**

   The Save As dialog box appears with the Templates folder already selected and the Save As Type box grayed out. You can only save this memo as a template.

8. **Give the template a name, and click Save.**

No matter how you got to the Save As dialog box and the Templates folder, notice that you can select one of the folders within the Templates folder to better organize the template that you're saving. Each folder represents one of the tabs in Word's New dialog box (refer to Figure 9-2). You can either create your own subfolders or use those that already exist, like Memos.

Communicating with the masses

Some philosophers believe the computers are killing the personal letter that for hundreds of years was the cornerstone of high intelligence and snooty literacy. We say, sure, that's happened, but business letters sure look a lot cooler. Oh, yeah. Microsoft Word 97, for example, makes it a cinch to create great-looking company letters and letterhead that say at least one thing about your company — you know how to create great-looking letters.

The meaningful words and catchy twists of phrase are up to you. But if you'll allow us, we'll show you how to create a snazzy business letter using a Word template:

1. **Choose File⇨New from the Microsoft Word menu bar.**

2. **In the New dialog box, choose the tab marked Letters & Faxes.**

3. **To preview one of the Letter templates, click the template's icon.**

   A bird's-eye view of the page appears in the Preview windows on the right side of the dialog box.

4. **If you like the template, click OK.**

   Word then generates a page based on the template you chose.

5. **To edit the different parts of the letter, click the areas that say** [Click Here and Type...] **on the page.**

   After that text is highlighted, you can type your own text for the various areas using the keyboard.

6. **To edit the body of your letter, select all the text in the letter with your mouse (see Figure 9-6), press Delete and begin typing.**

7. **You can Save the letter using File⇨Save, and print it using File⇨Print.**

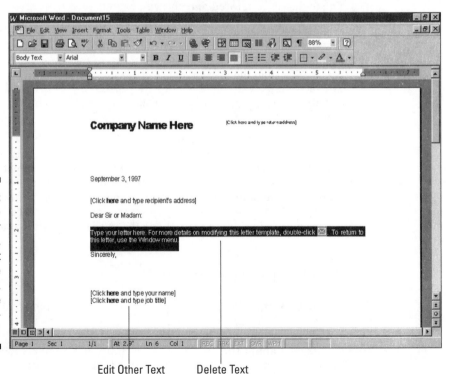

Figure 9-6:
Edit the letter template, and fire it off to the printer. You're communicating!

Edit Other Text   Delete Text

As with other templates for memos, faxes, and envelopes in Word, the Microsoft programmers created predefined styles that correspond to different parts of your letter. You can use these styles in the pull-down menu in the Formatting toolbar to change entire paragraphs to a particular letter style, like a Heading, Salutation, or Signature Line.

Creating letters with Ms. Wizard

The Letter Wizard allows you to quickly construct a complete shell of a business letter using one of Word's built-in designs. The wizard walks you through all the steps, giving you another five minutes or so of your life back, that you can chalk up to computerized productivity.

To create a letter:

1. **Choose File⇨New from the Word menu bar and then select the Letters & Faxes tab.**

2. **Select the Letter Wizard icon in the New dialog box and click OK (or double-click the Letter Wizard icon).**

   A new letter appears in the Microsoft Word editing window.

   Depending on your Word preferences settings, either the Office Assistant or a normal dialog box appears, asking you how many copies of the letter you expect to send.

3. **Choose to Send one letter in the thought bubble that appears over the Office Assistant.**

   The Letter Wizard finally appears, as shown in Figure 9-7. True to form, this wizard works almost completely unlike all the others.

4. **With the Letter Format tab selected, type a Date Line and choose the page design and letter style from their respective pull-down menus.**

   Your choices are pretty self-explanatory. Choose an overall design style like Contemporary or Professional. Then decide how you like your letters formatted: Block style (with everything aligned to the left), Modified Block (with the signature over on the right side like your grade school teacher taught you) and Semi-block, which looks pretty traditional.

5. **When you're done, click the Next button or the Recipient Info tab.**

   In both cases you move on to the next section where you enter information about the person to whom you're sending this letter.

   If you're using preprinted letterhead, you can select the check box in this part of the wizard labeled Pre-printed Letterhead. Then tell the wizard where the letterhead elements appear on the page and how much room to leave blank before printing your letter.

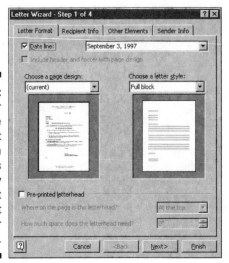

Figure 9-7:
The Letter
Wizard, like
most
wizards in
Office 97, is
completely
different
from most
of the other
wizards.

6. **You can use the Address Book to add the name of a recipient, or manually type the name and address in the available text boxes.**

7. **Choose a salutation either from the menu or by clicking the radio button next to the sort of salutation you want.**

   If you typed a name for your recipient, the wizard automatically generates what it considers to be appropriate salutations.

8. **Click Next, or the Other Elements tab.**

9. **To include one of the special lines in the header of your letter, select the check box next to its description and then fill in the line in the associated text box.**

10. **At the bottom of the wizard dialog box, you can type in the Cc: text area to add *carbon copy* recipients for this letter.**

11. **Click either the Next button or the Sender Info tab to move on.**

    Here's the final screen.

    If you typed your name and address elsewhere in the myriad cubbyholes of personal information that Windows and Office use to keep tabs on you (not that there's any possibility of wrongdoing, mind you), that information automatically appears here.

12. **You can select the Omit check box to keep your address for the return address on the letter.**

    Otherwise, you can edit the name and address.

13. **You can also use the check marks and menus to add a closing to your document, and the Preview window allows you to witness your creation.**

    If you ever wondered if you can use *Intelligently Yours* or *Best Beware* as a complimentary closing, you may look to this wizard for guidance.

14. **When you're done, click Finish.**

    Word returns you to the document editing window,

15. **Highlight all the phony body text and press Delete.**

    Now you can start typing your own letter.

16. **At any time, you can save using File⇨Save or print using File⇨Print.**

Creating a letter template

We'll make this quick because creating a letter template is remarkably similar to the way you create a memo template. You have two ways you can make your letter a template that can be used for subsequent correspondence sessions:

✔ With the finished letter (or the finished shell of a letter) onscreen, choose File⇨Save As. In the Save As dialog box, choose Word Template from the Save as type menu and give the template a name. All the tips and tricks outlined in the earlier section, "Building your own memo template," apply to creating a letter template.

✔ Choose File⇨New if you haven't yet created a new letter. Before you select one of Word's letter templates, or the Letter Wizard, select the Template radio button in the Create New section of the New dialog box. Then create a new letter, as outlined in the previous two sections.

Crisis scenario #1: What will you put the letter in?!

After you finish the letter, by gum, you need an envelope. We don't know how many people we meet who keep an old IBM Selectric hanging out for the express purpose of typing envelopes. Maybe doing that works for you, too. Let us say this: Envelopes printed on laser and inkjet printers look really good, professional, and all that. Keep typing if you want to, but you only need a few minutes to set up a nice little envelope template that you can use for life.

You can create an envelope two basic ways: on its own or along with a letter you created. We start you off with the second example, first — in the tradition of confusing academic writing.

Envelopes and letters living together

Here's how you create an envelope along with a letter:

1. With the letter open onscreen, choose Tools➪Envelopes and Labels.

The Envelopes and Labels dialog box appears (see Figure 9-8).

Depending how you created the letter — and sheer, random chance — you may have certain aspects of your envelope (Delivery address/ Return address) automatically filled in.

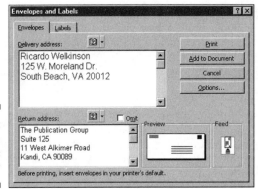

Figure 9-8: A knight in wizard's clothing?

2. Fill in the Delivery and Return addresses by typing in their respective text areas.

You can also use the address book buttons to access your Exchange or Outlook address listings.

3. Next, click the Options button.

4. With the Envelope Options tab selected, choose envelope characteristics like envelope size, whether you want a delivery barcode printed, and what font you want to use for the various parts of the envelope.

5. Click the Printing Options tag.

6. Tell Word what printer you want to use and how you'll feed the envelope into the printer.

7. Click OK when you're done setting options.

8. **Back in the Envelopes and Labels dialog box, the last step is a two-prong decision point:**

   - Click the Add to Document button, which makes the envelope page zero of your letter document (so it stays part of the document when you save).

   - Choose to Print the envelope immediately.

The stand-alone envelope

The other way to create an envelope is to begin with the Envelope Wizard in Word's New menu item. Just as you can with letters and memos, you can quickly generate a custom envelope with the automagical help of a Microsoft wizard. (Why do we have this nagging feeling that we need to reread *Brave New World*?)

In the words of the immortal Lawrence Welk, "And-a-one-and-a-two":

1. **Choose File⇨New from the Word menu bar.**

2. **In the New dialog box, click the Letters & Faxes tab.**

3. **Select the Envelope Wizard icon and click OK.**

   Depending on your settings, a dialog box or the Office Assistant pops up to ask you if you want to create a single envelope or one from a mailing list.

4. **Choose to Create one envelope.**

   The Envelopes and Labels dialog box, discussed in the previous section, appears onscreen. To create envelopes from a mailing list, see Chapter 10.

5. **Go nuts.**

   Not literally, unless you've already committed to CreditShielder, allowing you to go completely insane while never having to worry that your credit card minimum payments are covered for life. Instead, we simply mean that you should complete the envelope as detailed in the preceding section, "Envelopes and letters living together." Oh, and try to have some fun while you're at it.

Creating the Perfect Fax Cover Sheet

Early in the 20th century, monopolies were the rage. Busting the trusts that had become part of American business took a Big Stick president and Oliver Wendell Holmes. The economy recovered — after a little downtime, followed by a rather instrumental war — and thrived on traditional principles in a market unfettered by competition. Then the Japanese approach took over, as Demming, Z Corps, and Management By Walking Around all came and went.

Why this history lesson? Because, especially in North America, businesses are once again taking a new approach to gauging success. In the early years, profit and dominance measured success, followed by profit-sharing and employee satisfaction. We once even measured success by the aggregate of individual productivity within an organization.

All that has changed. These days, the mantra in American business is unmistakable, straightforward, and, ultimately, attainable. *The best fax cover sheet wins.* No other yardstick exists.

Fax cover sheet templates

It's hard to imagine that you want to spend too much time on this, but if you took our advice earlier in this chapter, maybe you're not even reading this part. Instead, your hired assistant is reading it for you, so we're not even talking to you right now. You may as well just ignore what we're saying. (Sheesh! This time, we're even confusing ourselves.)

Here's how you use a fax cover sheet template:

1. **Choose File⇨New from the Word menu bar.**

2. **Choose the Letters & Faxes tab in the New dialog box.**

3. **Click one of the fax templates to see a Preview of the fax cover sheet.**

4. **If you like what you see, click OK.**

   If you're creating a cover sheet that you want to make a template for all your future fax cover sheets, make sure that you choose the Template option under Create New in the New dialog box.

   A new document is created using the fax template as a guide.

5. **Click any of the** [Click here and type...] **entries to edit your fax cover page.**

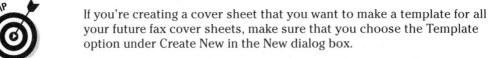

6. **To type notes for your fax cover sheet, highlight the paragraph text below the address section, and press Delete.**

7. **Now, type your message.**

8. **Choose File⇨Save to save the file, or to save it as a template if that's your objective, and choose File⇨Print to print this cover sheet.**

Remember that you can print directly to your modem and send a fax that way if everything is properly configured in Windows. Just choose your fax modem from the Printer Name menu in the Print dialog box.

Fax cover sheet via wizard

You may be hard pressed to believe this, but a wizard exists to assist you in creating a fax cover sheet in Word. We know what you're thinking — "Does the value never end?!" That's right, you may not have known when you signed on for your copy of Office 97, but a fax cover sheet wizard is included *at no additional cost*. But wait, there's more.

Actually, the Fax Wizard aides in not only creating a fax cover sheet but also faxing a completed document and cover sheet. You'll really be sending an electronic facsimile of a computer document in *no time at all*.

How much would you pay for that? (You caught us — we write infomercials in our downtime. You didn't think Todd paid for that bass boat just by writing computer books, did ya?)

Here's how you create a cover sheet with the wizard :

1. **Choose File⇨New from Word's menu bar.**

2. **In the New dialog box, select the Letters & Faxes tab and then select the Fax Wizard icon.**

3. **Click OK.**

   The Wizard starts up, but if its first screen is any indication of its power, we're all in trouble. All it says is that the wizard assists you in creating a cover sheet, but we already knew that!

4. **Click Next.**

5. **Decide if you want to send a document and if you want to send a cover sheet with it, and use the radio buttons to make your choices.**

6. **Click Next.**

   If you don't see the document you want to send in the wizard's menu, close the wizard, open the document you want to fax, and restart the wizard. Sorry, that's what you have to do.

7. **Choose the fax program that you want to use to send this fax, or choose to print the fax, and then click Next.**

   Microsoft Fax is the default fax program choice because it has *Microsoft* in its title. (And it comes with Windows.)

8. **Type the names and phone numbers of your intended recipients, or choose them from the Address Book button, and then click Next.**

9. **Choose the style for your cover sheet, and click Next.**

10. **Type a little information about yourself to add to the page.**

    If you typed yourself in an Exchange or Outlook Address Book, or if you want to pretend someone else is sending this fax, click the Address Book button to choose an entry from the Address Book.

11. **Click Next to be heartily congratulated by a computer program, or if you don't need that much positive reinforcement, click the Finish button.**

Your fax cover sheet is created. Edit as desired by clicking on the [Click here and type...] entries, and then typing appropriate replacement text. To send the fax, choose File➪Print from the Word menu bar. You'll notice, in the Print dialog box that the wizard has already set your Printer Name to either a fax driver or a printer, depending on your choice from within the wizard.

You can also choose the save the fax cover sheet by choosing File➪Save.

Creating Your Own Business Cards and Labels

Ah, the business card. In American business, these little lines of communications into the outside world are often sacred symbols of middle management: You haven't arrived until you're held in high enough esteem to warrant a piece of card stock with your very own name on it, along with the company logo.

If you're in business for yourself, forget that tired line. Business cards are advertising, name awareness, and worth giving to every employee. Plus, they're pretty easy to create for yourself in Word. They're not raised-letter, full color testaments to your ability to jockey favor with the vice president, but even black-and-white business cards can be stapled into a prospective customer's Rolodex.

Of course, Word has a business card wizard, but it's a bit buried, so follow along carefully.

Note two things. First, when we say *business card* in this section, realize that the same instructions can be used for creating labels, folder labels, stick-on addresses, and diskette labels. Second, the wizard in Word is smart enough to set up your page so that it works with those labels and business cards that are designed for computer printers and that you can buy at the office supply story. Avery made most of the boxes of these fancy little card stocks lying around our office. Each Avery-type card style has a little number and general instructions included that tell you how to set up the wizard in Word and other applications.

Here's how you create your business cards:

1. **Create a new, blank document by choosing File⇨New, the General tab, and the Blank template.**

   Inhale. Good! Exhale.

2. **Click OK.**

   A blank page appears.

3. **Choose Tools⇨Envelopes and Labels from the Word menu bar.**

4. **In the Envelopes and Labels dialog box, click the Labels tab if it's not already selected.**

5. **Click the Options button.**

   The Label Options dialog box appears.

6. **From the Label products menu, choose the name brand of the business card sheets that you bought at the office supply store.**

   If you don't see your brand, choose the brand that's recommended by the instructions that came with your business cards, or try Other, which may include your product.

7. **In the Product number listing, find and select the type of business card or label that you want to print and then click OK.**

   Some of the cards on the market will want you to play with Word's default settings. You find those by clicking the Details button.

8. **Click the New Document button in the Envelopes and Labels dialog box.**

   In most cases (assuming you're printing on a sheet of cards or labels that is fed through a laser or inkjet printer instead of a dedicated label printer), you'll now you have a new document that is broken up into boxes that are just the right size for business cards.

9. **In the upper-left box, design your business card.**

10. **After you design the card, move the mouse pointer to the left edge of the card.**

    The mouse pointer turns into a right-facing pointer.

11. **Click the mouse button to select the entire card.**

12. **Now, using Edit⇨Copy and Edit⇨Paste, you can paste the business card design into all the other boxes in the document.**

    You're ready to print.

13. **Use the File⇨Print command to print this page.**

    You may want to print a test page first on regular paper to make sure everything is lined up. (That business card stock can be a tad expensive.)

14. **If you're satisfied, feed the card stock into your printer.**

    Check your printer's documentation to determine whether the card stock should be fed face up or face down.

15. **Use the Number of copies entry in the Print dialog box to select how many pages of cards you want to print.**

Check your document carefully before printing many sheets of those expensive cards or labels. Be especially sure that you have everything lined up correctly. For best results, you want to create a document with one complete page of cards or labels, and then print it multiple times (no warranties are expressed or implied).

Chapter 10

Creating Sales and Marketing Material

. . . .

In This Chapter

▶ Keeping in contact with contacts

▶ Discovering reasons #1 and #2 to create a database

▶ Creating a newsletter, just like GigantaCorp's

▶ Making brochures the easy way (but you still have to fold them)

. . . .

*I*f you believe the core values statement at your company, you're in business to respect diversity, maintain personal integrity, and support community partnerships. The mission statement is just as helpful: Expand the corporate envelope of proactivity through teamwork, resilience, and targeted growth.

On the other hand, you also have to consider the whole issue of serving customers and making a profit. If you're interested in these lesser known topics, perhaps you want to take a gander at this chapter, in which we talk about ways to make your small business seem a little more like a big business. How do you make your small business look big? With sharp, professional-looking sales materials and efficient marketing strategies, of course. Sure, hang on to those core value statements, but also learn how to create a newsletter and contact logs, too. If you use Office 97 and the lessons in this chapter, Microsoft will soon quiver at the sound of your company's name — trust us.

Keeping in Contact with Contacts

You have a few ways to tell if you're a highly effective person. Take this quiz, for example:

1. **When your significant other says, "Honey, tonight is your night to make dinner," do you:**

   a. Prepare the meal first thing in the morning, before leaving for the office.

   b. Make Rice-a-Roni at 6 p.m. and serve it with day-old chicken.

   c. Order a pizza.

2. **When you need to call that guy from the trade show, do you:**

   a. Flip around in your Rolodex because you're sure you wrote it in there somewhere.

   b. Thumb through two dozen sticky notes that you've been scribbling on since the office Christmas party.

   c. Find the info instantly, thanks to Outlook.

Though we're of very little help about the whole dinner thing — Todd eats pizza four days per week — maybe we can try to get your contact log in order. Outlook is a great program for managing contacts, exporting the information to other applications, and managing vitals like phone conversations, meetings, and correspondence.

Storing contact info in Outlook instead of my current method, an old shoebox

If you're new to Outlook, you probably don't already have a comprehensive database of contacts. Using Outlook as your central warehouse for contact info is in your best interest because you can use that information in many ways. From Outlook, you can perform all kinds of tasks, including:

- Sending e-mail
- Visiting your contact's Web page
- Calling your contacts
- Tracking phone calls and other correspondence
- Tracking time spent on phone calls and other correspondence, such as for billing purposes
- Creating mail-merged documents

Creating contacts

Switch to the Contacts view by clicking the Contacts button in the Outlook bar and you'll see a virgin white expanse that someday, if you play your cards right, will be filled with information about your contacts. To create a new contact, do this:

1. **Double-click anywhere on the Contacts module.**

2. **Fill in the details.**

   Yeah, this isn't rocket science. Just fill the stupid thing in (see Figure 10-1). For details, check out Chapter 5.

   The Contacts module has four tabs. The most important information is on the General tab, where you can input the contact's name, address, phone numbers, and e-mail addresses. Fill in as much detail as you want on the General and Details tabs. (You use the Journal tab later in this section.) You can even create custom fields on the All Fields tab.

3. **When you add all the information, click the Save and Close button in the toolbar.**

The first entry is one Microsoft added, called Welcome to Contacts. To delete it, or any other contact, just click the entry and press your Delete key.

Figure 10-1:
Use the Contacts page and you have the benefit of all your contact data in one place for phone calls, logs, and even mail merge in other Office programs.

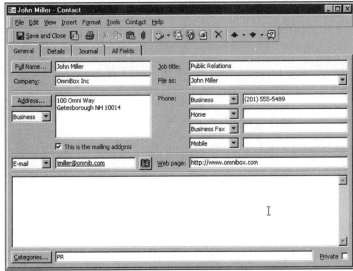

Getting organized with categories

When you get more than a few dozen contacts, you may want to change the way they're displayed so that you can easily locate specific entries. Changing the view is easy and fun (okay, it's only fun if you also enjoy creating your own Windows wallpaper, but don't start splitting hairs).

The first thing you need to do is assign categories. Categories (like co-workers, bowling buddies, editors, and probation officers) help you segment your contacts into easy-to-manage groups. You can create your own categories and assign them to individual contacts. Flip to Chapter 5 for details on how to assign, edit, and delete categories.

Finding a needle in a contact list

Dave has about 300 individuals in his Contacts database. Even when you use the alphabet tabs on the right edge of the window, finding the right entry can be an arduous task. Half the time, you may not even remember the person's name. Instead you may remember something nebulous, like that she's an editor at *Floppy Disk Weekly*. That's where the search tool comes in handy. To perform a search, try this:

1. **Click the Find Items button in the toolbar.**

   It is on the right side, to the left of the Help button. The Find dialog box appears, as seen in Figure 10-2.

2. **Type a word or two in the Sear͟ch for the word(s) box.**

3. **Click the drop-down In menu and choose frequently-used text fields.**

4. **Click Find ͟Now.**

You can, of course, search for any of the specific fields, like a name or phone number, but we've found that this is the most effective way to search. This way, you don't need to worry about whether you typed the key word you're looking for on the Company or Job Title text boxes, for example, when you originally created the entry.

Using your contacts

Now that you have a fairly good idea how to create, manage, and find specific contacts, take a look at how to get work done with them. Let's face it — as small business people, we all spend an awful lot of time communicating. In fact, we're fairly sure that we spend almost as much time on the phone as we do goofing off with the latest computer games. If you want to be able to spend as much time blasting ships from the Zorf Galaxy as we do, make sure that Outlook holds the information for all your important contacts.

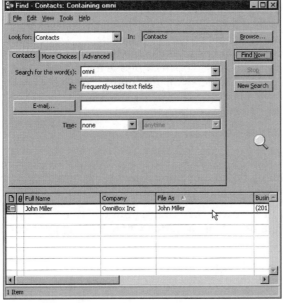

Figure 10-2:
The easiest way to search is by looking in frequently-used text fields, though you have other ways to look.

Sending e-mail

After you type e-mail addresses for your contacts, you can easily send the messages right from the Contacts view. Just do this:

1. **Select the contact entry to which you want to send a message.**

2. **Click the New Message to Contact button from the toolbar.**

   The button looks like an envelope.

3. **If you have multiple e-mail addresses for this person, delete the unwanted ones from the** To: **line.**

Deleting those extra addresses each time is a hassle. Unless you have a really good reason to type more than one address for your contacts, just type one address. You can always include backup addresses in the Notes section of their Contact information.

Surf their Web site

Because the Contacts format allows for a Web page Uniform Resource Locator (URL), you can view your contacts' page just by selecting the appropriate contact entry and clicking the toolbar button marked Explore Web Page (it looks like the Internet Explorer Web page icon). Your browser starts and automatically opens the designated Web page.

Maintaining phone logs

In addition to handy tools like e-mail and Web pages, Outlook dials the phone for any contact that has a phone number. When you're on the phone with your contact, Outlook also opens a phone log that records how long you were on the phone, and lets you take notes. Here's how:

1. **Right-click the desired contact.**

2. **Choose AutoDialer from the Context menu.**

   The New Call dialog box opens.

3. **If you originally typed more than one phone number for this contact, select the appropriate phone number.**

4. **If you want to keep a record of the phone call, be sure to check the box for Create new Journal Entry when starting new call (see Figure 10-3).**

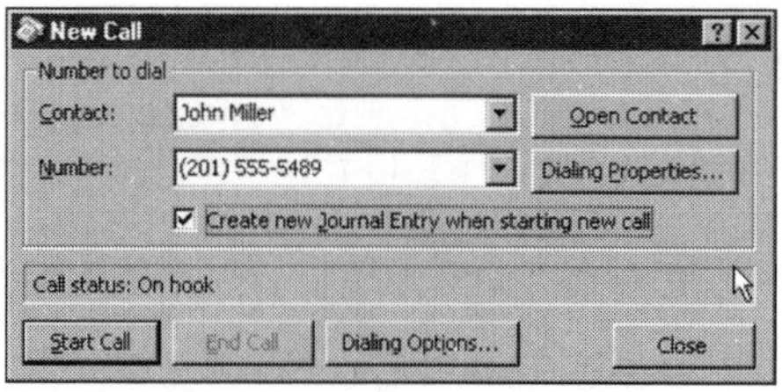

Figure 10-3:
The Journal
lets you
make a
written
record of
your
conversation,
along with
the time
and length
of the call.

5. **When you're ready to place the call, click the Start Call button.**

   When the number begins dialing, the Call Status dialog box opens.

6. **Click the Talk button, pick up your phone, and wait for an answer.**

7. **If you chose to record the call in the Journal, type any notes you want in the large text box.**

8. **Click Save and Close when you are done with the call.**

You may at some point need to look back at your phone logs for billing or other reference purposes. Here are two ways to see these entries — use the one you like best:

✔ To see a sequential list of all the Journal entries for a particular person, go to the Contacts view, find the appropriate entry, and open it. Click the Journal tab, and you see all the phone logs and other journal entries that refer to that individual, as shown in Figure 10-4.

✔ To see all the Journal entries in a particular time frame, the Outlook Journal view is more appropriate (see Figure 10-5). From there, you can compare the work done with one individual against others in the same day or week.

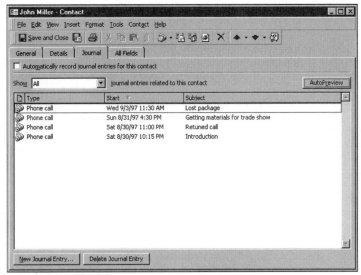

Figure 10-4:
A phone log
in the
Journal.

Managing Projects with Outlook

A recent survey showed that the average worker places over 12,000 telephone calls every day, and that doesn't include personal messages. If you're dubious about the accuracy of our poll data, don't be. Continuing a proud tradition we like to call *zero-based research,* we made the number up.

Nonetheless, we think you get the point that people are busy. Computers, originally designed to make our lives more complicated, can, surprisingly, be used for just the opposite purpose. Specifically, you can use Outlook to track the status of people, calls, projects, and activities with ease. In fact, Outlook is great at keeping you on top of all your daily activities.

Here's a common scenario: Imagine that you need to complete a short-term project that involves a dozen vendors. Some vendors you know, and others you don't. You need to take detailed notes on many phone conversations, and track many e-mail messages that you conduct with each of them.

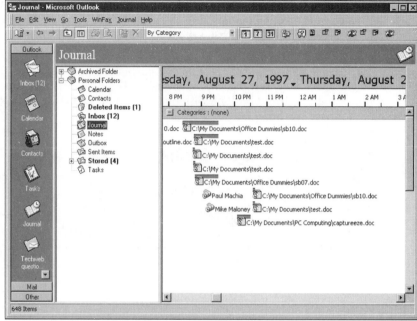

Figure 10-5:
Track all
the work
from the
Journal's
timeline
view, or go
straight to a
Contact
entry and
see the
Journal
entries.

You can get through this project in many ways. A common method is to scrawl notes on a tablet (paper, stone, over-the-counter ibuprofin, your choice), and eventually develop a rather extensive collection of notes on different pieces of paper. Sure, you may try to organize the stuff and keep all the information together, but eventually something important gets lost. Or you eventually forget to take notes on a critical call and forget which vendor is throwing in the free color TV with every box of MiracleWidgets.

That's why you use Outlook to manage your contacts on a project-by-project basis. Here's what you do to get ready:

1. **Create a category that describes your *projet du jour* (that's French, we're told, for *project with soup*).**

   Specifically, choose Edit⇔Categories, and use the Master Category List button to add a new category. Click New and enter the name of the category you're adding.

2. **When you add new contacts to Outlook for this project, assign them to the project category you just created.**

3. **Go back to existing contacts, and assign them to this category, as well.**

4. **Edit the Journal options so that it registers e-mail for the contacts in your project.**

5. **Choose Tools⇔Options, and click the Journal tab.**

6. **Select E-mail message on the left, and the name of each contact in your project on the right.**

And now for the steps that make this all worthwhile: You define a view so that everything, except the current project's contacts, is hidden:

1. **Choose View⇨Filter, and click the More Choices tab.**

2. **Select the category that represents the project and click OK.**

3. **Save this view for easy selection in the future.**

4. **Choose View⇨Define Views.**

5. **Make sure <Current View settings> is selected and click the Copy button.**

6. **Name the view (Project is probably a great name, unless you have a lot of projects — then be more specific, as in Figure 10-6), and click OK.**

   You can change the display settings before saving, but they're probably okay as is.

7. **Click OK.**

Now here's the payoff. When you want to work on a project, choose the view you just created from the drop-down View menu, and you see only the contacts that belong to the project's category. You can open a specific contact and drill down to the individual calls and e-mails you exchanged. If you take good notes on the phone, you have a complete record of everything you did in the project.

Figure 10-6:
Create a view in Outlook for each of your projects. That way you can switch to those contacts involved with that job with just a mouse click.

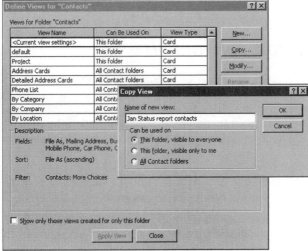

Keep these things in mind when you work with contacts:

✔ When you place a call to a contact, switch to the Contacts module and open the entry for the person you are calling. Click the Journal tab and double-click in the display window. Take notes on the call and close the dialog box when you're done.

✔ When you send an e-mail to the contact, a copy of the message automatically appears in this Journal display.

You can assign the same contact to more than one category. That means one contact can belong in several projects and display properly no matter which project you happen to be working on.

Reasons #1 and #2 to Create a Database: Mail Merge and Labels

Sometimes the title says all you need to know. For example, consider *The Old Man and the Sea*. That one covers both the main character and the plot, with a fairly high level of detail. Another one is *Aliens*. You just know when you sit down to watch that movie that the movie is about, well, aliens. Any suspicion that it's about just one alien is dispelled almost immediately. This section's heading leaves little to the imagination as well. Here we talk about mail merging things like envelopes and labels, which is a good thing because as the title also says, you have few other reasons to maintain a database that are so compelling as the mail merge.

Mail merge envelopes: Using the Outlook contact list

If you're a fairly dedicated user of Outlook, you can easily grab the data in the Contacts module and merge it into Word for mass mailings. (If you don't keep your addresses in Outlook, this section may convince you to start.) In fact, Word uses a very user-friendly dialog box, called the Mail Merge Helper, to walk you through each step. The Helper has three main sections:

✔ **Main document:** This is where you specify what kind of document you want to create, such as a letter, envelope, or label. You can also edit the document in this section.

✔ **Data source:** This is where you tell Word where to get the names and addresses. You can use a database already created in Word, or grab an external phone list, for example, from Outlook.

✔ **Merge the data with the document:** The final step — this is where you actually insert each name and address into a different copy of the main document.

Just complete each of those sections in sequence and you'll be all set. Say you want to print envelopes for a mass mailing. Here's what you do:

1. **In Word, choose Tools⇨Mail Merge.**

2. **Click the Create button and choose the kind of document to make — in this case, envelopes (see Figure 10-7).**

   You get a choice of creating envelopes in the active document or in a new document.

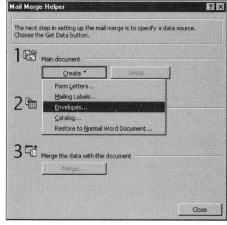

Figure 10-7:
The Mail Merge Helper is a great tool for creating mail-merged documents.

3. **Choose new document.**

   Now you get to choose the data source. The data source is the file that contains all your addresses.

4. **Click Get data and choose Use Address Book.**

5. **From the next dialog box, choose Outlook.**

   After a few moments, Word provides a dialog box and insists that you set up the main document.

6. **Click Set up main document.**

   The most important part of this procedure is that you need to ensure that the envelopes are set to properly feed into the printer.

7. **After the dialog box is configured for the way you load your printer, click OK.**

   Next, you need to design the layout of the address on the envelope.

8. **Use the Insert Merge Field button to add the name, address, and zip code for the addressee.**

   Don't forget to insert a space between mail merge fields that share a line, such as first and last name.

9. **If you want the postal bar code to appear on your envelope, select the bar code button, and select the field that has the addressee's zip code.**

   The finished product resembles Figure 10-8.

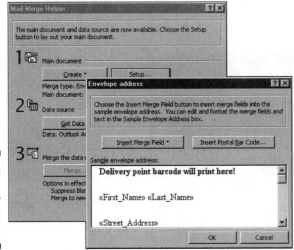

Figure 10-8:
Getting a
postal bar
code on an
envelope.

You can change the default return address from Word's Tools⇨Options menu. Just choose the User information tab.

Almost done — finally, you get to merge. Before you just jump right in and merge, however, you need to fine-tune the data. After all, you may not want to send this envelope to everyone in your Outlook database.

10. **Click the Query Options button, and you see a dialog box like the one in Figure 10-9.**

11. **Choose whatever criteria you want to limit your printouts with.**

    For example, you may have entries in Outlook without complete addresses. Instead of wasting paper, you can set the Filter Records tab so that it looks like this:

    • **Field:** Postal Code

    • **Comparison:** Not blank

    • **Compare to:** <blank>

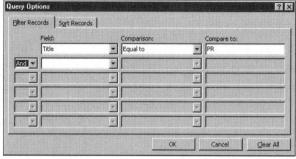

These settings make envelopes for Outlook entries that have zip code entries. You can also try this one:

- **Field:** City

- **Comparison:** Equal to

- **Compare to:** Colorado Springs

These settings create envelopes for your friends, customers, and associates in Colorado Springs.

12. Finally, click the Merge button.

If you plan to use the same merge file again, save it to a new Word document from the Merge dialog box. Otherwise, you can merge the envelopes directly to the printer.

Merging a form letter

Whew! That one had many steps, but we think that you'll agree that the merging process is fairly simple. The other merge documents — like labels, form letters, and catalogs — work basically the same way.

One of the most important differences between the form letter and the envelope is the rather free-form style available to you. The post office doesn't much care for liberally organized, eclectically arranged envelopes, but you can do anything you want with the form letter. In fact, if you select the form letter option, you get a blank page in which to craft your letter.

Keep in mind that when you're creating a form letter, you needn't just include simple address information. You can embed merge fields throughout the document, to personalize it as much as you want. You've probably seen letters that say:

> *Dear Mr. Stauffer,*
>
> *Congratulations! You are among just 200 million others to receive this exclusive notice!*

This type of letter is created with merge fields. This hasn't stopped Todd from saving all the letters he gets in big shoe boxes under his bed, and for two reasons: First, he's a lonely guy who doesn't get the volumes of fan mail Dave regularly boasts about; second, he has really big feet.

When you create a form letter, you'll probably find yourself using the Mail Merge toolbar (see Figure 10-10) in Word. Here's what you'll need to do:

1. **Choose Tools⇨Mail Merge.**

2. **Click the Create button and choose Form Letters from the drop-down menu.**

3. **If you're using the Outlook Address Book for mail merge addresses, do that next by choosing Get Data.**

   You can't insert merge fields until the database is available.

   Word tells you that you haven't created any merge fields and drops you back to the blank page.

4. **You can now craft your letter and use the Insert Merge Field button in the toolbar to add merge fields.**

5. **When you finish the letter to your satisfaction, you can click the Mail Merge Helper button in the toolbar to get the familiar Mail Merge Helper dialog box back.**

6. **Finish the process using the same concept as we used for envelopes back in "Mail merge envelopes: Using the Outlook contact list."**

You can turn the Mail Merge toolbar on and off any time you want. Just right-click in the toolbar area of the screen and either select or deselect Mail Merge from the menu.

You may often want to use the same sort of form letter. Be sure to save it to the hard disk with merge fields intact when you're done with it.

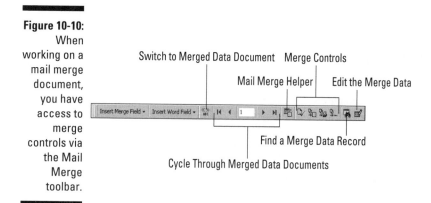

Figure 10-10:
When working on a mail merge document, you have access to merge controls via the Mail Merge toolbar.

Switch to Merged Data Document   Merge Controls

Mail Merge Helper   Edit the Merge Data

Find a Merge Data Record

Cycle Through Merged Data Documents

Merging data by category, date, or other wacky criteria

"Okay, cool," you say: Using the filter control, you can print letters just for people in a particular zip code, state, or with certain names. But what if you want only to send letters to people filed in your Outlook category called *Weird, Rambling Hate Mail?*

Or what if your business is a veterinary clinic? You probably have vaccination reminders that you need to send to specific clients on a monthly basis. How can you set Word's filter criteria to do that?

You can set such special filters the same way as we set filter criteria back in "Mail merge envelopes: Using the Outlook contact list," but with one big difference: You can't just import the Outlook Address Book directly. When you perform a direct import, you don't get all the fields that Outlook actually stores. You don't get categories, for example.

But there's a way arond this importing issue. When you're ready to merge, do this:

1. **In Outlook, go to the Contacts module and choose File➪Import and Export.**

2. **Choose Export to a file and save it as a Microsoft Excel file on your hard disk.**

3. **Switch back to Word, and when you're ready to import the addresses into your mail merge project, select Open Data Source.**

4. **Select the file you just exported from Outlook.**

   Now when you create your document, you have more fields available to play with.

You can create documents for everyone in two different categories, for example, by setting the filter this way:

- ✔ **Field:** Category
- ✔ **Comparison:** Equal to
- ✔ **Compare to:** Friends

Or this way:

- ✔ **Field:** Category
- ✔ **Comparison:** Equal to
- ✔ **Compare to:** Enemies

All your friends and enemies — at least those you put in those categories, receive this document.

We want to make sure that you understand the way Boolean operators work in filters. No, Boolean operators are not what you get when you dial 411 in the smaller American Protectorate islands in the Pacific. Boolean operators let you combine information, so you can be more selective.

In the case of the example we just used, if you want all the people listed in the Friends category and all the folks in the Enemies category, you need to use the Boolean operator **or**. That tells the mail merge engine to include anyone in the Friend category **or** the Enemy category. If you use **and**, an entry would have to be in the Friend **and** the Enemy category to be included (a much smaller group because not many people are likely to be listed as both a friend and an enemy). See the difference?

Okay, back to the vet clinic example. You have many ways you can print just those clients who need vaccination reminders this month. Try the way you like best. Here are some examples:

- ✔ Design a dozen categories, one for each month of the year. Then set the filter for the appropriate month.

- ✔ In an arbitrary field (like Categories or Account), use the numbers 1 through 12 to represent months. This way you can use Boolean operators like *greater than* and *less than* to print several months at a time.

Don't forget that you can assign several categories to each item in Outlook. So you don't waste the category field by assigning a month to a client, you can also tag the client as a dog owner, a carrot eater, and a bicycle rider.

You don't use Outlook at all? Well, Word can maintain its own mail merge database. Just choose Create Data Source from the Get Data button, and save the resulting file to your hard disk. You can build up your own mail merge database in Word, and load it using the same Open data source item that you used earlier when loading addresses from Outlook in "Mail merge envelopes: Using the Outlook contact list."

Creating Your Own Newsletter, Just Like GigantaCorp Does

Desktop publishing can sometimes seem intimidating, and many people simply don't have the artistic skills to create professional publications (although sometimes we wonder if melting some crayons and tossing them at a piece of paper may result in a *Wired* magazine cover). Some publishing tasks, however, are simple to accomplish, even if your greatest artistic creations involve creatures with no more than three fingers. The key is to use Microsoft Publisher 97 and the built-in wizards associated with your task at hand.

We have worked with people who have only limited computer knowledge but have managed to put together quality brochures using Microsoft Publisher. Publisher 97, included with the Office 97 Small Business Edition, is even more powerful for creating quick, attractive newsletters. Publisher 97 offers an array of choices that you can use to create a newsletter that exactly meets your needs. You won't need much time or talent — in fact, you just create a new document.

Walking through the wizard

The Newsletter PageWizard Design Assistant helps you create just the look you want. All you have to do is answer a few questions. To create your brochure:

1. **Choose File⇨New.**

2. **Choose the PageWizard tab and then double-click the Newsletter icon.**

   You get a suite of choices, like those in Figure 10-11.

3. **Now choose the basic design that you believe will result in the sort of image you want to project.**

   Sorry, no newsletter template is based on *Wired*. In fact, they don't use Publisher to make that magazine — they lay it all out by hand, cutting up strips of paper and arranging them using rubber cement. Those Bohemians.

4. **In most cases, you need to select the number of columns that you want your newsletter to have.**

   A few designs are hard-wired (by Bohemians) for a specific number of columns, and can't be changed.

Figure 10-11:
The
PageWizard
walks you
through the
design
process,
allowing you
to select
various
traits for
your
brochure.

The most common newsletter layout has three columns. A newsletter with four columns tends to be difficult to read (on 8¹/₂-x-11-inch paper), and one with only a single column presents a dense horde of text that looks busy. We recommend that you stick with two or three columns.

What would your newsletter be without stories? The last few steps set up your newsletter layout.

5. **Choose how many stories you want on the first page, the name of the newsletter, and so on.**

   Don't fret — this stuff is easy to change after you start editing the document. Answer each question in turn.

   Finally, you can actually edit the newsletter.

6. **Click the Create It! Button.**

   You can use the Back Arrow button at the bottom of the screen to move backward through your design choices.

Creating a professional, non-Bohemian newsletter

Professionals tend to follow a few basic rules when they create serious publications — rules that the Publisher 97 templates generally adhere to and are a good idea for nondesigners to live by.

✔ **Minimize font use:** Most designers swear by the use of two or three fonts at most: a serif font (like Times, for text), a sans serif font (like Helvetica or Arial, for emphasized elements), and maybe a decorative font for personality and uniqueness.

Filling a brochure with Publisher's inexhaustible supply of fonts does not make the layout more creative. The layout just looks as though the designer has recently discovered Publisher's inexhaustible supply of fonts.

✔ **Write to size:** Although the rambling nature of this particular narrative may seem to break this rule, in desktop publishing, you need to write the correct number of words to fill a particular space. If your story ends and you can't add more text to fill the space, try to rearrange other elements (like headlines or images) to fill the space that's left. Take a quick look at your daily newspaper and notice that they rarely leave blank space when a story ends — articles are always the correct length to fit the allotted space. Otherwise, the document tends to look somewhat unbalanced.

If your article ends and you haven't actually said anything, that's a different story. Change the title so that it looks like a *thought-provoking exploration of the subject,* and then your readers will think they need to draw their own conclusions.

✔ **Be consistent:** If a particular heading is in a certain font at a certain size, put all similar headings in that size. Do the same thing with body text and other elements, and don't be too quick to change a font size if something doesn't fit. First try editing and writing better.

✔ **Be conservative:** Look at the original document after the Design Assistant is finished with it, and get a feel for how the newsletter works. Where are images placed? Does the document seem to have a certain sense of balance? Do certain elements draw your eye to them? Notice these elements, and do your best not to destroy or move them while you're editing.

You can break the rules, as long as you first know what the rules are. Master the art of creating conservative, understated documents, and then experiment with wacky fonts or Bohemian ideals in moderation. (Once again, *Wired* comes to mind.)

Cleaning up the template

Depending on the template you use, and how you answered the Design Assistant's questions, you may now need to do a quick run around your brochure to see if the Assistant typed any text or created any elements that look a bit odd. Particularly important are titles and other text that the Assistant may have typed automatically. In Figure 10-12, for example, the default style for the newsletter's name is a bit bland. The style was created with Microsoft WordArt (a tool in Office for creating fancy text), and you can modify its appearance by double-clicking the text. Use the toolbar to change the text attributes. Figure 10-13 shows just one of the many things you can do to WordArt text from the drop-down choices.

A thought-provoking exploration about managers

An office manager encountered a sheep rancher with a field of sheep and said, "If I can guess how many sheep you have may I have one?"

Thinking this impossible, the rancher agreed to the office manager's request. The man quickly replied, "You have 1,795 sheep."

Amazed, the rancher accepted defeat and let the man have his pick. The office manager slung the animal over his shoulder and turned to leave.

"Wait," called the rancher, "If I can guess your occupation, can I have that animal back?"

"Sure," said the office manager.

"You're a middle manager," the rancher said at once.

Equally amazed, the manager said, "How did you figure that out?"

"Well," said the rancher, "Put my dog down and I will tell you."

Publisher doesn't have multiple levels of Undo like other Office applications. Save your work frequently to ensure that you don't make a disastrously large number of changes to something you like.

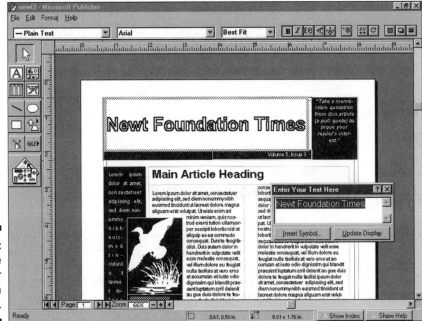

Figure 10-12:
The newletter name is a little boring.

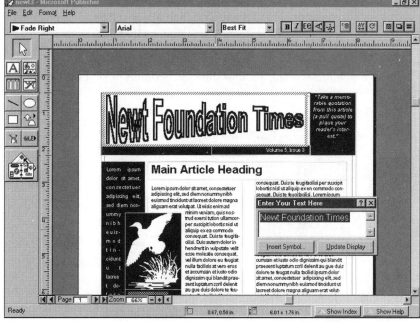

Figure 10-13:
Experiment
with
WordArt's
many
options for
creating
interesting
headlines
and banners.

Word and Publisher: A marriage made in Redmond

Although you can type directly into Publisher, often doing so is kind of a pain, particularly if you're sitting on thumbtacks. What's easier is to sit on a relatively flat surface and work in Word. Then pour the finished product into Publisher. To do that, just right-click the desired column in Publisher and choose Insert Text File from the drop-down menu. You can also take a story out to Word for editing by choosing Edit⇨Edit story in Microsoft Word.

Picking images

After you complete all the text for your brochure, move on to the images. The Design Assistant offers some placeholder images (generally clip art images) that almost certainly have nothing to do with your newsletter topic. (One of Dave's Original Hair Remedy newsletter prototypes, for some inexplicable reason, includes a lot of airplane clip art.) If you like these images, feel free to leave them, but changing them is a simple matter.

To change an image, select the image in the Publisher window and choose Insert➪Picture File from the Publisher menu if you have your own image file to add, or Insert➪ClipArt to use Microsoft's Clip Gallery library, shown in Figure 10-14.

You can also load the Clip Gallery by right-clicking a selected image, and choosing Microsoft Clip Gallery Object➪Replace from the pop-up menu.

Figure 10-14:
Adding an image with the Microsoft Clip Gallery or a scanner, digital camera, or even the Internet.

To add a clip art image from the Gallery:

1. **Choose Insert➪ClipArt.**

   The Clip Gallery appears.

2. **Select the image in the Gallery window, and select the Insert button.**

   You can view clip art images in various categories by selecting the category name on the left side of the screen. The images change as a result of your selection.

   You can also explore the tabs at the top of the Gallery window to change between clip art images, and Microsoft's library of photographic images.

   After you select an image, Publisher asks you if you want to change the frame to fit the picture or the picture to fit the frame.

3. **If you like the frame the size it is (as the Design Assistant originally placed it), choose Change the Picture to Fit the Frame and click OK.**

   The image appears in your document at the original size of the frame.

4. **To resize the image, click it and choose one of the resize boxes.**

To maintain the image's *aspect ratio* (so that it doesn't look unnaturally tall or wide), hold down the Shift and Ctrl keys while you resize the image.

Adding cool special effects

Now that you have mastered the basics, here are some other tricks you can try to make your newsletter look good:

- ✔ **Add drop caps to the start of each article.** *Drop caps* are large first letters that signal the start of a story. To include a drop cap, click the story you want to affect and choose Format⇨Fancy First Letter. Then pick the style of drop cap that you want.

- ✔ **Wrap text around an irregular picture.** By default, Publisher wraps text around the image frame, which is obviously just a boring rectangle. You can wrap text around the image instead, if you prefer. Just click the image and choose Format⇨Picture Frame Properties. Click Wrap Text Around Picture Only.

- ✔ **Add a shadow to a picture or text box.** This, in moderation, can look very spiffy. Just click the frame you want to modify and choose Format⇨Shadow.

- ✔ **Add a background to a text box.** You can draw attention to specific text boxes by adding a colored background. In general, you want to make this background a very light grayscale tone — just enough to see, but not enough to make the text hard to read. Click the text you want to draw attention to and choose Format⇨Fill Patterns and Shading. Then choose the background you like.

- ✔ **Add automatic text that tells readers what page the story is continued on.** Betcha didn't know Publisher can do this, huh? Just select the text frame and choose Format⇨Text Frame Properties. The bottom options are Include "Continued On Page" and Include "Continued From Page."

Finishing up

Review your newsletter one last time and then head over to the File menu and choose Print. This allows you to print the page and get a feel for how things are working. In the Print Proof dialog box, you have some options, including the opportunity to choose not to print your images for a faster proof or to display the *print marks* (crop marks, registration marks, publication info, and so on) on the final printed page. Make those decisions and then click OK to begin printing.

If you want to see your progress on the screen, a single menu command allows you to drop out all the hidden lines and frame borders so that you can see basically what the page looks like on paper. Choose View⇨Ignore Background, and the full power of your brochure design appears onscreen, without all the annoying background lines mucking things up.

Using mail merge with Publisher

The time will come when you want to mail your newsletters, and Publisher has its own built-in mail merge facilities. Though we would love to say that mail merge is just as easy in Publisher as it is in other Office applications like Word, this just ain't so. Granted, mail merge is not that tricky, but Publisher doesn't hold your hand quite so tightly as Word. Say you want to print mailing labels directly on the newsletter. You probably won't want to keep a separate merge database in Publisher — after all, you already have one in Outlook. So, here's what you do:

1. **Export your Outlook Contacts to an Excel file by choosing File⇨Import and Export.**

   See the section "Mail merge envelopes: Using the Outlook contact list" earlier in this chapter for details.

2. **Choose Mail Merge⇨Open Data Source.**

3. **Choose Merge Information from a File I already Have.**

4. **Find the Outlook Excel file, and select it.**

5. **Tell Publisher to use the sheet called Contacts.**

   Immediately, you get the Insert Fields dialog box.

6. **Lay out the merge fields in the newsletter to your heart's content.**

7. **When you're done, click the Close button to close the dialog box.**

8. **Choose Mail Merge⇨Merge.**

   If you're a voyeur, or just interested in the results, you can use the Arrow keys to see the merge data in your newsletter.

9. **Choose Mail Merge⇨Filter or Sort.**

   Use the filter options to include just the entries you want. Again, for details on using filter criteria, see "Mail merge envelopes: Using the Outlook contact list," earlier in this chapter.

10. **When you're as happy as a bug, choose File⇨Print Merge.**

Do you have a funny joke that uses the word *merge* in a family-oriented way that we can print in the next edition of this book? If so, send it to radiopeak@aol.com. Sorry, we don't pay $500 per joke — what do we look like, *Reader's Digest*?

Creating Brochures the Easy Way (But You Still Have to Fold Them)

Guess what? You can use Publisher to create brochures, fliers, forms, and other documents that can enhance your company's professional image. The basic procedure for creating any Publisher document is the same as creating a newsletter. Here are some things to keep in mind:

✔ **Don't get carried away.** Often, the best choices are the more conservative designs, with names like Classic or Traditional.

✔ **Minimize clip art.** Use some graphics to splash action onto the page, but make sure that you don't overdo it. Make sure that every image is on the page for a reason and that it doesn't crowd the text.

✔ **Use a spot color if you can afford it.** Spot color adds a single color to designated parts of your document. You need to go to a professional printer to add a spot color, but clients (and potential clients) typically spend twice as much time looking at color pages as grayscale ones. Our eyes are drawn to color. Beware of two spot colors, though. The second color can add a third (that's 33 percent, or one third, not a third color, which wouldn't really be all that bad) or more to the total cost of the print job.

✔ **Eventually, you want to fold this brochure — or you become known as *that person that hands out flat brochures.*** Odds are good that people will start throwing fruit at you, too. Anyway, if you resize the width of a particular text frame, make sure that the text frame is not overlapping one of the folds of your brochure, or it may end up looking unprofessional.

You can usually stop people from throwing food at you by yelling at them — especially if you accuse them of being Bohemians and threaten to send them to Colorado Springs.

To print or not to print

Given your access to a program like Publisher, you may now believe that you can do all your publishing in-house. After all, why spend the money to go to a professional publisher? This all centers on quality, quantity, and cost.

Take, for example, GoPilot Publishing, publisher of *Tap*, the "#1 Resource for PalmPilot and WorkPad Users." An eight-page newsletter dedicated to 3Com's handheld organizer, *Tap* needs to be both high-quality and cost-effective to print. The actual print quantity is not out of the ordinary for a small business: According to editor Rick Broida, *Tap* needs to print about 21,000 pages a month. "It costs about $1,000 with spot color," Broida reports. "That makes it attractive to buy a high-volume laser printer and do the work in-house."

In-house printing won't work for color output. Only a professional printer has the resources to give you color. Color laser printers are still low-resolution devices (no more than 600 dpi), cost at least $4,000, and are extremely slow (3 ppm or less). The cost of consumables is high as well. Thus, any document that is printed in quantity, and requires color (even spot color) needs to go to a professional printer.

GoPilot can print its newsletter without color, though. Says Broida, "We can purchase a high-volume printer for about $1,500, about the same as a one-month run of the journal." What does that buy GoPilot? "Long-term cost savings, plus more control over quantities — no more over- or underruns," says Broida. On the other hand, in-house printing has its disadvantages. You can expect 2400 dpi resolution at a professional print shop, whereas lasers offer no more than 600 or 1200 dpi. Plus, you need to do your own collating, and you have to contend with printer maintenance problems.

What did Broida decide to do? "I'm going to stick with print services for now," he says. "A company with more modest printing needs, like a four-page newsletter, perhaps, may do well with in-house printing. But 20,000 pages is a bit higher volume than I want to contend with right now. Plus, I get higher-quality output and spot color."

Chapter 11

Reporting Your Profits in Fun and Exciting Ways

. . . .

In This Chapter

▶ Reporting budgets with style

▶ Mapping stuff

▶ Exploring your data

▶ Getting data from your accounting software into Excel

. . . .

*I*f you're running a small office or home business, there's nothing more pleasing than reporting your profits. From personal experience, we know that a spreadsheet can become just a bit more fun than usual when you're talking about all the money you've made from hard work rendered. Even if accounting isn't exactly your forté (perhaps because you know more appropriate uses for the word "forté"), you can use Excel and the Financial Manager (if you have the Small Business Edition of Office 97) to perform some amazing feats of numerical manipulation, interpretation, and regurgitation.

Of course, your interest may lie in taking only the most rudimentary of data elements and turning them into stunning charts, graphs, and reports that include lots of confusing words — especially if you have something other than profits to report. Fortunately, you can do that too. Using the magic of *OLE* (Object Linking and Embedding — or Office's Little Egotrip), you can embed spreadsheet data and charts in other documents (like a report created in Word) and come up with wonderful reports for your employer, clients, or investors.

In any case, this quick little chapter roots out some of the more esoteric capabilities of Excel and the Financial Manager. You'll soon be using Excel as a real business tool — even if (like one of your authors) you took Business Calculus at the local junior college during summer break to avoid being forced to take an entire semester of it at the university.

By the way, welcome to Chapter 11. We couldn't have picked a less appropriate chapter number than this one for discussing how profitable your business has become, eh? Sorry about that.

Reporting Budgets with Style

To begin reporting your budget, you're first going to need to, um, create a budget. How you do this is up to you, with a few caveats. After all, you want to create a budget that is imminently "graphable," the authors said, as if the corporate world needed more made-up words. Here's some advice for making a spreadsheet work as a graph:

- ✔ **Don't try to squeeze too much information into one graph.** If you were to create a monthly budget, for example, begin by creating a single month with a few, basic comparisons. It's best to enter basic information one sheet at a time and then build comparisons from that data. If you want to take the totals and compare them to other months, for instance, you can do that elsewhere.

- ✔ **Create summary cells.** Doing so makes the chart much easier to read and more sensible. Now you can chart just the totals of each budget area, for instance, or chart a single area completely.

- ✔ **Add some visuals.** Using lessons put forth in Chapter 3, it's easy to add dividing lines, colors, fonts, and alignment to make things easier to read.

If you're a real fan of templates, you may have noticed that Excel doesn't come with many. But that doesn't mean they don't exist. In fact, some are included on the Microsoft Office SBE CD-ROM, and they're hidden, just to make the hunt that much more rewarding. On the CD-ROM, look in the directory **\Valupack\Template\Excel** and copy the templates to Office's Excel template directory, probably located at **C:\Program Files\Microsoft Office\Templates\Spreadsheet Solutions**. Office Pro users can download templates from http://microsoft.com/officefreestuff/excel/ on the Web or try out the templates we've included on this book's CD-ROM.

Summarize, summarize

Remember the Peter principle: People rise to their level of incompetence. That is, when management decides that you're very suited to a particular level of responsibilities and set of tasks, they, in their infinite wisdom, give you a new level of responsibilities and a new set of tasks. It's only when you've finally been promoted into a job that you're incapable of doing that they leave you alone — usually in that position.

Anyway, that's why executives require "executive summaries." You're bound to be forced to create summaries for your data, just as in most other business reports. And just in case your boss (client, investor) is competent but busy, summaries can go over really well in your final presentation.

Now our example budget is pretty reportable as it stands, but we could do one better by creating actual summary cells that appear outside of the budget spreadsheet itself. Obviously, there's no one correct way to do this, but what we'd suggest is that you remember to use the whole sheet to your advantage — if you have data in one place, that doesn't mean you can't rearrange it to make it work better in another place. In the example, we'd like to see very clearly what sections of our business missed their budgets, so we arrange the summary cells as shown in Figure 11-1.

Remember sheet links from Chapter 3? We want to do that same thing when creating this summary section — link directly to the cells in question. To do that:

1. **Click in the empty cell that you want linked to one of your existing cells.**

2. **Then click the "equal" sign in Excel's formula bar.**

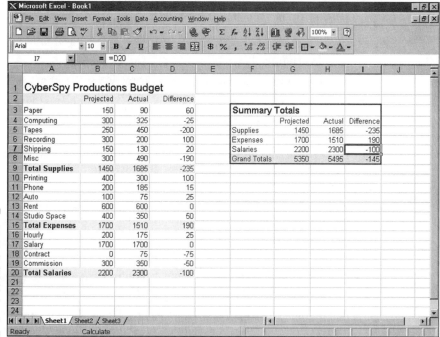

Figure 11-1: Create a summary section of your sheet for easier analysis.

   3. **Now click the cell you want to link to (like one of the totals cells that you're duplicating) and press the Enter key.**

      The cell is linked and will change when the values in the original cell change.

If you look carefully at Figure 11-1, you'll see that the selected cell has a formula that looks like **=D20**. That's a simple formula that links one cell to another. You can type a similar formula to link cells if you don't want to go through all the pointing-and-clicking described in the preceding steps (we don't want to wear you out in case you're going to the gym later).

Charting, of course

Now, with the summary data well in hand, it's a simple matter to create a chart using the Chart Wizard in Excel. You've seen this before in Chapter 3, but to recap:

   1. **Highlight the summary data you've created in your budget. Choose Insert⇨Chart to start up the Chart Wizard.**

   2. **With the Standard Types tab selected, select the type of chart you'd like to create.**

      This example uses a Column chart.

   3. **Select the subtype that you'd like used for your chart.**

      In this example, it's a 3-D Clustered Column chart.

   4. **Make sure that the range of data selected for the chart is correct.**

      If it's not, you can edit it directly in the Data range text box or click the small chart icon to return to the spreadsheet and use the mouse to select a new range of data.

You'll probably find that you get a better-looking chart if you don't include your Grand Total values, as they tend to skew the values upward and make the chart look unbalanced.

   5. **Still in Step 2 of the wizard, decide whether you want the data arranged in series by rows or columns.**

      Just play with it. You can see in the preview windows which version is better. Click Next when you've decided. (See Figure 11-2.)

   6. **Now in Step 3 of the wizard, you have the opportunity to customize the appearance of the chart.**

      Each tab at the top of the Chart Wizard allows you to change some other aspect of the chart. When you've gotten through all these options, click Next.

Figure 11-2:
How the data is arranged can make a big difference. In this example, arranging by columns makes for a better chart.

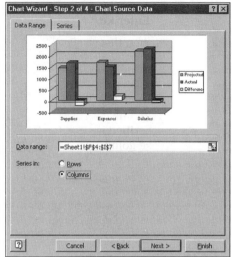

7. **Finally, you decide to place the chart as an object in the current worksheet — that's makes it a bit easier to get to. Make you're decision and click Finish.**

The chart appears in your document, and it's as ugly as one of those dogs with the pushed-in face. (Maltese? Mongrels? Something like that.) You can do something to change that, though (the chart, not the dog), by customizing the chart using Excel's chart formatting tools.

Formatting your chart

If you've got a chart that has some problems, you need to dig in and work on it a little bit. The Chart Wizard has an amazing ability to take in tons of information, figure out the correct data points, faithfully plot your data in a way that seems almost to read your mind, and then plop it on the chart with the same amount of interest and care that Dave would put into the liner notes of a Mel Torme album (see Figure 11-3).

Each element in the chart is individually selectable (just click different parts of the chart to see what we mean). You can click and drag elements around within the chart, resize elements (including the entire chart), or even edit many of the text elements, like the chart's title and the axis labels.

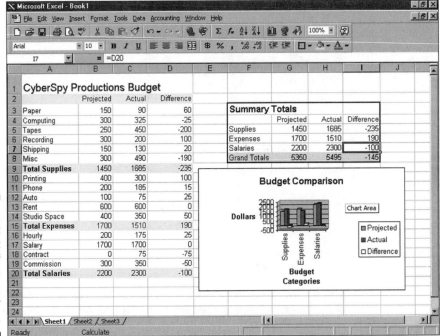

Figure 11-3:
The Chart
Wizard just
sort of
drops this
lump of a
chart on our
spreadsheet.

Right-click formatting

Most of the tools you can use to format your chart are available by right-clicking on the chart. The key is, you need to click in exactly the right place. To start, you can right-click on the entire chart and set some global formatting options, as follows:

1. **Right-click very close to a corner of the chart's box, away from other elements.**

   A pop-up menu appears.

2. **Choose Format Chart Area from the menu.**

   If you see some other options at the top of the menu, you right-clicked in the wrong part of the chart.

3. **In the Format Chart Area dialog box, choose the Font tab. Pick a Font, Font Style, and Size.**

In our experience, you can sometimes fix the whole chart by just changing the font size — make it smaller by one or two points. Click OK immediately and the chart sort of "pops" into place.

4. **Click the Patterns tab.**

   Now you can choose a border, background color and/or experiment with Fill Effects to get a patterned background for your chart.

5. **Click OK to make the changes take effect (see Figure 11-4).**

   Other elements can be formatted in this same way. Try right-clicking on different elements in your chart to see the different Format ... Area options you can alter.

Toolbar formatting

You can also format individual elements using the toolbar. For example, select one of the table Axis titles (in our examples, they're "Dollars" and "Totals"). In the toolbar, you can change the font, font size, font style, and so on, just as if you were working in Word.

Putting it all together (Ole!)

There's one quick way to put all your data and charts together in Excel — just drag the chart back up to where you've created your data and summaries; then drop it into place in the worksheet.

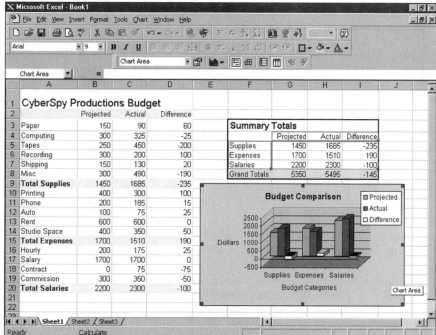

Figure 11-4: Changes take effect after you close the Format Chart Area dialog box.

But that's certainly not all you can do. Are you ready to test that Peter Principle stuff on yourself? You might just get a promotion for this next little trick: adding a chart to a report in Word. To do this, you're going to make use of Microsoft's OLE — Object Linking and Embedding — technology, which allows you to take elements from one Microsoft program (and some others) and drop it into another program. For example, you can take a chart from Excel and drop it into Microsoft Word.

But that's not all that's cool about this. After all, you can already cut and paste, right? The difference with OLE is that it doesn't just paste an image into your Word document. The chart (or spreadsheet data) that you place in Word is still an Excel object, meaning that you can double-click it in Word and edit it with Excel's tools (that's the embedding part). Plus, the data always stays current, even if you change the original chart back in Excel (that's the linking part).

Embedding an Excel chart in Word

The first OLE trick we'll perform is embedding an Excel object in a Word document — we want to talk about it first because we like it less. Embedding the object allows you to edit it using Excel's tools while it's still in Word, but it doesn't link the object to the original file, meaning that a copy of the chart is placed within your Microsoft Word file. The chart is still an Excel object, but any editing you do to the object changes only within the Word document — your edits don't affect the existing chart or spreadsheet. What's more, embedding the chart bloats the size of your Word document, making it less friendly for network or e-mail transmissions.

In fact, embedding is almost like placing an *image* of the chart or spread-sheet in the Word document. The only real difference is that Word is smart enough to allow you to edit the chart once it's been placed in Word. Word's toolbar will even change to look a bit more like Excel's.

In spite of the fact that it isn't our favorite use of OLE, embedding can be useful, especially if you want to change the data in a chart or spreadsheet without affecting the original. Perhaps you want to use the same data available in the example budget chart we've been creating, but you'd prefer to use a different chart type. That's easy enough to do with embedding, and it won't effect the original chart.

Here's how to embed an Excel object in a Word document:

1. **Open both your Excel workbook and a Word document.**

2. **In the Excel document, click once to select an object that you'd like to embed in the Word document (like a chart).**

Charts can be tough to select in Excel (you end up selecting just parts of the chart if you're not careful). Click very close to the outline of your chart to select the entire thing.

3. Choose Edit⇨Copy from Excel's menu bar.

4. Switch to Word.

5. In Word, Choose Edit⇨Paste from the menu bar.

6. The object appears, safely ensconced in your Word document.

Now you can move the object around, resize it, and change other properties using the Format⇨Object command in Word's menu. You can also edit the chart directly in Word, using Excel-like commands and toolbars. To do that, just double-click the chart (see Figure 11-5).

We defy you to name even one other computer book that uses both the word *ensconced* (ensconce: verb, to surround) and a reference to Mel Torme in the same chapter. No need to thank us; we're always trying to give you, the reader, that extra, unexpected value.

Excel-Style Toolbars

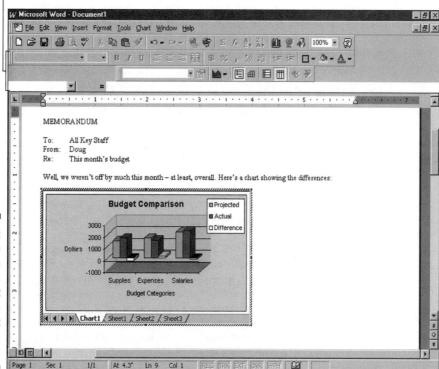

Figure 11-5:
Double-click an embedded Excel object and you can edit it right there in Word.

You can change options for the chart as well using an interface similar to the Chart Wizard. Just choose Chart⇨Chart Options from the menu bar.

Linking a chart in Word

The other method used for adding objects to Word (and other Office 97) documents is linking, which is similar to embedding, except that the object maintains a link to the original data. In our example, you can link a chart from Excel to a Word document. The chart appears in Word, but any changes to that chart occur in the original Excel document. Instead of changing Word's toolbars when you double-click the linked object, the original document is loaded in Excel for editing.

Linking has certain advantages over embedding:

✔ Any changes in the original document also change in the linked object (so a report that includes the object won't become outdated with the object's spreadsheet changes, for instance).

✔ The containing document remains smaller because the object isn't completely embedded in the document.

✔ Editing of the objects occurs in the original application, which may be less confusing than using, for example, Word to edit an Excel object.

Here's how you link to an Excel chart (or similar object):

1. **Open both your Excel workbook and a Word document.**

2. **In the Excel document, click once to select an object that you'd like to embed in the Word document (like a chart).**

3. **Choose Edit⇨Copy from Excel's menu bar.**

4. **Switch to Word.**

5. **In Word, Choose Edit⇨Paste Special from the menu bar.**

    The Paste Special dialog box appears.

6. **Choose the Paste link option and click OK.**

    The object appears in your Word document, as shown in Figure 11-6.

Now, with the chart in your Word document, you can move it around and resize it just as you would an inserted image. The only difference comes when you double-click the chart. The result? The chart's original document is loaded into Excel and Excel appears on your screen. (If Excel isn't already loaded, it launches and then opens the document.) You can change the data in Excel, recalculate the spreadsheet (to update the chart), and the chart changes not only in Excel, but in Word as well. If the Word document isn't currently loaded, the link is changed the next time you launch the Word document.

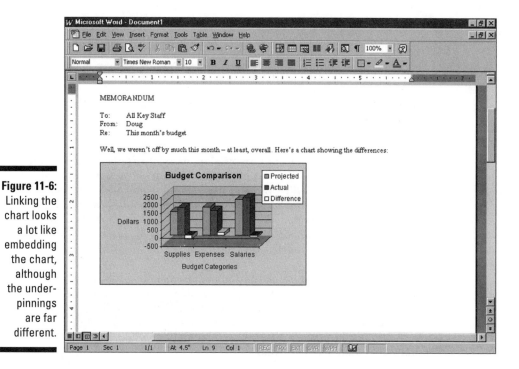

Figure 11-6:
Linking the chart looks a lot like embedding the chart, although the under-pinnings are far different.

People Like to See Maps with Little Dots All Over Them — Really

Todd likes to call this concept "Designing by committee," and he believes his pet concept to be applicable much more often than it really is.

You see, it's his contention that some actually interesting and brilliant (okay, maybe just brilliant) computer programmer is usually responsible for the first few iterations of a software program that changes our lives. Remarkable and laudable people were responsible for creating the first spreadsheet program, the first desktop publishing program, and the World Wide Web.

Then, in The World According to Todd (soon to be a major motion picture starring Harry Connick, Jr. in the lead role), a big company swoops down, buys the small brilliant company, and begins to design by committee. When no one can come up with an interesting idea, the committee simply tosses in eight or nine not-so-interesting ideas.

Enter Microsoft Map. It's amazing that Microsoft engineers have this much free time on their hands, but apparently it's the case.

The worst part, admits Todd, is the fact that Microsoft Map is pretty cool, even if he does insist that it's "bloatware."

Mapping Excel data

What does it do? Consider Microsoft Map an extension of Excel's built-in ability to create charts. Instead of pie or bar graphs, though, Map uses actual geopolitical satellite imagery-based outline maps to graph your data. Though it sounds like the waste of time, there are actually some uses for this tool. Consider the possibility of easily and quickly creating a map of your sales forces' states or regions and then showing, on a map, where your company's sales are the strongest.

By way of example, the following steps show you how to create a simple map that tells you how a company's exports (in this case, the company exports happiness) are doing over in Europe. This example does two things. First, it shows you the benefits of using Microsoft Map. Second, it very effectively tests the authors' ability to recall the names of a convincing number of countries in Europe.

To create a simple map of data:

1. **In Excel, enter a range of data that can be displayed graphically on a map.**

   In most cases, that means a series of city, state, or country names in one column and numerical data in the second column (see Figure 11-7).

2. **Now select the range of data by highlighting all the relevant cells on the sheet.**

   You'll get some interesting results if you include any header cells that you create for your charting data. You don't have to include them, but if you do, Microsoft Map will attempt to label the map with your headers.

3. **To begin creating the map, choose Insert⇨Map.**

4. **The cursor changes to a cross hair. Click and drag to draw a place on your worksheet for the map. Release the mouse button when you feel that you've created a large enough space.**

5. **The Multiple Maps Available dialog box may appear. In it, choose the map that seems to best represent what you want shown; then click OK.**

6. **The map appears, with Microsoft Map's best guess at the requirements of your data, as shown in Figure 11-8.**

Next up, edit that puppy and make it useful.

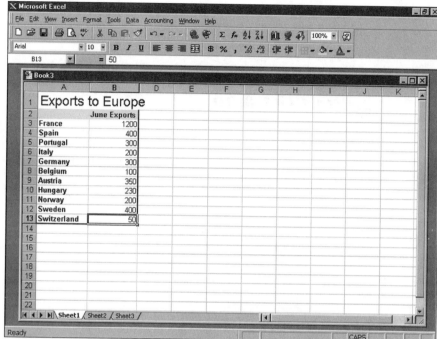

Figure 11-7:
The data for tracking exports to Europe — the formatting is just to trick you. All you need are names and numbers.

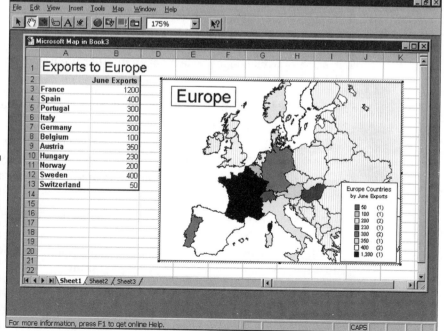

Figure 11-8:
And the map appears. (We've tweaked it a bit for clarity here on the page.)

Here's a good tip for one of those times that Rover starts to ailing and the vet makes a particularly painful suggestion. When you tell your kids about them, just say, "Sorry, that puppy's been edited." (See Footnote 1 at the end of the chapter.)

Editing the map

The Microsoft Map control is a great place to start the editing process, giving you access to the different types of colors and fills for representing your data on the map. To change the way your map looks, just drag one of the format buttons from the left side of the control window into the formatting box (see Figure 11-9).

Figure 11-9:
The
Microsoft
Map control
can be used
to change
which data
is displayed
and how it
looks.

Data Buttons

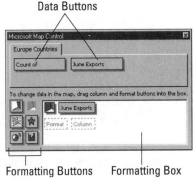

Formatting Buttons   Formatting Box

At the top of the window, you have access to a number of other tools in the toolbar, some of which might be familiar from other programs. From left to right along the toolbar, here's what you can accomplish:

- **Select Objects.** Use this tool to select and move the entire map or element within the map.

- **Grabber.** Use this tool to move the map around within its frame borders (so that you can see other parts of the map if some of it is hidden).

- **Center Map.** Click this tool and then click the map to center it in the frame.

- **Map Labels.** Click this tool and then click on the map to label the countries, provinces, or states.

- **Add Text.** Click this tool and then add text boxes and your own text to the map.

✔ **Custom Pin Map.** Click this tool and then click in the map. You're asked to create or open a custom pin map. (A pin map overlays the current map, allowing you to make notes or annotations that can be displayed or hidden separately from the shaded map.) Then click the map to place your pin, and then type a label or note for the label.

✔ **Display Entire.** Click this tool to return the map to it's original 100-percent size if you've changed it.

Have you noticed that the maps pictured in recent figures didn't quite show every bit of every country? That's because they've been "zoomed" in their frames. You can use the size menu in the Map toolbar to change how much zoom is used to display the map. Make it big enough to see the important parts, but don't worry about countries or provinces that aren't affected by your data.

✔ **Redraw Map.** Click this tool to redraw the map if anything gets mucked up.

✔ **Map Refresh.** Click this tool to update the map if you change the associated data.

✔ **Show/Hide Microsoft Map Control.** Click this tool to hide or view the Microsoft Map control window.

Aside from these tools, you'll find that nearly any element within the map can accept a right-click of the mouse, allowing you to change certain properties (like the font used) or allowing you to hide the element altogether. If you right-click the map itself, you get another option — Add Feature. This menu item allows you to add (or delete) levels of detail from the main map. Details include things like more countries, oceans, major cities, highways, and other details.

Different Views for Your Data

Let's be fair here. In many large *Fortune* 500 companies it's perfectly reasonable to lose an employee or two every once in a while — and it doesn't help that those employees will often continue to accept their paychecks while sitting in a quiet corner office laughing at management and playing with Microsoft Office. It happens. We can't keep track of everyone, right?

We hope your streamlined organization isn't susceptible to this sort of thing. But even if you're a one-person home business, you can still pretend, every once in a while, that you're that forgotten employee on the company (or government) dole. What's the best way to do that in Microsoft Office? They're called PivotTables.

What's a PivotTable?

For years, Microsoft has fought to get people to stop creating databases in Excel. "We have Access; we have FoxPro; we'll buy dBASE if you really want it," says Microsoft. And still people don't listen. They understand Excel. They enjoy using it, and their company isn't sure what they're doing anyway, so it might be dangerous to make a ruckus about requisitioning a copy of Access.

Finally, Microsoft gave in and came up with PivotTables. Basically, a PivotTable is a reporting mechanism for dealing with database-like data. PivotTables allow you to take a typical 2-D spreadsheet (with rows and columns) and report the information in it in many different, flexible ways. As an example, Figure 11-10 shows a database-like spreadsheet.

Using a PivotTable, this data can now be reported in much more interesting ways, as shown in Figure 11-11.

PivotTables automatically generate a number of summary fields, including subtotals and totals. You may instantly recognize that this feature makes the table not only much easier to digest, but it makes creating charts from this data easier too.

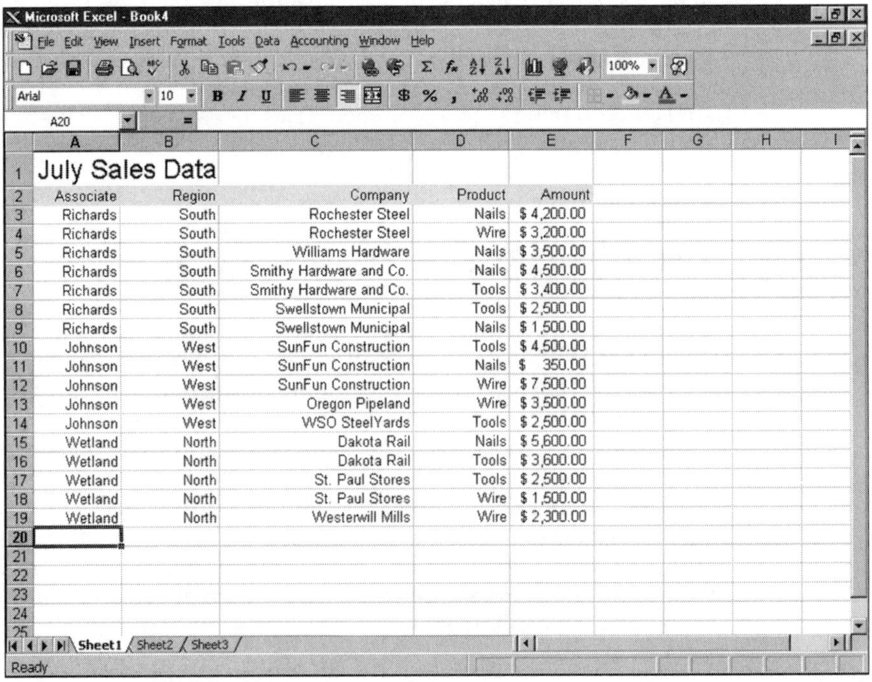

Figure 11-10: Some folks insist on using Excel to store database info. But that's cool.

	Associate	Region	Company	Product	Amount
1	July Sales Data				
2	Associate	Region	Company	Product	Amount
3	Richards	South	Rochester Steel	Nails	$ 4,200.00
4	Richards	South	Rochester Steel	Wire	$ 3,200.00
5	Richards	South	Williams Hardware	Nails	$ 3,500.00
6	Richards	South	Smithy Hardware and Co.	Nails	$ 4,500.00
7	Richards	South	Smithy Hardware and Co.	Tools	$ 3,400.00
8	Richards	South	Swellstown Municipal	Tools	$ 2,500.00
9	Richards	South	Swellstown Municipal	Nails	$ 1,500.00
10	Johnson	West	SunFun Construction	Tools	$ 4,500.00
11	Johnson	West	SunFun Construction	Nails	$ 350.00
12	Johnson	West	SunFun Construction	Wire	$ 7,500.00
13	Johnson	West	Oregon Pipeland	Wire	$ 3,500.00
14	Johnson	West	WSO SteelYards	Tools	$ 2,500.00
15	Wetland	North	Dakota Rail	Nails	$ 5,600.00
16	Wetland	North	Dakota Rail	Tools	$ 3,600.00
17	Wetland	North	St. Paul Stores	Tools	$ 2,500.00
18	Wetland	North	St. Paul Stores	Wire	$ 1,500.00
19	Wetland	North	Westerwill Mills	Wire	$ 2,300.00

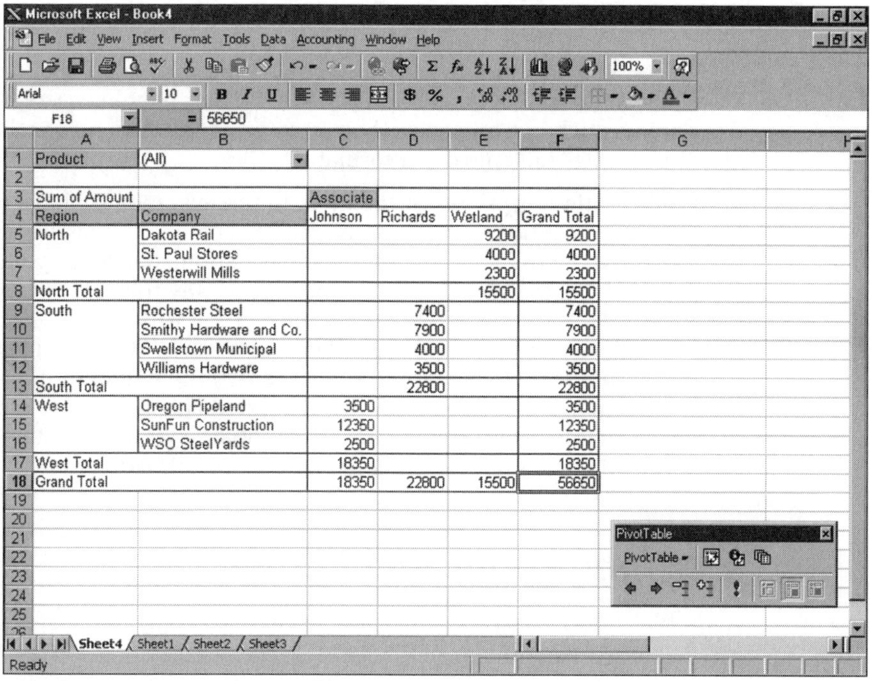

Sum of Amount		Associate			
Region	Company	Johnson	Richards	Wetland	Grand Total
North	Dakota Rail			9200	9200
	St. Paul Stores			4000	4000
	Westerwill Mills			2300	2300
North Total				15500	15500
South	Rochester Steel		7400		7400
	Smithy Hardware and Co.		7900		7900
	Swellstown Municipal		4000		4000
	Williams Hardware		3500		3500
South Total			22800		22800
West	Oregon Pipeland	3500			3500
	SunFun Construction	12350			12350
	WSO SteelYards	2500			2500
West Total		18350			18350
Grand Total		18350	22800	15500	56650

Figure 11-11: A PivotTable reports spreadsheet data in more useful ways. In this case, we can see who sold nails, in what region, and to which customers.

Choosing your data

To begin, you need to enter or import database-style data that will work well with a PivotTable. This task will probably take a bit of data entry on your part, although Excel can also import data using Microsoft Query for the PivotTable. And then there's always the "hire a kid" option. Or call Mel Torme — we hear he's a whiz with Excel.

How will you know if data is good for a PivotTable? Here are some indicators:

- **Lots of redundant information.** If your Excel spreadsheet repeats some values over and over again (like "nails" and "fencing" in our example), then it's ripe for summary by PivotTable.
- **An obvious comparison.** In the example data, it's clear that we may easily want to compare the performance of our sales associates. This makes for a better PivotTable because it's clear that something (like each salesperson's success) can be measured and compared.

✔ **More than one comparison.** Although each PivotTable results in just one report, you can create more than one PivotTable from the same data. So if we want to also compare the performance of each region in our database, we can create another PivotTable to see that relationship, which is a lot easier than re-entering the data on another spreadsheet page in some other format.

✔ **Subrelationships within the data.** In the example, we have individual customers who all fit into some regional category, making for a more effective PivotTable. Anytime you have subfields within your data in a spreadsheet, a PivotTable may be a good way to report that data.

If your data seems well suited to a PivotTable, enter it on the page in a basic, tabular format, much like tables in Access (if you've read those chapters). Each column is a field, and each row represents a single record in the database. You'll want a heading for each column before you start; then just fill in the information for each individual record or instance.

Beginning the PivotTable

With the right kind of database at your disposal, you can begin to walk through the PivotTable process. You use a wizard to help you create the PivotTable, but you need to rely on your own daring, resourcefulness, and sense of ruthless adventure to create the relationships among the fields you've created.

To create a PivotTable:

1. Highlight a range of your database table, including the column names.

2. Choose Data⇨PivotTable Report from the Excel menu bar.

The PivotTable Wizard appears. The default value of `Microsoft Excel list or database` is fine on the first screen.

3. Click Next.

4. Two choices:

- If you preselected the range of records you want to use for the PivotTable (including the column names), then just click Next again.

- You can click the Collapse Dialog button on the left side of the Range text box if you'd like to return to the spreadsheet for a moment and reselect a range. Click Next when you've entered a range.

5. In Step 3 of the wizard, build the PivotTable report.

You do this by dragging the named field buttons from the right side of the wizard's window to one of the listed elements (Page, Column, Row, or Data). This is where you need to be fairly sure of the relationships you want to build for your data (see Figure 11-12).

6. Click Next when you've built the table.

In our earlier example, the Page variable holds Product data so that the entire page table can be changed to reflect one or another of the products. The regions are divided into rows, with each customer representing a subcategory of its respective region. The columns are broken down by the name of each sales associate so that their individual sales success can be noted. The actual data in the chart is the amount (presumably in units) sold by each associate to each customer — and in each region.

7. Choose whether you'll use an existing worksheet (and choose which one in the pop-up menu) or choose the New worksheet option for this table.

8. Click Finish.

Second Field Is a Subcategory of the First

Figure 11-12:
Just drag fields around to create a PivotTable report. (This example is the same as the report created for Figure 11-11).

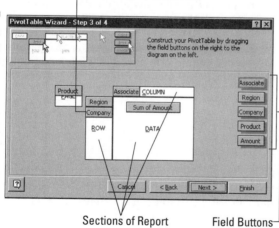

Sections of Report   Field Buttons

When the table finally makes its appearance, you may have to tweak it a bit to make it legible — just drag the columns around a bit to make them wide enough to read. Then sit back and soak in the data, or copy the entire PivotTable out to Word, PowerPoint, or Publisher as an OLE object for your reporting pleasure (as described earlier in this chapter).

As we mentioned before, all those totals generated by a PivotTable can be tasty morsels to the charting connoisseur. After you have all those totals generated, you might want to simply link them to a small chart of "totals" cells somewhere just outside of the PivotTable, like we did earlier in this chapter in the section "Summarize, summarize." Then create a chart based on that data.

The Small Business Financial Manager

According to information that Microsoft gave us (designed, by the way, to convince members of the press of the merits of the SBFM), the Small Business Financial Manager is designed to help folks take advantage of tools within Excel, even if they don't have time to learn the intricacies. Sounds cool. And it is. The SBFM allows you to quickly perform some impressive financial management tasks, even if you don't have a financial analyst hanging around in your accounting department ready to pop together these reports for you.

The financial manager is actually an "application" of sorts that runs on top of Excel, using sophisticated macros and scripting to make dialog boxes appear and importing functions launch. (That also explains why the financial manager is so darn slow.) But, like any application included with Office, you can launch the SBFM from the Start Menu. It then appears in Excel.

To use the SBFM (actually sounds a little like a jazz radio station doesn't it? "Soft Blues FM, 106.3 on your radio dial"), you just click one of the three buttons. In descending family-tree sort of order, these buttons do the following:

- **Import.** This button allows you to import accounting data from your accounting program into Excel so that it might be manipulated and reported by the SBFM tools.

- **What-If Analysis.** Use this button if, after you've imported the accounting data, you want to work with that data in order to generate "what-if" scenarios, where altering variables in your spreadsheet can tell you how to, for instance, become more profitable or cut costs.

- **Reports.** Use this button if, with your accounting information imported into Excel, you want to use the SBFM to generate many different financial reports, including balance sheets, income statements, cash flow analysis, and other such information.

Importing accounting information

If your business relies on a popular accounting software package, you'll probably be able to get it to work with SBFM. All it takes is a (fairly) quick import of the data to get rolling with what-if scenarios and reports. SBFM can import from Peachtree Accounting, QuickBooks, Simply Accounting, One-Write Plus, DacEasy Accounting, and a number of other packages.

You can find updates and other free downloads related to the Small Business Financial Manager Microsoft's Web site. The current URL to SBFM's home page is `http://microsoft.com/excel/sbfm/`.

To import accounting information into Excel from your accounting software, follow these steps:

1. **Launch the Small Business Financial Manager from the Start menu.**

   The Small Business Financial Manager sheet appears.

2. **Choose to Import data and click Next.**

   The Import Your Accouting Data dialog box appears. (You can also get to this step by choosing Accounting⇨Import Data from Excel's menu.)

3. **Next, either you can have the wizard search your entire computer ("My Computer") for accounting data, or you can choose to look in specific folders.**

   If you select the In specific folders option, use the directory tree to find the specific folder you'd like to have searched. Click the Add folder to list button for each folder you want searched.

4. **Click Next.**

5. **After searching the specified folders or computer (it can take a while), the wizard asks you to choose the data to import or update. Do so and then click Next.**

6. **Select the data file to load.**

   If the Import wizard comes up with more than one accounting data file, you need to select the file you want to work with.

7. **Click Next.**

8. **Next, decide what you want to do with the data.**

   You can create a financial report, perform a what-if analysis, or remap the data if the Financial Manager has trouble figuring out how to import the data. Choose the option you like and click Finish.

Don't worry if you want to both see a financial report and also perform a what-if analysis. You'll have the opportunity to do both because the Financial Manager simply drops you back at the main screen again.

Use the Import option to bring the Financial Manager up to speed on changes in your business's accounting data since the last time you used it.

What-if analysis

After you've imported (or updated, if necessary) data into the Small Business Finance Manager, you're ready to perform some what-if analyses on that data. With this feature, you can build different scenarios that allow you to determine how your business can be run differently — from a financial perspective:

1. **To begin, click the What-If Analysis button on the SBFM interface or choose <u>A</u>ccounting⇨<u>W</u>hat-If Wizard from the Excel menu bar.**

2. **Select the company you want to perform the analysis on (if more than one loaded) and click Next.**

3. **Either open an existing what-if analysis, or give the new one a name.**

   Select an existing what-if analysis from the pull-down menu, or click the New button and type a name to create a new analysis.

4. **Then choose the span of data that you'd like to use for the analysis from the pull-down menus.**

5. **Click Next.**

   The Save As dialog box appears (if you're creating a new scenario).

6. **Give the workbook a name and save it.**

You're greeted by the What-If Analysis Overview worksheet. From here, you can see what impact your what-if strategizing has versus your actual data for the time period specified. In order to change the analysis, choose one of the analysis items (like Profitability, Expenses, or Buy versus Lease). Each analysis area has its own wizards and dialogs to help you generate a what-if scenario that revolves around that area. Then, back in the Overview worksheet, you'll see the results of your what-if estimates and analysis.

Creating Financial Manager reports

One other advantage to the SBFM comes in the form of reports. Many of the financial reporting statements that larger companies take for granted can be quickly generated from your accounting data, without too terribly much input (and time) from you. To create a report, follow these steps:

1. **Click the Report button in the SBFM toolbar or choose Accounting⇨Report wizard from Excel's menu bar.**

2. **In the Create a Financial Report wizard, choose the type of report you want to generate from the Financial Reports menu and choose the Company data from the pull-down menu.**

3. **Click Next.**

4. **Select the type of report. Make your choice and click Next.**

   Within most of the major report categories (balance sheet, sales analysis), you have options for how the report should be laid out.

5. **Choose the end date for the reporting period you're using to generate the report. Click Next if you can. If you can't, just click Finish.**

   Different report types will end a bit early, requiring no more info.

6. **The final step allows you (with some reports) to generate a report based on a previously-created what-if scenario. Then click Finish.**

   For example, you may be creating a projection based on last month's sales that assumes that some variables will change. To create a cash flow statement based on that what-if scenario (so that you can show your investors how much things are going to improve), choose the what-if scenario in this step.

Excel and the SBFM templates go to work on your data, generating the final report (see Figure 11-13). You can now edit the report if you'd like (perhaps to perform a more informal what-if scenario), or you can save, print, or do whatever else you'd like with this report. It's yours to do with what you will — plus, it looks pretty good.

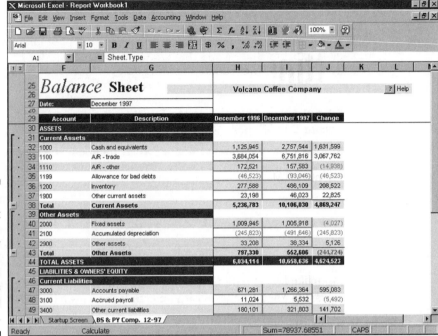

Figure 11-13:
A report
that's been
completely
generated
by the Small
Business
Financial
Manager.

Footnote #1: No animals were harmed in the production of this chapter.

Chapter 12

Putting Stuff on the Web

. . . .

. . . .

*I*f you're like Dave's parents, you're one of the few who haven't heard of the Internet yet. Even the former Soviet state of Muscovy is wired for the Internet — credit cards in hand — and is ready to connect to your Web site to buy whatever the heck you sell.

What? You don't have a Web site yet? You're making lots of Muscovites very unhappy. Perhaps you should read this chapter. We'll shut up now so that you can go ahead and read. If you have any questions, we're right here.

Why the Web?

Ah, the Internet. That great bastion of computer sales that has convinced most Americans that they should put off buying that new car to finance a high-speed ISDN line. And yet for some businesses, the Internet is like those turn-of-the-century perpetual motion machine gimmicks. No one can prove anyone is making money from the Net, yet everyone is revving up to get there.

ISDN stands for Integrated Services Digital Network, and it's a high-speed phone line that you can use to exchange data on the Internet at about four times the speed of a 28.8 Kbps modem.

Actually, we don't mean to scare you. Some folks really are making money from the Internet. Companies that would benefit from maintaining a virtual storefront include

- ✔ **Companies with regional exposure:** If you sell across a state line or across the country, consumers expect you to have a Web site. This way, customers can easily see products and services without making a phone call or traveling to a store. The Web also serves as a storefront magnifier, so you can do more business without having more locations or employees.

- ✔ **High technology companies:** A Web presence is a way to demonstrate you're techno-savvy while you broadcast your products and services to your ideal market segment — people who are technology oriented.

- ✔ **Niche industries:** Are you the only company in the world that sells hamburger patties shaped like the state of New Jersey? A Web site is a unique way to promote and sell that product far beyond the bounds of what you can do regionally.

- ✔ **Professional service businesses:** Your site gives potential clients the ability to research your services in an objective manner and compare what you offer to other Web-present businesses.

Who doesn't necessarily need to be on the Web?

- ✔ **Local retail:** If your potential client base is not Web-savvy or too small to warrant a Web presence, you should probably just save your money.

- ✔ **General purpose retail:** If you have no way to distinguish your products or services on the basis of price, performance, or other marketable criteria (other than your store's physical location), you may not have a compelling reason to set up a Web site.

- ✔ **Too busy or indifferent to maintain the site:** Don't overlook the ongoing investment required to maintain your site. If you don't update the content for six months, you demonstrate a lack of credibility. If you include contact mechanisms, like an e-mail address, you must check the incoming e-mail frequently. Not doing so is worse than not having a site at all. In other words, if you're presenting an unfriendly site, you don't need a site at all.

Web sites aren't just for clients, either. You can use a Web site for corporate training, internal information, and continuity while you're on the road. Just plug into the Net while you're on a business trip, for example, and you have access to documents stored on the server back home.

Have we convinced you yet? If so, read on. Otherwise, skip to Chapter 13, but don't say we didn't warn you when you go out of business early next week.

Getting Your Business on the Internet

Congratulations on your decision to join the Internet. You need to do two things right away:

- ✔ Raise your right hand and say, "I swear never to say the words *Information Superhighway* in front of Todd or Dave." It's just too darned clichéd, and we're tired of hearing it.

- ✔ Run out right now and buy all the other books Dave and Todd wrote about the Internet. Hey, we've got mouths to feed. In particular, you might be interested in Todd's *HTML Web Publishing 6-in-1* and Dave's *Internet Explorer 4: Browsing and Beyond*.

When you have those preliminaries out of the way, get serious. You have to decide how to handle the content, the Web pages themselves, and the delivery mechanism (the server and Internet access). Read on to find out about both of these in more detail.

Coding for dollars

Someone has to create your Web site — that's a given. You can hire someone to do it, or do it within the company. Last year, we probably would have said, "Let Acme Web Coders write your Web page. HTML (Hypertext Markup Language — the codes that are used to format Web pages) is a hassle, and no good beginner tools are out there to really automate the process. Hiring these folks is $500 well spent."

Wow, how times have changed. Unless you want to create the Web equivalent of Mount Rushmore, today Todd's answer is "What? Are you nuts? Pay someone to do something that you can do just as well for free? That's why you bought this book! Get with the program and create it yourself!" Dave would say the same thing without the exclamation points.

In other words, your business probably has enough graphic talent and writing skill inside its four walls to make a Web site. Add the Microsoft Office suite into the mix, and you have a fairly easy solution. Now you only need the professionals if you want some really complicated stuff, like Microsoft Active Server pages, dynamic databases, or obscure CGI scripts. Office can't do this stuff for you.

You can get knee-deep in jargon and acronyms pretty quick when you're learning about the Web. CGI scripts, for instance, are little computer programs commonly used to retrieve information from Web surfers when they visit your page. Other stuff — like Active Servers and dynamic HTML — are Microsoft innovations that make the Web a bit more television-like and interactive. In general, as a beginner you don't need to worry about any of it.

The essential tools

What do you need to create a Web page from start to finish? Here's our recommended list:

- **Microsoft Office:** You can combine elements from each of these programs to make a good site. No single Office program can do it all, but all the Office applications together make a formidable tool.

- **A graphics program:** You probably need a stand-alone paint program like Corel PhotoPaint or Paint Shop Pro to make logos, buttons, or other images for the site. Microsoft Photo Editor, which is bundled with many Microsoft applications, may be enough to get you started.

- **An FTP client:** You need a way to get your completed Web pages from your local hard disk to the Great Hard Disk on the Net. FTP (you know, *file transfer protocol* — stop looking at us like we're geeks) is the traditional way to do that.

- **A few good books:** Sure, this book is great — one of the best. You should buy copies for all your friends, family, and co-workers. The world of Web publishing is so different from print publishing, however, that we suggest you get a good book or two on the subject.

Those are the basics. If you really get into this whole Web thing, here are other tools you may want to have around:

- **A Web site management tool:** This is a program that helps you manage your site with tools for doing things like repairing hyperlinks, and tracking to-dos as you work on your site.

- **A real HTML editor:** You can supplement what you do in Office with a real WYSIWYG (*What You See Is What You Get,* now stop it already!) HTML editor. Some great ones are around. FrontPad comes with Internet Explorer 4.0 and is free; FrontPage 98 and HoTMetaL 4.0 are phenomenally powerful and easy to use. But danger, Will Robinson: They cost money.

- **Animated GIF editor:** You need a program that can combine separate images into an animated GIF if you want a rotating logo, dancing rabbits, or any other cute and clever animation on your site. The GIF Construction Set, available at better public FTP sites everywhere (such as www.download.com), is a popular choice.

Setting up shop

So you're sure you want to create your own Web site, but you're not out of the woods yet. On the bright side, an axe-wielding murderer is not in the woods close behind you. The other major decision you have to make is how you want to host your site. Here are the major hosting options (in other words, how to get the Web site on the Internet):

- Place your site on an Internet Service Provider (ISP) server.
- Place your site on a commercial online service, like AOL.
- Host the site on your own server and connect to the Internet through a full-time connection to an ISP.

The last option, to do it yourself, is probably the least attractive. To do that, you need to arrange with an ISP for this kind of Web hosting and use server software to prepare the computer for Internet duty. Microsoft makes Personal Web Server software available with programs like FrontPage 98, but it is complicated to set up and use. You also need to design a system that can handle the number of *hits* (visitors) you expect your site to take. A 28.8 Kbps modem connection to the Internet, for example, can't deal with more than a few dozen hits each day. The modem speed is too slow to handle even two people looking at your site at one time. Instead, you need to get an ISDN line, at a minimum.

Because we're working backwards up the list, we'll talk about AOL next. Using AOL is fine, except for two principal disadvantages: There's a stigma associated with AOL among many professionals that costs your business credibility, and AOL charges quite a bit extra for business services that include your own domain name and reports on access by users. Though the basic Web space is free, your free Web address is always a subdirectory of the AOL URL, such as `members.aol.com/username/`, which is a mouthful.

A *domain name* is part of your Web address and signifies the name of the network server computer on which your Web site is stored. Most large companies register their corporate name as their domain with an organization called InterNIC (your ISP can do this for you). So Microsoft is found at `www.microsoft.com`, and CNN is at `www.cnn.com`. For $100, you can register your business domain name and then pay an ongoing fee to an ISP to host that domain. Not only is your site easier to find, but also you don't need to change your Web address if you later change your ISP. You will have to pay a small fee to the new ISP to take over host duties, however.

Which leaves you with our recommended option: Pick an ISP and let them host your site. Just remember to shop around and include at least one name-brand national ISP as a gauge for current pricing. Make sure you stir up a little heated competition. Check your local computer magazines (usually they're free on the newsstand) or the Business section of your local newspaper for ISPs.

While you're evaluating different ISPs, ask them these questions and compare what each tells you:

- ✔ How painless and inexpensive is setting up a custom domain name?
- ✔ How much server space do I get?
- ✔ How many e-mail accounts do I get?
- ✔ Do you forward e-mail to other accounts?
- ✔ What are the various costs? Do you charge for bandwidth? In other words, do I have to pay for the privilege of allowing others to visit my site?

> ✔ What are your reliability, maintenance policies, and redundancy precautions? Do you let me know when you're *going down* for planned maintenance?
>
> ✔ Do you have any kind of hotline for tech support during off-hours?
>
> ✔ Do you support Microsoft's FrontPage extensions or have other special services, like help with custom CGI scripts?

This stuff may seem overwhelming, but it really isn't much worse than reading up on cars before you go auto shopping. You can learn a lot about an ISP's site hosting policies just by reading their Web page

Turning Anything into HTML

You don't have to know HTML or be a programmer to create good-looking Web pages. The current crop of software, including Office 97, does a pretty good job of turning your random scribblings into Web pages. In fact, creating a Web page from your work-in-progress is just a menu item away in most Office applications.

Saving a Word document as a Web page

To create a Web page from your current Word document:

1. **Save your work as an ordinary Word 95 or Word 97 file so that you have a copy with all the Word formatting intact.**

2. **Choose File⇨Save As HTML.**

That's all you need to do. Pretty simple, huh? You can easily use Word as a Web page designing program, and save your finished product, ready for posting to the Internet.

You should periodically check for updates from Microsoft that improve Word's Internet features. Every once in a while, enter Word's Internet mode (save a file as HTML) and choose Tools⇨Autoupdate. Word visits the Microsoft Web site and installs any new features.

Getting started on the Web

Ross Hunter is the Director of Marketing Services with Matrix Media, a Denver-based 3-D animation and graphic design studio that performs, among other things, Web development. We asked Ross how he and Matrix would advise new Web designers. He had a lot to say:

"Start small. Make a minimal investment, and leave yourself time to figure the Web out — but don't stop once you start. Plan to grow your knowledge base and Web site gradually and continually.

"Determining a minimal investment for getting a site on the Web is like asking how much a house costs. You can do it all yourself for $50 a month for hosting and access, and $50 a year for a domain name. That's all you need in money; the rest is time and effort. To have two or three thousand dollars to spend over one year is useful, but that's to build an entry-level site, do some basic promotion, pay for hosting, and have a few hundred left over for unexpected extras.

"Don't let an ISP build your site. Figure your costs as separate items: site creation, hosting and access, maintenance, and marketing. Own your site so you can move it to a different host. Own your domain name so that your moves are seamless for visitors. Budget for a new site in one year, and figure what results constitute break-even for you along the way.

"Unless you plan to pay people to do things for you, budget your time. You need to spend time on the Web to learn how to work the Web. All the resources you need are on the Web, but you have to be prepared to spend the time to learn from them. I recommend spending a minimum of fifteen hours a week for surfing through the Web.

"Promotion is important. Try to find an inexpensive consultant who can outline all your options because you have many. Understand that your goal is not to become visible to the whole Web, but only to your customers. Study the sites of your competitors. Take a close look at a Web directory like Yahoo! (www.yahoo.com) to see what categories your competitors are in, and submit your own site to those categories."

Here are some of the most common methods of promotion:

- **Make multiple submissions to hundreds of engines and directories:** Save money by doing this yourself.

- **Create E-mail lists:** Several million people voluntarily want to be informed of news in their topic of interest, and many allow commercial announcements.

- **Send press releases:** You can find sites with advice on writing a good press release, and that send the releases for a few hundred dollars.

- **Make reciprocal links:** Offer to link a site from yours if they'll link yours from theirs. Don't be pushy if they don't want to cross-link.

- **Track your visitors:** You eventually want to know where your visitors are coming from (which of your promotional efforts is paying off the best). Ask your ISP to provide you with daily log files of all the activity at your URL (your Web site address), including click-through figures that tell you where someone just came from on the Web, if they have this info. This way, you can tell what prompted visitors to come to your site.

Saving an Excel spreadsheet as a Web page

While we're on the subject, you can also save an Excel spreadsheet as a Web page, but doing so is ever so slightly more complicated:

1. **Start by choosing the range of cells that you want to include in your Web page.**

   You can actually include more than one range. You have the opportunity to select those additional ranges in Step 3, so hold onto your britches and just choose one range for starters (see Figure 12-1).

2. **Choose File⇨Save As HTML.**

   The Internet Assistant wizard appears. This dialog box lets you choose any number of ranges from the current spreadsheet and include them on the Web page (see Figure 12-2).

3. **Click Add, select a range, and click OK. Repeat this process until you select all the ranges that you want to include.**

   Change their order, if you have more than one, with the Move Arrow buttons.

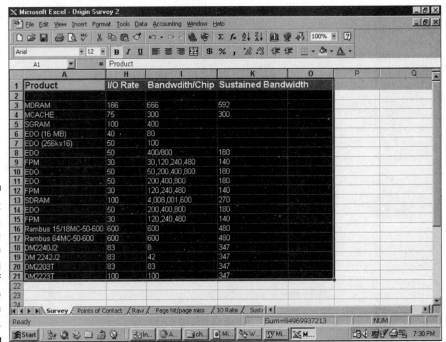

Figure 12-1: Start saving an Excel file to the Web by selecting a range of cells to include on the page.

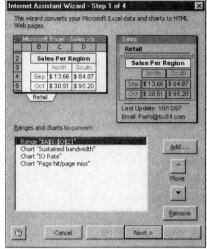

Figure 12-2:
Arrange
your tables
in any order
with the
Move Arrow
buttons.

4. Click Next.

The next step in the wizard appears. Here you get to decide whether to create a new Web page or insert this in an existing HTML document.

5. Choose Create an Independent, Ready-to-View Web page.

We talk about how you insert a range of cells in an existing Web page later in "Inserting Excel spreadsheets as tables." This process is a bit more complicated, and we don't want you to get hurt right now.

6. Click Next.

The next wizard step appears. This dialog box determines the page's appearance.

7. Fill in the sheet with any preferences you have, such as drawing a horizontal line above or below the spreadsheet.

8. Click Next.

Finally, we get to the dialog box in which we save the new HTML document.

9. Choose Save the File as an HTML file, and give the file a name.

10. Click Finish.

Voilà! The file is saved to your hard disk.

You can now open either the Word or Excel files you just created in Internet Explorer or another Web browser like Netscape Navigator (though Microsoft pays us $10 every time we use their browser as an example) and see what you created (see Figure 12-3).

NOTE

It's a joke, people. Microsoft doesn't really pay us $10 every time we mention their browser. In fact, we're pretty sure Microsoft doesn't even like us. Todd, in particular. In reality, Netscape pays us every time we mention their browser. Netscape, Netscape, Netscape.

Netscape, Netscape, Netscape.

Saving a Publisher document as a Web page

Most of the time, you wake up on a bright, blustery Tuesday morning and say, "By golly, I'm going to make a Web page in Microsoft Publisher today." Sometimes, though, you may create a brochure, newsletter, or some other pedestrian marketing tool, and then decide that publication would make a great Web page. If the latter is the case, the process is childishly simple. Just choose File⇨Create Web Site from Current Publication. In the blink of an eye, your publication is a Web page that you can then save using the File⇨Publish Web Site to Folder command. For more details on that, see the next section "Combining All Office Applications for Great Web Sites."

Figure 12-3:
Spreadsheets become tables in Web pages.

Survey Results

This chart identifies the major rated criteria for each of the computing processors.

Product	Density	Interface	Page Hit	Page Miss	Row Access	I/O Rate	Bandwidth/Chip	Memory Sys Width	Sustained Bandwidth
MDRAM	4,5,8,9,10,16 Mbit	SSTL	12	55	30ns	166	666	32,64,96	592
MCACHE	1,2 Mbit	LVTTL	30	30	30ns	75	300	32,64	300
SGRAM	8 M	LVTTL	24	84	54ns	100	400	32,64	
EDO (16 MB)	16M	LVTTL	15	80	50ns	40	80	64	
EDO (256kx16)	4 MB	LVTTL	15	80	50ns	50	100	32,64	
EDO	1 M	TTL			50ns	50	400/800	64	180
FPM	4 M	TTL, LVTTL			50ns	30	30,120,240,480	64	140
EDO	4 M	TTL, LVTTL			50ns	50	50,200,400,800	64	180
EDO	16 M	TTL, LVTTL			50ns	50	200,400,800	64	180
FPM	16 M	TTL, LVTTL			50ns	30	120,240,480	64	140
SDRAM	16 M	LVTTL			50ns	100	4,008,001,600	64	270
EDO	64 M	LVTTL			50ns	50	200,400,800	64	180
FPM	64 M	LVTTL			50ns	30	120,240,480	64	140
Rambus 15/18MC-50-600	16/18Mbit	RSL	20	50	27ns	600	600	8,9	480
Rambus 64MC-50-600	64Mbit	RSL	20	50	27ns	600	600	8	480

Combining All Office Applications for Great Web Sites

If you want to, you can use just one Office application to whip up a Web site. You can use either Word or Publisher and create an attractive site. You may be missing out, though, on some cool things you can do by combining forces with the entire Office suite.

Designing the site on paper

Before we jump right into applying the mechanics of Publisher, Word, and other Office applications, you need to have an idea of what you want your Web site to look like. You may want to sketch your idea on a piece of paper (a napkin, handkerchief, and the hood of a neighbor's car also work). You may feel like jumping into designing the page without a plan, but trust us — you'll be thankful later that you have a grand plan for unifying the site as a whole.

Decide what pages your site will have, and draw lines among them to indicate how they'll connect with hyperlinks. Decide what the theme of each page is: home, corporate information, new products, and so on. Publisher's wizard may limit your site somewhat, but at least start out with a clear vision of where you're going.

HTML design elements may also have a significant effect on the shape your site takes, as shown in Figure 12-4. Consider these in your design:

- **Advertisements:** Will your site include banner ads at the top of pages?

- **Frames:** Will your site be constructed from frames? If so, Word and Publisher won't cut the ketchup. You need to code your site by hand or use a graphic HTML designer like FrontPage 98 or HoTMetaL 4.0.

- **Navigation:** How will your visitors move around in your site? One common method, for example, is *sidebar navigation*. A narrow strip of color runs down the left side of the screen, and buttons or text links reside there for easy navigation.

Creating a Web page with Publisher

Publisher is a very easy place to begin creating Web pages because of its handy Wizards. In fact, Publisher can create an entire, interlinked site in minutes — then it's up to you to add the content.

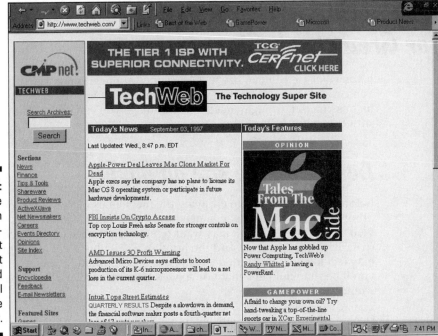

Figure 12-4:
This site
has an
adver-
tisement
banner at
the top and
navigational
aids in the
sidebar.

Here's how to get started:

1. **Start Publisher and choose the Web Site wizard from the PageWizard dialog box.**

   The PageWizard Design Assistant leaps into action.

2. **Feel free to experiment, but choose a Business site because we're, uh, creating a business Web site.**

   The next wizard step lets you choose how complicated your site will look.

3. **Most useful Web sites have more than one page. Choose Multiple Pages.**

   Next, you get to choose what kinds of information you want to incorporate into your site.

4. **Select all the options that you want your site to include.**

   The next step displays a variety of styles you can use to give your site a particular look.

5. **Choose the style of Web page that you want your site to display.**

   Choose carefully because the style is a fundamental part of the page's design and is difficult to change by hand.

6. **Choose a background style.**

   Textures look good but can take the longest to load. Experiment!

7. **Choose a style for the navigation buttons that visitors use to move around your site.**

   We suggest that you pick both text and graphics. Graphics alone are confusing, and text alone is plain and boring.

8. **Give your home page a name, and complete the remaining steps by providing contact information if you want this info to appear in the site.**

9. **Click Create It! to generate the site.**

   Your new Web site — or at least the shell for it — appears in Publisher.

You're done! Now you flesh out your site with graphics and text (see Figure 12-5). You can check out Chapters 4 and 10 for information on the many formatting and editing tools in Publisher.

Figure 12-5: Publisher creates attractive sites quickly. Just pour in text and graphics and add special touches.

Fine-tuning your Publisher Web site

Some tools specific to the Internet come in handy while you edit your Web page.

Creating links on your site

We're talking about *hyperlinks,* not sausage or golf links. This hasn't stopped Todd from smearing maple syrup all over his computer screen and screaming for more pancakes (and his seven iron), but let's move on and leave him to his odd little hobby.

Hyperlinks are what make the Web go 'round. You can easily connect your Web site to other locations on the Internet or to other pages within your own site with these clickable links. The site that Publisher made for you probably already has links. Scroll down until you find some underlined text and then right-click it. Choose Hyperlink from the pop-up menu. You probably see that the page is linked to another page in your prototype site. You can change it to another location with just a mouse click.

Now you get to create our own link from scratch. Say that you have some text on the page and want to make one of the words a link to the CNN Web page, www.cnn.com. Here's what you do:

1. **Select the word you want to turn into a hyperlink.**

2. **Choose Insert⇨Hyperlink.**

   The Hyperlink dialog box appears.

3. **Select A Document Already on the Internet and type its address in the Address (URL) of the Internet Document box (see Figure 12-6).**

   If the site is saved as a favorite in Internet Explorer, you can also use the Favorites button to choose the site.

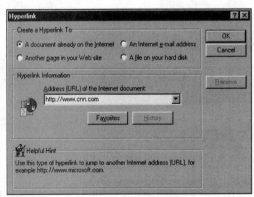

Figure 12-6: Hyperlinks connect different pages in a site and across the Internet.

You can also turn graphics into links, using the exact same procedure. Select the image and then choose Insert⇨Hyperlink.

Changing the background

You may not be able to tell exactly what you're getting yourself into when you select a background color or texture in the wizard. With Publisher, you can easily modify the background once you can see it in its full glory. To modify the background, choose Format⇨Background and Text Colors. A dialog box with other options appears, and you can choose from any of the textures via the Standard tab. If you want a solid color in the background, select [None]. Then switch over to the Custom tab, where you can choose any background color that you like.

Previewing your work

When you want to see your Web site in a Web browser, choose File⇨Preview Web Site. Publisher sends your masterpiece to Internet Explorer, where you can see exactly the way it all looks and works. You can test the links, for example, and make sure they do what you expect.

Saving your work

When you want to save your Web page, Publisher has more ways to save than the Australians have cute, endearing names for dingos. You can save the file as a Publisher document so that you can edit it again. To get it on the Internet, however, you need to save the document as a Web page. You have two more options:

- ✔ Save the document directly to the Web using the Web Publishing Wizard.
- ✔ Save the Web page to your hard disk and put it on the Internet later.

We typically recommend that you save it to your hard disk and only put it on the Web when you're finished. If nothing else, it's faster that way because a 28.8 Kbps connection to the Net can make even just a few files take forever to upload. If you want to save it to your drive, just choose File⇨Publish Web Site to Folder.

Posting your site to the Web with the Web Publishing Wizard

Sure, you can use a vile, computerized demon called FTP to upload your site to the Web. But then you're just contributing to the delinquency of the Internet. Instead, you may want to try the Web Publishing Wizard, which automates much of the process for you. Just follow these steps:

1. **Choose File➪Publish to Web.**

   The Web Publishing Wizard dialog box appears.

2. **If this is your first time using the wizard, click New to create a new Web server.**

3. **Type a descriptive name and then complete URL to the computer that will receive your uploaded files.**

4. **Next, specify the FTP server.**

   It isn't always the same as the Web server, so ask your ISP for details.

5. **Click Finish.**

   Your Web site is magically sent to the Internet for you. (This isn't really magic. Getting Dave to update some of the jokes on his personal Web site every few months. *That* would be magic.)

After your first experience with this wizard, you can just select the descriptive name of your Web server, and the next step is the Finish button, thereby avoiding all that nasty mucking around with FTP names and stuff. If you've dealt with FTP clients, we think that you may agree this is easier.

Word: The great HTML editor

You may not think of Word, your trusty word processor, as much of an HTML editor. The fact remains, however, that you can create some attractive pages using Word. Here are several ways to get started in Word:

- ✔ Open an HTML file, such as one you already started in Publisher, or one you saved from the Internet.
- ✔ Use Word's Web Page wizards and templates.
- ✔ Open or create a Word document and save it as HTML.

Using Word to fine-tune a Web page

After you created the guts of your Web site with Publisher, you may want to bring it into Word and finish it off. When you're there, you find a number of tools to help you create a spiffy looking page.

If you installed a minimal version of Office 97, you may not have the Web enhancements installed. Go find your Office disc and run the setup program again to wedge those extra features onto your hard disk.

Try some of these on for size:

- ✔ **Cool backgrounds:** Change the background of a Web page by choosing Format➪Background. You can select a solid color or pick a graphic background using Fill Effects.

Word or Publisher: Which to use?

Both Word and Publisher can be used to design a Web page, so which one should you use?

Publisher can create a set of linked and related pages — a Web, in essence, of pages. Word doesn't have that ability; it can only make one page at a time.

Publisher's Web creation wizard is more sophisticated than Word's, so it makes more attractive and involved pages.

Word, using the Conversion Wizard, can take a batch of Word documents and convert them immediately to HTML. That's great for taking your store of existing files and getting them published on the Web quickly. Publisher can't do that.

Word can create sophisticated layouts using tables as a dense mesh to hold text and graphic elements in place on the page, exactly where you want them. Publisher's table feature can't store graphics in cells.

Word can import Word or HTML files for editing. Publisher can't read HTML files, so you have to make a Publisher copy of the file to reload in the program for later editing.

If you have a graphic background that you want to use, choose Format⇨ Background⇨Fill Effects, and click Other Texture. You can make an attractive color sidebar that loads very quickly by creating, in a paint program, a single-pixel-high image that has a colored strip as wide as you want the sidebar to appear. The browser simply repeats the colored strip vertically, all the way down the page.

✔ **Graphic Bullets:** Word uses graphic bullets while working in HTML mode. To insert a bullet, choose Format⇨Bullets and Numbering to choose a bullet style that you want to use. A bullet is automatically inserted at the insertion point. The Bullets button doesn't stay on like it normally does in Word. Click the Bullets button in the toolbar for each new line you want to add (see Figure 12-7).

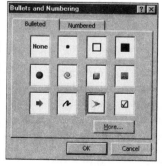

Figure 12-7:
Word uses
a variety
of eye-
catching
bullets.

You can't use the Bullets button to remove a bullet like the way Word usually works. Because the bullet is a graphic, you need to select the bullet and press Delete.

✔ **Hyperlinks:** Hyperlinks in Word work similarly to Publisher. Select the word or image you want to transform into a link and choose Insert➪Hyperlink. Type the URL of the page you want to link to in the top of the dialog box.

✔ **Save as a template:** Okay, this isn't as cool as graphic bullets, but you can design a page layout and save it as a template so that all the other pages in the site look uniform and standardized.

You can link to a particular part of a Web page using bookmarks. Click the start of the line you want to link to, choose Insert➪Bookmark, and give the location a name. Later, when you create a link, you can reference the bookmark in the bottom of the Hyperlink dialog box. Visitors that click that link go to the designated page, but the page also scrolls right to the bookmarked location.

Using tables as a page layout tool

One of the most frustrating things about traditional HTML (by *traditional,* we mean back, oh, three years) is the fact that function was considered more important than form. In other words, using HTML, you can't position things in completely arbitrary locations on the page, because the original architects of HTML didn't care about that kind of thing. These days, Web page designers takes aesthetics much more seriously, and the lack of page layout controls has become a liability.

New revisions to HTML, including Cascading Style Sheets and Dynamic HTML, eliminate many of these problems by making it easier to "lay out" a Web page like a print document. That only works for browsers that recognize these features, however. Until all browsers everywhere can read pages designed with these enhancements, the basic HTML problem remains.

That's why many Web pages are designed with a thin digital mesh that holds everything rigidly in place — text, images, and so on. That *mesh* is a simple table, and the table's cells glue the page's parts in place. Word is a great tool for designing Web pages this way: Just insert a large table into the page (perhaps ten cells wide), and insert text and images as needed in cells to create your layout.

In most cases, you want a page layout table to be completely invisible in the Web browser. After all, it's just holding the various pieces in place. To control the visibility of the table, right-click on the table and select Borders. The Borders and Shading dialog box appears. Make sure that you select None, and the table will become invisible.

Adding forms to your Web page

One of the spiffiest things you can do to your Web site with Word is add forms. What are *forms*? They're controls that let Web visitors enter information into your site and send it to you. Here are a few things can you do with forms:

- ✔ Do marketing surveys
- ✔ Perform online purchases
- ✔ Solicit e-mail addresses for mailings and newsletters
- ✔ Receive site feedback

These are just some suggestions. The neat thing is that forms allow two-way communication: Not only do visitors read what you put on your site, but they can give you information as well.

Before we go too far and get your hopes up that you're about to receive the magical keys to the Internet, we have some news. Actually, we have good news, bad news, and no news at all. Here they are:

- ✔ **Good News:** You can easily add form elements to your Web page, and make the site look like the navigation console for the Starship Enterprise.
- ✔ **Bad News:** None of your controls will actually do anything without some advanced scripts that you need to write.
- ✔ **No News At All:**

That's right, Microsoft had a secret meeting one day, which unfolded something like this:

Bill: Okay, Ted, how's our Word project coming along?

Ted: Just great, Bill. We've added forms, so you can put cool push buttons and things on the screen. They look really neat-o.

Bill: What do the buttons do?

Ted: Well, um, nothing, actually. You see, the user has to create sophisticated scripts that attach actual functions to each of the buttons.

Bill: And they're easy to write, these — scripts?

Ted: Well, um, no. Actually, they're fiendishly complicated.

Bill: And we haven't included any, um, scripts that the average user may commonly need?

Ted: No.

Bill: Okay. *[Presses big red button, dropping Ted into vat of boiling oil.]* What's next on the agenda?

Which brings us back to the problem of what to do with your buttons. Here are a few solutions:

- If you use a program like FrontPage 98, Microsoft automates a lot of form scripting, using tools called WebBots. Using these WebBots, you can add forms without knowing anything about scripts.

- If you want to learn to write scripts (or pay someone to do it for you) you need to use a programming language like PERL to create CGI scripts for your site. This certainly isn't trivial, and you'll probably need to buy a book to learn how.

- And then you have the easy way, which is the one we show you. If you're brave enough to do just a tiny bit of mucking about in your Web page HTML, you can have form results sent to you via e-mail. This only works well for a fairly low-traffic Web site, but it will get you going.

Creating the form

Before you get to all that, though, you can actually create the form in Word. Start by sketching out the kind of form you want to make. In this example, we make you use a table to format the form so that you can get a feel for what working with tables for page layout is like. Open up your Web page and find a place where you want to insert the form:

1. Insert a 3-x-3 cell table in the Web page (see Figure 12-8).

You don't need a table to create a form, but we'll use the table to improve the formatting.

Figure 12-8:
Tables make great page layout grids.

2. **Our form asks visitors for some personal information: their name and e-mail address. So type** First, Last, **and** E-mail **in the left-most cells.**

   Now add some form elements.

3. **If it isn't already, turn on the Control Toolbox.**

   Just right-click in the toolbar region of Word, and choose Control Toolbox.

4. **Place the cursor in the top-middle cell, and choose the Text Box control from the toolbar.**

5. **Do the same for the last name and e-mail address.**

6. **Let's also find out if our mystery visitor is a Mr. or a Ms. Place the cursor in the upper-right cell and click the drop-down box.**

   A drop-down control is added to the cell.

7. **Add a button the user can push to send all this wonderful data to us. Place the Submit button in the lower-right cell (see Figure 12-9).**

Well, by golly, you created a form! Save your work. You can see what your cool new form looks like in Internet Explorer by choosing File⇨Web Page Preview. If you need to, you can drag the borders of the table around to

Figure 12-9:
The finished form in Word.

change the size of the cells. Based on the table we made at the same time you were doing yours (I hope you weren't peeking), we'd make the label text one level larger and bold it.

Oh, and one other thing — our drop-down menu is empty. Here's how to give the menu some preset data:

1. **In Word, select the drop-down control and click Properties in the Control toolbar.**

2. **In the DisplayValues form, type all the options, separated by semicolons:** Mr;Ms;N/A

3. **Click the Properties box's close button.**

Now you can save and preview the page. The drop-down control displays the options you typed (see Figure 12-10). When you're happy with what you made, roll up your sleeves, and dive into a little HTML.

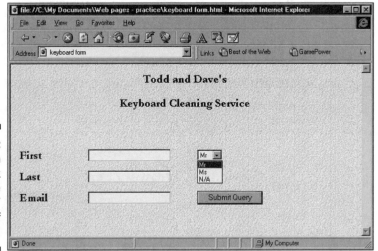

Figure 12-10:
Our form doesn't look bad for five minutes' worth of work!

Making the form do something

Now you're going to modify the form so that it e-mails the results back to you. This is the easiest, cheapest way to use a form, and it also works.

1. **Choose View⇨HTML Source.**

   If you're anything like Todd, right now you're saying, "Golleeeee! There's more HTML here than there is hair on Dave's head. Er, rather...." But we're not concerned with most of it. scroll down to the start of the form, signified by the <FORM> tag. You can even search for the tag, if a lot of lines exist, by choosing Edit⇨Find.

When you get there, modify the <FORM> tag so that it knows to e-mail the results to you.

2. Replace the <FORM> **line with this:**

```
<FORM METHOD=POST ACTION="mailto:me@myemail.com">
```

where me@myemail.com is our clever little way of saying, "Insert your own e-mail address here, bozo."

Note: The publisher, IDG Books Worldwide, Inc., wants to formally announce that they do not sanction nor do they share the sentiment offered in the above statement. They would never call our readers, customers, and friends bozos under any circumstances. Frankly, some of the blue suits up in corporate are still a bit sheepish about calling you people Dummies.

3. Now you need to name each of the form elements, so find the first one, which should look like this:

```
<INPUT TYPE="TEXT" WIDTH="46">
```

4. Change it so that it looks like this:

```
<INPUT NAME="first" TYPE="TEXT" WIDTH="46">
```

5. Name each of the elements in turn.

The name is relatively unimportant (as long as you remember what it means).

The drop-down box looks a bit different — it uses the <SELECT> tag. After you name it, it looks like this:

```
<SELECT NAME="PREFIX">
```

After you give each element a name, you're done.

6. Click Exit HTML and save your work.

Now you can test your creation. Preview the page in your browser, type some data, and click the Submit button. Internet Explorer creates an e-mail message and sends the data to you. The actual data looks like this:

```
FIRST=Dave&PREFIX=Mr&LAST=Johnson&EMAIL=mymail@mydomain.com
```

Inserting Excel spreadsheets as tables

Earlier in this chapter we looked at how to turn an Excel spreadsheet, or just a group of spreadsheet ranges, into a Web page of its own. Now it's time to see how to take a spreadsheet and insert it into an existing Web page, such as one you've been crafting in Publisher or Word:

1. Open the Web page in Word and choose View⇨HTML Source.

2. **Find the location in the page where you want the table to appear and insert this tag:** `<!—##Table##—>`.

3. **Save the file.**

   You see the insertion point for the table.

4. **Choose the range of cells that you want to include in your Web page.**

   You can include more than one range, but just start with the first one for now.

5. **Choose File⇨Save As HTML.**

   The Internet Assistant Wizard appears. This dialog box lets you choose any number of ranges from the current spreadsheet and then include them on the Web page.

6. **Click Add, select a range, and repeat until you have all the ranges included.**

   Change their order, if you have more than one, with the Move Arrow buttons.

7. **Choose Insert the Converted Data into an Existing HTML file.**

8. **Specify the file in which you want to insert the table.**

9. **Specify the name of the new HTML file.**

   You can overwrite the file that you stuck the `<!—##Table##—>` tag into, or create a new one.

10. **Click Finish.**

You only have to face one challenging step in this procedure. If you've never toyed with real HTML, you need to find the location for the table in the code. Doing so isn't that hard, though. Just scroll through the code and look for landmarks, like headings and text that you recognize. For the most part, HTML is just a bunch of tags that describe to the Web browser how to display text and graphics on the page. Hey, you've made it through our jokes thus far, so we know that you can figure out some HTML.

Part III
Making Your Business Work Better

The 5th Wave®   By Rich Tennant

MEN

PRINTER PAPER

In this part . . .

Teamwork and smooth communication are the keys to good business, right? Or maybe it's backstabbing and deception? No matter what your company culture, Office can not only help you get stuff done, but it can also help you get other people to get stuff done. Chapter 13 shows you how Office makes it easy to share documents, and Chapter 14 shows you how Office can make an intranet truly useful.

Chapter 13

Synergistically Leveraging the Utility of Collaborative Techniques: Sharing Stuff

. . . .

In This Chapter

▶ Using comments and revisions to share documents

▶ Using Word's sharing features

▶ Sharing spreadsheets, too!

▶ Group scheduling and delegating tasks

. . . .

*O*ffice 97 can make your office work like a well-oiled machine. No, not all slippery and dangerous to operate if you're sleepy, but rather a picture of efficiency. Each of the Office 97 applications is designed like a corporate volleyball game to encourage group interaction.

This chapter gives you all the tools you need to charge into the office and energize your officemates into a cohesive, dynamic, and effective troupe of team-oriented, high-five delivering go-getters — or your money back. (This offer is not valid in New York, New Jersey, Wisconsin, Florida, any states that are roughly square, states that charge a sales tax, Minnesota, California, or any state that George Washington slept in.) Get ready to learn all about sharing documents, making annoying comments on other people's work, and delegating tasks using Outlook.

Using Comments and Revisions to Share Documents

This is another good news, bad news sort of thing. On the bright side, you're the team leader for creating a big, high-profile report that is sure to net you some working weekends and unpaid overtime. On the gloomy side, you'll need to work fairly closely with a few folks who want to share their opinion about your writing style, including Grumpy George and Nit-Pick Sally. Oh well, you can't win every time.

The traditional way to share a document, still practiced as recently as last week in offices that we personally worked in, is to follow these steps down to the letter:

1. **Write your document in painstaking detail and then print it.**

2. **Forward the paper document to your supervisor or team member for comment.**

3. **Receive the document back with The Pen's Blood all over it.**

   Comments are wedged into corners, varying from hard to read, to completely illegible, and covering every bit of white space on the page.

4. **Take these comments and, in office parlance, *fold them into* your document.**

   In reality, this clever and inoffensive pseudo-cooking term disguises the fact that you have to re-create your document by typing all the edits back into your original product.

5. **Lather, rinse, repeat.**

   After all, Nit-Pick Sally wants to be sure all her suggested commas are in the document, and she's sure to think of new comments in the second round. If you're lucky, you only have to do this one or two more times.

A better way does exist, though: Quit and become a freelance writer. You get to write whatever you want without fear of editing, plus you'll be rich, and people of the opposite sex will flock to you. At least, that's Todd's experience. Dave is the scourge of editors everywhere and lives in abject poverty. But you get the idea.

You can also introduce Office's revision tools to your office. Using the capabilities in Office, you can do things like

- ✔ Save incremental versions of your document to create a dynamic audit trail of changes.

- ✔ Mark changes to a document so that you can see who suggested what, and accept or reject the changes one at a time.

- ✔ Mark documents with sticky notes and audio comments.

- ✔ Turn comments into tasks using Microsoft Outlook, and then delegate those tasks back to the smarty-pants who raised the issue to begin with!

Using Word's Sharing Features

Of all the Office 97 applications, Word has the widest array of tools for sharing documents and tracking changes. With Word, you can pass the document around and let multiple users add their two cents. It's a great way to start arguments in the office.

Tracking changes made by pesky co-workers

So, you still pass printed documents around by hand? Then you should learn all about the Track Changes tool. The changes coin has two sides, if you'll excuse the cliché. One person makes the changes; we'll call her the editor. The poor sap who wrote the thing to begin with has to later incorporate the changes. That person is the author.

Note: We're actually trying to wean ourselves from clichés in general. Here's a way to have fun with the book when you're bored: Using a highlighter, circle all the clichés you can find, and try to guess whether Dave or Todd wrote them. ***Hint:*** Dave often mangles his clichés, like *six of one, half-dozen in the bush.*

From the editor's point of view

If you are going to enter suggested changes into a document, do this (if you're the boss, never mind the *suggested* part. You'll just enter changes):

1. **Open the Word file.**

   You can get it from an intranet, e-mail, or a floppy disk. How you get it doesn't much matter.

2. **Choose Tools⇨Track Changes⇨Highlight Changes.**

3. **Select the Track changes while editing check box.**

   Make sure that Highlight changes on screen is also selected (see Figure 13-1). Close the dialog box.

Figure 13-1:
The
Highlight
Changes
dialog box.

4. **Pretend you're using a red pen and just go nuts: Delete text, insert text, move text, and so on.**

   As you make changes, a revision line appears in the margin, and the text you change looks different than the original text (see Figure 13-2).

5. **When you're done, save the file.**

Deleted Text   Different Editor Appears in Another Color

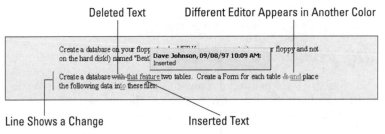

Figure 13-2:
Hold the mouse over a change to see who contributed it.

Line Shows a Change   Inserted Text

If you want to move a block of text from one part of the document to another, as you may do if you're reordering sections in a chapter, you deselect the Track Changes While Editing check box while you cut and paste the chunk of text. Otherwise, a huge section of the document is marked with a change where none really exists — you didn't change the text, after all, you just moved it. Use a comment, discussed later, to indicate that you moved the text.

Any number of people can make comments before the document goes back to its owner. Each editor's comments are uniquely identified — just hold the mouse over some edited text, and a text balloon appears to show you who was responsible.

From the author's point of view

All good things must come to an end. As we said, eventually the document finds its way home to the poor sap who has to find a way to tell Grumpy George that *titillating* isn't the best way to describe the CEO's new marketing strategy. Here's what you can do with a revised document when it lands back in your inbox:

1. **Choose Tools⇨Track Changes⇨Highlight Changes, and make sure that Track changes while editing and Highlight changes on screen check boxes are selected.**

   They're selected automatically unless someone deselects them before you get the document.

2. **To open the Reviewing toolbar, right-click the toolbar region of the screen and choose Reviewing.**

3. **Click the Next Change button, and Word zooms you to the first change that someone typed.**

   You now have two choices (see Figure 13-3):

   - **Accept Change:** This makes the witty, insightful revision a permanent part of your document because it's such a logical and compelling complement to what you already wrote.

   - **Reject Change:** This deletes the revision and reverts the appearance of the document to the way it looked before that untalented heathen soiled your fine work.

Figure 13-3:
Use the
Reviewing
toolbar to
make
changes
to the
document.

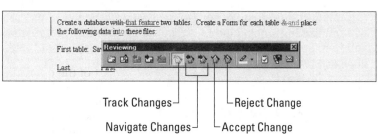

Track Changes ⎤   ⎡ Reject Change

Navigate Changes ⎦   ⎣ Accept Change

4. **Use the Next Change button to maneuver through your document, accepting or rejecting comments as you see fit.**

Accepting all the changes at once

You don't have to make a snap judgment and accept or reject comments on the spot. You can use the Next Change button to sift through the document and then go back to make changes later. One common way to deal with changes is to read, muse, edit, and finally accept all the changes at once:

1. **Browse the document with the Next Change button and review the suggested changes.**

2. **If you don't completely agree with a suggested change, modify it, or if you don't like a revision at all, delete it.**

   Your change takes precedence over the underlying change.

3. **When you're done, choose Tools➪Track Changes➪Accept or Reject Changes (see Figure 13-4).**

4. **Choose Accept All.**

Figure 13-4:
The Accept
or Reject
Changes
dialog box.

You can use the View buttons on this dialog box to see what the document looks like. Without the tracked changes visibly marked that way, you can proof the document without lots of revision marks getting in the way.

All the changes in the document are implemented, including the changes you make to the changes — if you follow our logic. The advantage to using this method is that you're sure to deal with all the revisions in the document without leaving any behind by accident. Be sure that you review them all and that you're happy with the results because after you accept all the changes, they are part of your document.

Using comments in a document

Sometimes you may want to leave a comment in the document without actually changing anything. This is an easy thing to do. It's called a *Comment*. Of course, you can use Changes (see the earlier section, "Tracking changes made by pesky co-workers") to leave comments, too, but that's a sloppy way to manage the document. Consider this: If Dave sends Todd a chapter and embeds a comment like, "What was that crack about my hair in the last chapter? You'll be bald long before me, jazz-boy," using Changes, Todd can't just use Accept All to incorporate all Dave's changes into the chapter. Otherwise, an odd comment is wedged into the text that doesn't belong, and Todd has to first delete the sentence.

Plus, using Changes to reference a specific part of a sentence isn't always easy. Consider, for example, that you want to send comments back to Grumpy George about his use of the word *titillating,* but you don't want to change the word. Using Comments, you can attach a comment to the actual word with a note, "Perhaps you can think of a more accurate word, George."

Including comments in a document

Here's how you add a comment to a document:

1. **Select the word, phrase, or other group of text that you want to add a comment about.**

2. **Choose Insert⇨Comment.**

   You can also use the Comment button in the Reviewing toolbar. A comment window opens at the bottom of the screen.

3. **Type whatever comment you want.**

4. **When you're done with the comment, click the Close button.**

   The comment looks like the one in Figure 13-5.

Comments don't always have to be terse emotional outbursts. You can format the comment with bullets and do many of the things you can do in an ordinary Word document. If your colleague just made an erroneous assertion, such as "The sun orbits the earth," you can do more than just say, "No, Todd. I know you weren't a science major, but it's the other way around." You can actually include a hyperlink to an appropriate Web page, with a message saying, "New evidence contradicts your assertion. Please check out **this link** for details."

Perhaps you noticed the Sound Object button in the Comments window (the button looks like a cassette tape). That's right, you can also record audio comments. Just click the button and then click the Record button in the Sound Recorder window. When you're done, click the Stop button and close the window.

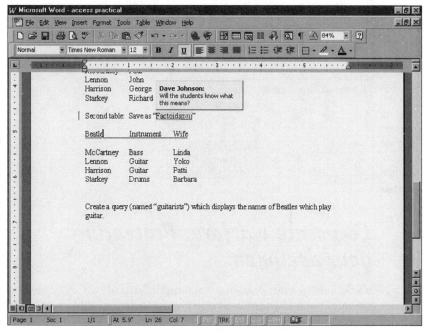

Figure 13-5: Comments are an easy way to draw attention to questions or comments about a specific part of the document.

Use audio sparingly. Despite the efficient compression scheme that Microsoft uses on audio (a statement, again, culled from Microsoft press releases on the subject), these audio comments can make your Word document dramatically larger. This is a concern if you plan to send the file via e-mail or Sneakernet (hand-carrying it on floppy diskette).

Viewing thoughtfully crafted comments

When you receive an edited file, you can easily find comments from your ever-thoughtful coworkers. Words with associated comments appear as highlighted text, and the culprit's initials appear immediately afterwards. Comments are numbered sequentially, as in [DJ1], [DJ2], and [DJ3].

You can change the name and initials that Word uses to identify your comments by choosing Tools⇨Options and editing the User Information tab.

Move the mouse over a comment, and a ToolTip displays the comment. You can use the Previous Comment and Next Comment buttons in the Reviewing toolbar to move among comments, or just click directly on a word that has a comment attached. Then you have two options:

- **Delete the comment:** You can click the Delete Comment button or choose Delete Comment with the right mouse button (see Figure 13-6).

- **Edit the comment:** Click Edit Comment to open the Comment window and add your own witticisms to the comment. In addition, look at the comment window to see if any embedded objects, like sound clips, are waiting for your review.

Figure 13-6:
You can delete comments using the right mouse button.

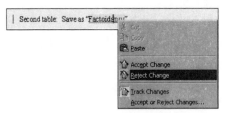

Corporate warfare: Protecting your document

If you'll make your precious document available on an intranet for group comment and changes, you don't want to send it off to war without any protection. We'd certainly hate to trust Nit-Pick Sally, for example, to remember to select Track Changes before she works on your document. If she gets halfway into your manifesto before she remembers — too late. You'll spend late nights rooting out all her dangling participles from your elegant prose. Here's what you do before you give your document its marching orders:

1. **Choose Tools➪Protect Document.**

2. **Select either Tracked Changes or Comments (see Figure 13-7).**

   Here's the difference:

   - **Tracked Changes:** Anything that anyone types in your document is automatically tracked as a change, which you can accept or reject at your leisure. The editor doesn't need to do anything to enable tracking. Heck, they can't *not* track changes — if that isn't not enough double negatives for you.

   - **Comments:** Sorry, Charlie. No changes of any kind are allowed — tracked or otherwise. Anyone can add comments, however.

3. **Type a password.**

   Now you're the only one who can disable the protection. Adding a password is like giving your document shields. Now if only it had phasers.

Oh, shock — a *Star Trek* reference in a computer book. How could that happen? Phasers are pretend laser-like weapons that can be the size of a ship (and able to destroy a moon), or a handheld gun (actually some phasers have a disturbing resemblance to little musical kazoos, or hand-held vacuums). This joke is funny because *Star Trek* spaceships have shields and phasers as defensive and offensive systems, respectively.

Figure 13-7:
Protect
your
document
from
unintentional
changes
with the
Protect
Document
command.

Protection also applies to you, the author. You use your password to dese-lect this feature, so don't forget that password! To turn it back off, just choose Tools➪Unprotect Document.

Changing the options for tracking changes

Everyone has preferences. In music, for example, some like Paul better, while others prefer John — heck, even a few Ringo holdouts are out there. We've heard, though this is entirely unconfirmed, that a few people even like jazz.

You can change the way Changes works to display your document the way that works best for you. Choose Tools➪Track Changes➪Highlight Changes, and click the Options button. Using this dialog box, you can affect the kinds of changes that are identified and the way they appear on-screen (see Figure 13-8). You can affect

- **Inserted Text:** Set the way changed text is displayed, such as with an underline or in italics.

- **Deleted Text:** If the editor deletes text, this text can be hidden from view, displayed as strikethrough text, or appear as a character that indicates text was deleted, without revealing the text itself.

- **Changed Format:** If the editor changes the text formatting, you can choose in what way you show that the format has changed.

- **Changed Lines:** This is simply a line in the margin that indicates that a change has taken place. You can change the way this line appears.

In each of the three change notifications, you can also set the color. Your color choices include

- **Author:** Each author gets a distinctive color so that you can easily tell at a glance who made the change. You can have up to eight authors (and if you have more than eight people reviewing your work, excuse us for saying so, you have too many cooks).

- **Auto:** All changes appear in your casual black.

- **Specific color:** Choose the color you want all the changes to appear in.

For deleted text, inserted text, and changed format, you have the option to hide the change from view or select another display mechanism. One possible way to display tracked changes is shown in Figure 13-9. Keep these tips in mind:

- **You generally want to see all changes to inserted text.** Underline is a good display option, except that the underline can interfere with intentional format underlines and the squiggles that Word uses to indicate spelling and grammar errors. Sometimes a new color suffices.

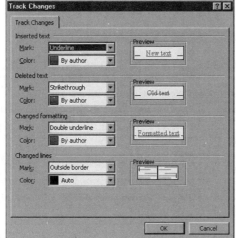

Figure 13-8:
Configure
the way
changes
appear
on-screen.

✔ **Hiding deleted text is usually easiest because you want to see the document the way the editor intended, without unwanted text disturbing the visual momentum of the surrounding text.** You may sometimes want to see what text the editor deleted, however. The first time you scan a document, for example, you may want to know what that clown (and we mean no offense to actual clowns, so please stop with the weird, rambling hate mail, already) deleted. Did Grouchy George kill a key paragraph, for example, that outlines your contributions to world peace?

✔ **If someone reformats parts of your document — like adding italics or an underline — you may not care to see Word's change marks, and you'll see the change visually anyway.** Sometimes format changes are critical to the overall document, though, such as when you're using a particular style that is later fed into a page layout program. Word hides format change markers by default, but you can enable them if you need to.

Change options are really intended for the guy who implements the changes, not the editor. Word remembers all the changes, even if a change is set to hidden while the edit is taking place. The viewer can later switch it from hidden to another view mode, and see everything that the editor did to the document.

Creating tasks from changes and comments

You receive all your comments and suggested changes back from your so-called friends, and many of their recommendations include actual work. Heck, they made comments like "Aren't these really '95 figures, not '96 ones?" Also, "I think we should get Production involved in this working group. Don't you agree?" (No, I don't agree, you weasel. If I wanted Production in the working group, I'd have already invited them.) Weasels, phasers, and clowns. Oh my!

Because you can't deal with all the comments immediately, you can easily transfer these action items to your normal day planner — if you use Microsoft Outlook, that is. Here's what you can do:

1. **Navigate to a comment or change that you want to document as a task for Outlook.**

2. **From the Reviewing toolbar, click the Create Microsoft Outlook Task button.**

   A New Task dialog box appears.

3. **Fill it out by entering the subject, due date, and any other details you want to record (we talk about this in Chapter 5 and show it here in Figure 13-10).**

4. **Click Save and Close.**

Notice that the task includes a shortcut to the Word file and pastes the selected text into the task window. You can also open the comment window and include the text of a comment in the task instead.

Sharing Spreadsheets, Too!

Excel has many of the same sharing tools as Word, but the tools work differently. You don't have versions to worry about when dealing with spreadsheets, but you can easily track changes to your shared workbook. If you want to send your spreadsheet around for group collaboration, just follow these steps:

1. **Choose Tools⇨Track Changes⇨Highlight Changes.**

2. **Select Track Changes while editing.**

Format Change as Double Underline   ⌐Deleted Text as Strikethrough

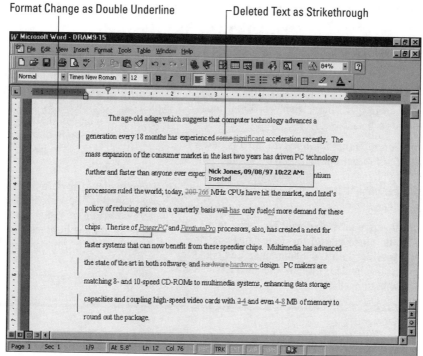

Figure 13-9:
A document with tracked changes enabled.

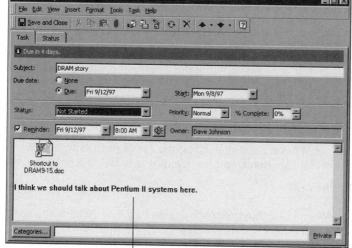

Figure 13-10:
Turn changes and comments into tasks and deal with them in Outlook.

Selected Comment from Comment Window

Rah! Rah! Teamwork!

If you're like 80 percent of office workers, you solicit feedback on projects, because you want to or you have to. Using Office 97, you can easily get others involved. Keep these pointers in mind:

✔ **Force Track Changes to be on using the Protect option.** People can accidentally forget to turn this on and make permanent changes to your work without intending to.

✔ **If you're providing your feedback to others, make use of the Comments tool to provide detailed comments.** Don't just type your ideas directly into the document with tracked changes.

✔ **Be polite.** Realize that pride of ownership can make people very territorial about their work. Offer suggestions as gently as possible, or they may be resistant to change. Remember that everyone says they don't have pride of ownership, but a caldron of possessiveness is steaming just under the surface.

✔ **If you're using revisions, remember to save the final document to a separate file when you're done, particularly if you're sending it in electronic form to a client.** Letting anyone see earlier, less polished versions of your work can be embarrassing.

---

3. **Select the options you want in When, Who, and Where, as in Figure 13-11:**

   - **When: All** tracks all changes. **Since I Last Saved** eliminates tracked changes every time you save your file. **Not Yet Reviewed** keeps tracked changes until you accept and reject changes. You can also track changes since a certain date that you specify.

   - **Who:** Choose whose changes you want to track, such as everyone, or everyone but me (we don't mean me as in the authors of this chapter. Microsoft isn't so paranoid about our tremendous influence in the computing industry that they design software limits with Dave and Todd in mind. *Me* means *you,* which isn't nearly as confusing as it appears in print.)

   - **Where:** Specify a particular range of cells to protect, or leave this option blank and track changes in the entire spreadsheet.

4. **Click OK.**

Unlike Word, enabling the track changes feature (which automatically enables worksheet sharing) disables a few other tools. You can't protect your worksheet using other levels of protection, for example. That makes sense if you want to track changes, or your coworkers need to be able to type in your sheet. Nor can you insert objects like clip art (stock images that you paste into documents) or create new macros (small programs that automate Word and Excel for you) that weren't resident in the sheet when it was first set for sharing.

Figure 13-11:
Tracked
changes are
a bit more
flexible in
Excel than
in Word.

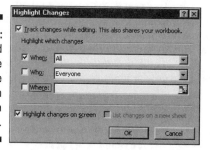

When users type changes to the worksheet, small marks indicate modified cells in the upper-left corner of the cell. If you hover the mouse over the cell, a ToolTip indicates who most recently changed the cell contents.

Resolving Changes

You can accept and reject changes in Excel almost the same way as in Word: Just choose Tools➪Track Changes➪Accept or Reject Changes. The Highlight Changes dialog box appears — but Excel's version has two major differences:

✔ After selecting Accept or Reject Changes, you get a choice of Who, When, and Where. This resembles the dialog box you used to turn tracking changes on to begin with.

✔ Excel keeps track of every change to a cell. If several different people have changed a cell, you're given a list of all the changes. As the spreadsheet author, you get to choose the one you want to use (see Figure 13-12).

Figure 13-12:
Excel
remembers
every
change to a
cell and lets
you decide
which one
wins.

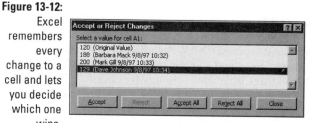

Viewing a history of your changes

Unlike Word, you can later review all the changes you make to a spread-sheet. Specifically, you can save all the changes accepted and rejected to a new sheet that lists specific data about who typed the change, and the old and new values of the affected cells. To create this history sheet, choose Tools⇨Track Changes⇨Highlight Changes. The Highlight Changes dialog box appears. Select List Changes on a New Sheet. This is great for creating an audit trail to resolve disputes at the Wednesday morning meeting.

The history feature only works after you at least once resolve the changes using Accept or Reject Changes.

Setting options for tracking changes

You can set a few important options for your shared workbook. Choose Tools⇨Share Workbook to get to the Share Workbook dialog box. On the Editing tab, make sure that the check box is selected that allows changes by more than one user at a time. Then switch to the Advanced tab (seen in Figure 13-13):

- ✔ **Track changes:** Make sure this is enabled if you want the ability to accept or reject changes. Ensure that the time period is long enough to cover how long the spreadsheet is going to be in use by your office.

- ✔ **Update changes:** If your spreadsheet is located on an intranet and you want access to it while others are working with the data, you may want to update the changes every few minutes instead of when the file is saved. That way you can see what others are doing and accept or reject their work in real time. The downside is that the data they type may not be complete until they save the file.

- ✔ **Conflicting data between users:** Make sure you get to decide who wins if different people enter contradicting values. After all, you're respon-sible for this thing, right?

Corporate warfare II: Protecting your spreadsheet

Just like your Word document from earlier in the chapter, you probably want to force others to work with Tracking Changes turned on. You can enable this super advanced digital force shield technology by choosing Tools⇨ Protection⇨Protect and Share Workbook. Select Sharing with Track Changes, and type a password.

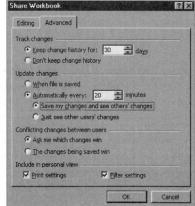

Fire phasers! Cutting off spreadsheet access

In Excel, you can also break a user's access to a network spreadsheet. You may do this if some clown (or weasel, perhaps) left the file open and departed the office for a long weekend and you need to perform file maintenance that is impossible with the file still open. To cut off that user from accessing your spreadsheet, choose Tools⇨Share Workbook and click the Editing tab. Then select the offending user's name and click Remove User.

The removed users can lose data if they haven't saved their work when you cut off their access, so only cut them off if you have to. Otherwise, it's just plain pernicious (and not in your personality, if we may say so), and they may later seek revenge by faxing you 100 sheets of pure black paper.

Adding comments to spreadsheet cells

Spreadsheets are complicated animals, and if you want your co-workers to fully understand what's going on, you need the ability to add comments to your numbers. Excel lets you attach comments to individual cells, not unlike Word's comments that get attached to specific text selections. Unlike Word, though, which has a handy comment window that displays all the comments in a document, Excel's comments are fully contained in their respective ToolTips. You can use comments for any reason you want — to communicate with other team members, explain a formula, or ask a question. To insert a comment:

1. **Right-click the cell to which you want to attach a comment, and choose Insert Comment.**

2. **Type text in the text box.**

Gee, we hardly needed to number that list. Notice that cells with comments have a triangle in the upper-right corner. If you pass the mouse over the cell, the comment appears (see Figure 13-14). You can make it appear permanently by right-clicking the cell and choosing Show Comment from the drop-down list.

Because comments are something you may choose to leave visible, you can format them to make them look more attractive. You can try out any of these little tricks:

- ✔ **Text in the comment box can be formatted:** Just right-click in the box and choose Format Comment, or use the toolbar controls like right, left, and center justify.

- ✔ **You can change the shape of the comment box:** From the drawing toolbar, choose Draw⇨Change AutoShape, and pick a different shape for the box. One possible result appears in Figure 13-15.

- ✔ **You can add a shadow or a 3D effect:** Choose the shadow or 3D button in the drawing toolbar, and select the effect you want to apply to the comment box.

- ✔ **Resize the comment box:** Use the drag boxes to change the size of the box, particularly because the comment doesn't automatically size itself to the text it's holding.

- ✔ **Reposition the comment box on the screen:** You can reposition the comment box for better visibility, and the comment box remembers the new position.

Group Scheduling and Delegating Tasks

A recent discovery by scientists in New Zealand reveals that dolphins advanced to the point of needing middle management and decided it simply wasn't worth the effort. Instead, they intentionally forgot all but the rudiments of their spoken language, decided once again to spend all their time in the water, and implemented severe salary caps for all their professional athletes.

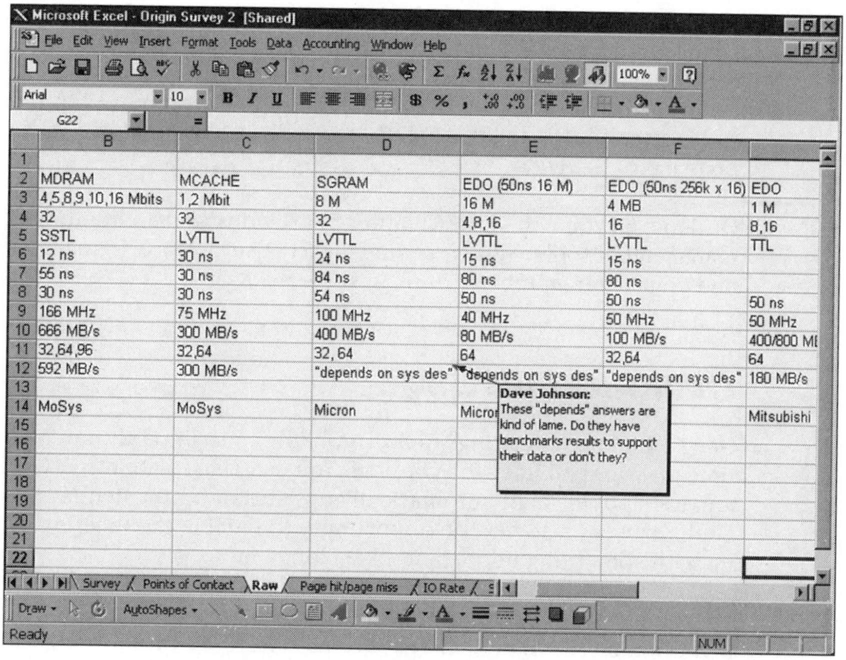

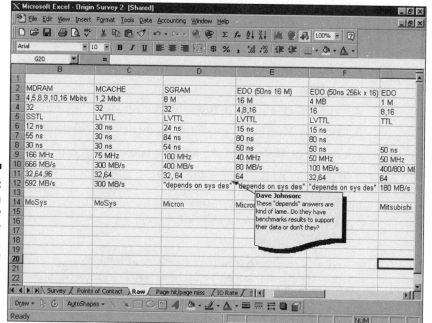

Figure 13-14:
An Excel comment from a helpful co-worker.

Figure 13-15:
You can beautify your comments, particularly if you plan to leave them visible.

Who can blame them? Managers have to deal with pesky things like supervising employees. We all know that nothing hampers productivity like having employees. Outlook makes handling employees a bit easier, though. After a few weeks with Office you may decide not to go join your flippered comrades after all (those little fish that people at Marine World throw to them taste nasty, anyway).

Outlook, as you can see in Chapter 5, provides quite a number of desktop management tools. You can conveniently use Outlook to manage your time, and your team members' time, in several ways.

Booking meetings

Need to set up a meeting? Refer to Chapter 5 to find out how you establish a time on your calendar for yourself. You can also invite other Outlook users, and the appointment automatically updates in both calendars. The other Outlook users also get the opportunity to decline the meeting if they're tied up with something important, like a long lunch.

For the meeting invitation to work properly, you need to send the meeting invitation message in Rich Text Format (RTF). In Outlook, click Contacts, find the individual, and select Properties. Choose Always send in Rich Text Format. Your invitees should respond to you in RTF also. If you don't use RTF, the message won't trigger the Calendar module to book the meeting.

When you're ready to create your meeting, do this:

1. **Switch to the Calendar mode and double-click the time for the meeting.**

2. **Type information like the subject of the meeting and its location.**

3. **Click the Meeting Planner tab, and click the Invite Others button.**

4. **Choose invitees from the address book (see Figure 13-16).**

5. **When you're finished with the form, click Send.**

When the recipient opens the message, the appointment appears in the Calendar. The recipient can choose Accept, Decline, or Tentative, as shown in Figure 13-17.

The invitee's response is automatically sent back to you. When you get the response, your calendar entry updates your meeting to reflect whether they've decided to attend. Figure 13-18 shows the meeting on the calendar. If you open the meeting and choose the Meeting Planner tab (see Figure 13-19), you can see who has responded to your invitation.

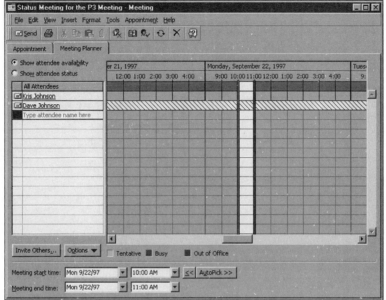

Figure 13-16:
You can invite any number of people to your meeting.

Respond to Meeting Request ⌐View Your Schedule to See If You're Free

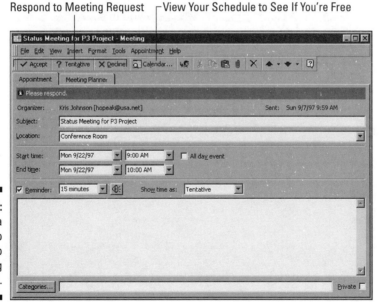

Figure 13-17:
Just pick a button to respond to the meeting invitation.

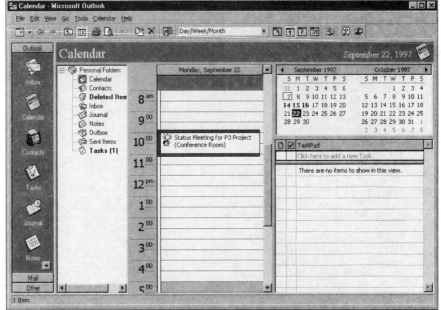

Figure 13-18:
The meeting, nestled comfortably in the Calendar module.

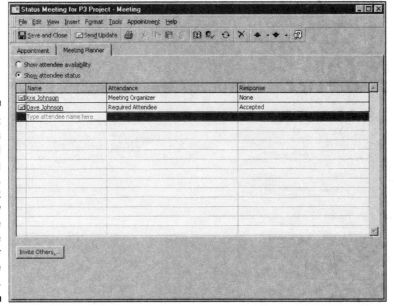

Figure 13-19:
Dave has accepted the meeting invitation, and Outlook automatically updated the Response status after getting the e-mail reply.

You can send invitations to people who don't use Outlook, and the message will arrive in as plain text. Not as fancy as automatically putting it in an appointment book, but they're at least notified of the meeting.

Delegating tasks

Do you have too much on your plate, or do you just want to keep on top of all the activities your people are working on? Either way, you can use Outlook to delegate tasks to other people. This is a great method for tracking the various high-profile activities that your team is working on. If everyone keeps their own copy of Outlook apprised of their status with a task, you find out automatically. Here's how to delegate tasks:

1. **Create a task by choosing File⇨New⇨Task.**

2. **Fill out the subject, due date, and other details. Then click the Save and Close button.**

3. **Right-click the task and choose Assign Task.**

4. **Decide who you want to reward with the honor of completing this task, and type the appropriate name in the To box (see Figure 13-20).**

5. **Type any other changes or notes and then click Send.**

Figure 13-20:
You can assign tasks in your calendar to others, and Outlook handles the details of updating status.

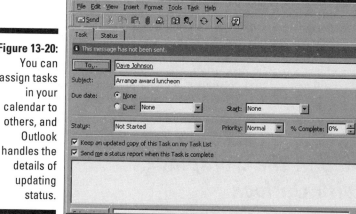

You're automatically notified when the task is complete if you select Send me a status report when this task is complete.

When the stuckee gets the message, the message is automatically entered in the task list when it is opened. The hidden message for the underling is *don't open the message,* but you didn't hear that from us. If you just received this task assignment, you actually get the opportunity to accept or decline the task, but don't kid yourself — if your boss took the trouble to send it to you, don't turn this one down. It's an opportunity to excel. Send the reply, and the boss's copy is updated to show you as the owner of the task.

For this assignment to work properly, send the task assignment in Rich Text Format, and the recipient needs to send mail back to you in RTF as well. Otherwise, the message won't trigger the Calendar mode to track the tasks.

Reporting task status

As you work through a task, you can send periodic status reports to the originator of the task. This way, the boss knows what's going on without you telling him or her about it in person, in which case you would probably just get more work to do. (This is called the *First Seen is First to Get the Work* theory of task assignment in the workplace.)

First, change the status of the task in the Calendar module. Set the percent complete, and mark any notes that describe what's going on. Then you can send a status report by right-clicking the task and choosing Send Status Report (and you thought it would be an obscure command). Just go ahead and send it — the message is an automated report on the status of the task. As soon as the boss opens this message, the task's status is updated in the calendar.

If a task is updated, such as with a new status, it appears in bold until you open it to inspect the change.

When the task is closed out, the task originator is automatically notified, and the task is completed on that computer, as long as the task was originally assigned with the Send me a status report when this task is completed check box selected.

Democracy in the workplace: Voting with Outlook

How many times have you needed to take a quick poll within the office but found that it was impractical to do? More times than you can count, we're sure — especially because you haven't had a great tool for actually counting the vote, until now. Outlook has a built-in Voting tool that lets you painlessly get feedback from your team members without even talking to them.

Avoid talking to your coworkers at all costs. Typically, talking leads to undesirable results, like additional work, catching the flu, and buying band candy and coupon books. Communicating through e-mail is much better.

You can use Outlook Voting for all sort of things:

- ✓ E-mail certification that everyone has taken their mandatory Interpersonal Communications Skills Training.
- ✓ Straw vote on the color of this year's trade show booth.
- ✓ Has everyone had a chance to buy band candy? Only a few cases left!
- ✓ How much are you willing to pay for Dave Johnson's autograph?

Voting only works if you send the message in Rich Text Format to each recipient.

To conduct an Outlook vote:

1. **Create a new e-mail message and address it to everyone whom you want to vote.**

2. **Fill out the message and subject.**

3. **Click the Options tab.**

4. **Select Voting and type the names of the buttons separated by semicolons (see Figure 13-21).**

   A few preconfigured buttons are already in the drop-down menu.

5. **Send the message.**

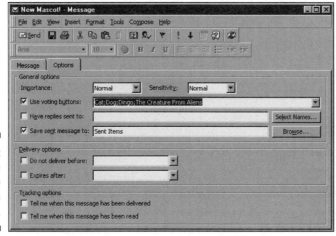

Figure 13-21: Use the Options tab to create an e-mail poll.

Recipients get a message with a row of buttons across the top. They can then cast their vote and return it to you like any other e-mail. Their vote is contained in the subject line of the reply, avoiding the need to open the message.

Do you want a quick tally of the voting results, but have lots — dozens or more — results coming in? Create a rule using the Rules Wizard to automatically divert various responses to different folders. You can send yes responses to one folder and no responses to another, for example, or check the number of items in each folder (displayed in the bottom left of the Outlook window) to see how many you received.

Chapter 14

Disseminating Information Using Office

• •

In This Chapter

▶ Playing with the ad-hoc office intranet

▶ Setting up a local home page

▶ Creating training materials

• •

*G*otta love that spell-checker in Word. Otherwise, we might not have gotten the word "disseminating" spelled correctly for this chapter. In fact, we considered a number of other names that would have gotten us around using "disseminate," but ultimately we decided it wouldn't be so hard to highlight the word and check the spelling. You might be surprised how often we struggle to find another word for a concept just because we forget about that silly command built into Word.

In this chapter, we want to quickly hit on some interesting little tidbits you can spend time on if you are the person responsible for getting employees up to speed in job training, if you're in charge of communicating with fellow employees, or if you're the designated answer-person. In short, if you're responsible for the human resources of your company (even if it's a small firm and you wear many hats), then you'll like some of the stuff in this chapter.

Most of what we want to discuss revolves around using Internet-related tools to distribute information within your company. We know that sounds like a contradiction, but it's nothing so bad as watching Dave try to play guitar. Trust us. In fact, you can set up Internet Explorer or another Web browser so that a quick corporate information page is not only available to your employees — you could make it the home page they see when they fire up the browser every morning. That way, you can communicate the latest to them quickly and without wasting paper.

You may want to put other things on your network to be browsed by employees, including HR materials, rules for doing business, reminders, reports, awards, and a suggestion box. You can even create an area where employees can pop-up their own comments, ideas, suggestions or hints for everyone else to see. It's a little like being a Webmaster (a computer whiz responsible for the day-to-day operations of a Web site), but, with the hints and teachings elsewhere in this chapter, putting together an intranet site of this magnitude just ain't that tough.

The Ad-Hoc Intranet

An intranet (for those of you who've been screaming, "Stop saying 'intranet' if you're not going to define it!") is simply a term used to describe the process of using Internet-style tools for disseminating information to a localized group of people. It's an internal Internet, if you will, which allows you to use Web browser to view documents that are internal to your company's operations. In many large companies, an intranet works a lot like the Internet does, anyway — using TCP/IP networking protocols, expensive server computers, and a vast array of Ethernet networking hardware devices to string everything together.

But an intranet doesn't have to be built like that. In fact, if your company uses any sort of networking at all (either the peer-to-peer networking built into Windows 95 or a server-based system using Windows NT, Novell, or a similar setup), then you can create your own intranet. All it takes is a shared folder somewhere on your local area network.

You may already be aware of the basics of how Web browsers, like Internet Explorer, work. Using an address called the Uniform Resource Locator (URL), you locate a particular HyperText Markup Language (HTML) document on the Internet, which is then read-into and interpreted by the Web browsing program. All documents on the Internet have a unique URL, allowing them all to be individually referenced through a special address.

Actually, Web browsers work because there's a tiny squirrel in your computer doing all kinds of advanced stuff to make it look like you're communicating with Sonya in Norway.

Well, this same URL scheme is applicable to your local area network. Using a slightly different protocol (Web pages on the Internet use the HTTP protocol, local pages use the FILE protocol), you can reference any individual document on your hard drive — or on a local area network. You can then load that file in your Web browser and view it. You'll have especially good luck if that file is an HTML document, one of which is shown Figure 14-1.

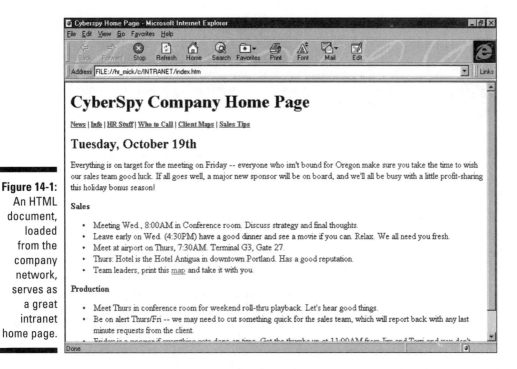

Figure 14-1:
An HTML
document,
loaded
from the
company
network,
serves as
a great
intranet
home page.

Deciding what goes on an intranet

Notice that you can set up an intranet for any number of reasons. As shown in Figure 14-1, the most immediate use for the intranet HTML document is for current news — news that brings the entire company together by sharing what everyone is doing and why (great for a small but growing office). The intranet document can also serve to cut down on paper because news like this is often sent around via memos instead.

But there are some other great reasons to use an intranet:

- ✔ You can place important HR documents, like the employee handbook or printable forms for leave-asking, in their own section of the Web site.

- ✔ You can store work-related documents, such as a telephone script, emergency sales hints, a contact list, and the company's internal list of phone extensions, on the intranet for quick access.

- ✔ You can place training materials that you'd like your users to have access to while they're working. This is especially worthwhile if you've created a help HTML document for an Access application you've created or some similar Office-oriented instructions you'd like to post for users to see.

✔ Put a map of the building (in larger offices) on your intranet, or include whatever other maps would be useful to your employees, including maps to customers and so that on.

Here's a great use for Automap (covered in Chapter 6). Save a route or pushpin file and place it on the intranet so that everyone in the office has access to it.

✔ Use your intranet for public archiving of records — like meeting minutes, old reports, product updates, and so on. Anything that could be worthwhile to your company, and would normally be stored in a filing cabinet somewhere, has a good chance of becoming an intranet document.

Creating the intranet

All you really need to do to create an intranet is create a shared folder somewhere on your company's network. This folder needs to contain the index page for your intranet site (the *home* page is often called the index page and is usually saved as **index.htm** or **index.html**) along with any subfolders you create for other files on the intranet. For example, you might create a folder that includes different files for different parts of your intranet — you might even make different employees responsible for updating different parts of your site. Figure 14-2 shows an example of how an intranet might look in Windows Explorer.

Figure 14-2:
An intranet's file structure on the network.

Choosing files

What files will you create? Exactly the same files you'd use for an Internet presence on the World Wide Web. In fact, you can use all the various Microsoft Office applications to create Web pages and similar files, as discussed in Chapter 12.

Essentially, you'll be dealing with three types of files:

✓ **HTML documents.** Even though these files aren't going to be placed the Web, you still want to save them with a **.htm** or **.html** filename extension, or use Word or Publisher to create HTML documents for y

✓ **Images.** Using either the GIF or JPEG specification, you can include images on your intranet pages. You can save these images in Word or Publisher (using clip art and similar images), or you can translate nearly any image to GIF or JPEG using Microsoft Photo Editor, included with some versions of Office SBE.

✓ **Office documents.** In most cases, Office documents can be read right from your intranet. In fact, using the latest versions of Internet Explorer, you can even view Office documents from within the Web browser window. So feel free to drop Office documents on your intranet as they are — especially if you've diligently upgraded the office's copies of Internet Explorer to version 4.

Using Netscape Navigator instead? You can easily set Netscape to respond to Office documents too. Just edit the Helper Applications (after choosing Edit⇨Preferences) options so that Navigator associates the appropriate file name extension (like .doc or .xls) with its Office application (like Word and Excel, respectively).

Loading an intranet page

After you have the pages and documents saved in the shared folder on the intranet, it's a simple matter to get other computers to load that page. As we mentioned early, this step uses a different protocol than the World Wide Web's HTTP. Instead, we use the FILE protocol. However, the rest of the address is still a URL, following this format:

FILE://name_of_computer/c/folder_name/filename.ext

For **name_of_computer**, substitute the network name of the computer where the shared folder resides. The "**c**" represents the drive letter on that computer where the intranet folder is. Next comes the name of the intranet folder (**folder_name**) and finally, the name of the document you'd like to load in your browser, along with its filename extension.

Here's an example of an URL to an HTML document you might load over your intranet:

FILE://hrsystem1/c/intranet/index.html

Of course, this would work with any document that your browser can recognize, including Office documents. Here's an example of a Word document:

FILE://maincomp/f/intranet/hr/policies.doc

Notice that, for the most part, the FILE reference is just a simple path name to the document you want to load, except that it uses forward slashes (the Internet convention) instead of typical Windows backslashes. Still, you can build a path to any file in a shared folder or subfolder just by adding folder names and slashes to the URL.

Setting the office home page

After you have your intranet in place, it's a great idea to run through the office (no scissors, remember) and change the home page setting in all the employees' Web browsers to the new index page of the Intranet. That way, employees will see the day's news, meetings, and other timely topics every time they fire up their browsers.

Here's how to set the home page in Internet Explorer 3.*x*:

1. **Enter the URL to the page in the browser and load the page.**

   Do this in the address box of your browser and then press Enter after typing. Most versions of Internet Explorer and Netscape will also allow you to open pages using the File⇨Open or File⇨Open Location commands.

2. **Select View⇨Options from the menu bar.**

   The Options dialog box appears.

3. **In the Options dialog box, choose the Navigation tab. Now, in the Page drop-down menu, choose Start Page. Then click the Use Current button.**

   In Internet Explorer 4, Microsoft moved this stuff around to keep book authors writing revisions and rolling in cash. Choose View⇨Options, and on the General tab, select Use Current in the Home Page section.

4. **Click the OK button to close the Options dialog box and set the home page.**

Don't forget that a good home page offers a number of features, which can include

- ✔ Office or company news
- ✔ Scheduled meeting for the day, week, and so on
- ✔ Links to archived documents
- ✔ Links to news pages for other parts of the business, if necessary
- ✔ Links to training and help materials
- ✔ Stock price, stock option information, and corporate financials
- ✔ Your company's favorite recipes for tapioca pudding
- ✔ Links to the Internet, if your employees have access

This last one can be pretty important. When you change your employees over to the company home page, you'll want to give them some links that help them get out onto the real Internet for searching, researching, or checking other Web sites. Create a few links to popular search engines and other important pages for your company, and suggest a good news page like CNN, Excite Live, or a similar service.

Using Netscape? In most versions of Netscape, you set the home page by choosing Edit⇨Preferences and choosing the Navigator item or tab. Then click the Use Current Page button in the Home Page section (or enter the URL to the home page if necessary).

Make the home page your wallpaper

In versions 4.0 and higher of Internet Explorer, the active desktop gives you the opportunity to add a page as the *wallpaper,* or backdrop, for your computer's desktop. The links to the home page are live, allowing you to click your wallpaper to open an Internet Explorer window and view other pages on the intranet (or on the Web).

To set a particular page as the wallpaper for your desktop, take the following steps:

1. **Right-click on the desktop and then choose Properties from the menu that appears.**

   The Display Properties dialog box appears.

2. **Click the Background tab and then click the Browse button.**

   The Browse dialog box appears.

3. **In the Browse dialog box, choose HTML Document from the Files of Type menu; then find the HTML file you want put on the desktop.**

4. **Click OK to dismiss the dialog box.**

The HTML document you've chosen appears on your Windows desktop as wallpaper.

Think that this whole Active Desktop is another bloated feature that Microsoft stuck in what should be a simple product? Sure it is! But, think about this: You can put important information and links right on your coworkers' or employees' desktop, where they'll see it every time they start their machine. That's handy.

Create Training Documents

One of the many reasons to create an Intranet is to put some help and/or training documents on the Web, especially if you've created any specialized forms or applications (using Excel or Access, perhaps) for you company. Whatever the case, though, it's a good idea to document your systems as much as possible. Along with a good intranet implementation, you can get your employees up and running more quickly if you make a concerted effort to create training materials. An example is shown in Figure 14-3.

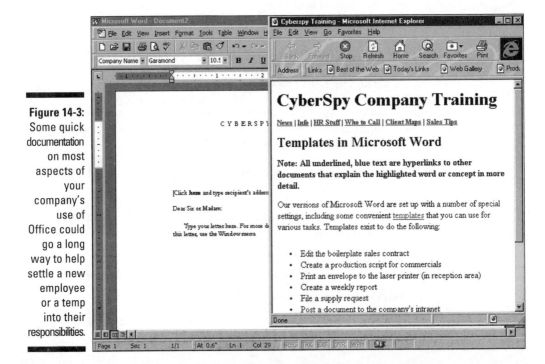

Figure 14-3: Some quick documentation on most aspects of your company's use of Office could go a long way to help settle a new employee or a temp into their responsibilities.

When you go to create online training or help materials, there are a few quick hints you should consider:

- ✔ Design each page of the lesson so that it appears in easily digestible chunks.

- ✔ Allow the user to click words and images to get a definition, better explanation, or a close-up view.

- ✔ Use bullets and numbered lists liberally (or just use them *a lot* if you're a member of the U.S. Republican Party; if you're a Libertarian, we figure you'll just do whatever you want to do).

- ✔ Create an easy-to-maneuver table of contents that makes it easy to begin a lesson or accomplish a task.

There's no question that writing documentation can take quite some time — it can be close to a full-time task. (In larger companies — or government offices — it is. Both of your caring authors have performed this task in large organizations on a full-time basis.) But a complete online training system is exactly the sort of thing your company should have if you're growing rapidly or if you use a lot of contract or temporary employees.

Here's a great reason to farm out documentation writing to a freelance writer rather than hire a computer tech for your company: We freelance writers work cheap, we're always on time, and best of all, we're much more fun than computer techs at parties!

Another reason to have an intranet is to post training material you've created in other programs — Publisher, Word, or even PowerPoint — so that everyone can get at them. Whether you're offering hour-long seminars on sales, data entry, or some other facet of your business, it's a great idea to post the notes or presentation for later reference. And because Internet Explorer can deal with many Office documents, you may not even need all the applications on every workstation.

Did you buy Office SBE for everyone? Well, then they don't have PowerPoint. But don't despair. You can always buy one copy of PowerPoint, create the presentation, and then deploy the free PowerPoint Viewer program (available for download from Microsoft's Web site and on the included CD-ROM) to everyone in the office. Now they can see the presentation over the intranet. Do not, however, simply install your single copy of PowerPoint on everyone's computer. That would be wrong, and Microsoft might not like it very much.

Training tips from the experts

Okay, we wrote these tips too. But we're pretty expert when it comes to these things, having both taught seminars and courses and written documentation over the years. And this training stuff isn't brain surgery, either, although there are some great tips to help you reach all your students.

First of all, the Office-related tip: When you can, use multimedia. Unless your students are in military basic training and you want to teach them how to keep themselves awake during class, there's no reason not to make your training sessions as interesting as possible. That means using images, presentation slides, sounds, and movies, and, where possible, hiring live stage actors to extemporaneously play out on a shadow-box stage the roles you cover in your discussion. (That is to say, inject some humor into the lecture. Notice, for instance, how much more awake you are when you read the funny things we write!)

Other tasty tips:

- ✔ The presentation mantra: Attention/Lesson/ Summarize/Remotivate. Get the students'

attention, teach them, summarize periodically, and remotivate. The best way to create a lesson and a presentation involves small chunks of lesson-giving, followed by summary and another funny line or multimedia attention-getter (or, best of all, have someone raise a hand and discuss an issue).

- ✔ Start with the test and work backward. If you have a particular skill-set or knowledge base that you want to impart, generate a test that accurately measures those skills. Then work backward to create the lesson. That way, you won't inadvertently test students over material they haven't been prepped for.

- ✔ Test and evaluate. Even if your lessons are Web-based, ask for feedback from employees, trainees, and anyone else who is exposed to the material. Every instance of better training tends to add to the bottom line in your company.

Part IV
The Part of Tens

The 5th Wave®   By Rich Tennant

IF BOB DYLAN HAD PURSUED A CAREER IN COMPUTERS

"PUT HIM IN FRONT OF A TERMINAL AND HE'S A GENIUS, BUT OTHER-WISE THE GUY IS SUCH A BROODING, GLOOMY GUS HE'LL NEVER BREAK INTO MANAGEMENT."

In this part . . .

*E*very *...For Dummies* book ends with a series of top-ten lists, and this one is no different. We present ten tips for using Office, ten cool downloads that make Office run better, and ten ways to put Automap to good use.

Chapter 15

Almost Ten Useful Ways to Use Office

In This Chapter

▶ Ten tips for making life with Office easier

A s we begin this chapter, it's difficult not to quote some very profound lyrics from the Throwing Muses' lead singer and lyricist, Kristin Hersh. For the most part, though, this is because that's the music that happens to be playing as this chapter is written. Nothing from *Limbo,* the current album, really has anything to do with Microsoft Office except, perhaps, in the most metaphysical of ways.

In any event, there are a lot of really cool ways to use Office — both obvious and not so obvious. Throughout this book, we've tried to bring everyday business applications to the forefront, rather than simply catalogue the mechanics of how to use Office 97. In this chapter, we've selected ten cool things you can do with Office that we haven't explicitly described elsewhere in this fine tome. Enjoy!

Hey, Kristin: It would be, like, totally cool if you autographed a copy of this book for Dave.

Automate Simple but Annoying Tasks

As with any program, there are probably certain actions that you do frequently in Office. In all likelihood, you don't want to do the same mindless task over and over again, but Todd isn't always around to do them for you. Consequently, Microsoft has built macro recorders into the Office applications. Using macros, it isn't difficult to create automated processes — little robots, in effect — that can run off and do your bidding for you.

To create a macro in Word, do this:

1. **Choose Tools⇨Macro⇨Record New Macro.**

   The Record Macro dialog box appears.

2. **Give your new macro a name.**

   If you want the macro to work with all your Word documents, choose **All Documents (Normal.dot)** in the Store Macro In drop-down menu. Otherwise, select the specific document that you want it to work with.

3. **If you want the macro to be deposited in the toolbar, click the Toolbar button and then switch to the Commands tab. Select the macro on the right side of the dialog box and drag it to the location in the toolbar where you'd like it to appear.**

4. **If you want to assign the macro to a particular keyboard shortcut, click on the Keyboard button on the Record New Macro dialog box or click on the Keyboard button at the bottom of the toolbar box.**

   Choose a keyboard combination that isn't already in use.

5. **When you close the dialog box, the cursor changes and looks like a little cassette tape.**

   Every mouse movement and keystroke you make is now recorded to the macro file.

   Before you start recording your macro, you should figure out exactly what mouse clicks and keystrokes the macro needs — and "script" it on paper so that you don't make mistakes.

6. **When you're done, click the Stop Recording button in the dialog box.**

Macros have almost unlimited use. You can use a macro, for example, to automatically open a document template and simultaneously open several toolbars that you use all the time.

Launch Your Favorite Programs from the Shortcut Bar

If you have the Professional edition of Microsoft Office, you can add your favorite programs, folders, and even data files to the shortcut bar. This is a handy way to start programs like QuickBooks, a paint program, an HTML editor, or other software you need frequent access to. Not only that, but you can add spreadsheets or databases you need immediate access to every day — and even a folder that's buried deep in your hard disk that you need to open all the time.

To add new programs and data files to the bar, just open the appropriate folder, find the program or data file in question, and drag it to the shortcut bar. You can then right-click the button and choose Rename to give the icon a more descriptive name. You can also right-click the bar and choose Customize, click the Buttons button, and rearrange icons or add a space between them.

Convert a PowerPoint Presentation into a Word Document

Your PowerPoint presentation looks great — heck, we showed you how to make it — but now the boss needs a written report based on the pitch you gave the other day. And you thought no one recognized excellence. (Otherwise, they wouldn't be *In Search of Excellence* to the tune of millions of copies, right? If someone finally found some excellence, you'd think they'd just write another book.)

 It's easy to take the presentation from PowerPoint and drop it into Word in a single mouse click. With the slide text as an outline, you can then craft a nifty report that captures all of the report's main ideas and overall pacing. All you need to do is open your presentation and choose File⇨Send To⇨ Word. A dialog box offers you a choice of ways to export the data, but choose the bottom option — Outline.

This technique is great for writing student guides based on an existing PowerPoint presentation. Also, this process works both ways. You can export a Word document directly to PowerPoint using the Send To command.

Publish Training Documents Online

If your job description includes training new employees, perhaps you've grown tired of constantly clear-cutting forests just to reprint and distribute welcome books, corporate policy binders, and company benefit primers. There's an easier way: Take your Word products and publish them on the company LAN (local area network). You can do it in either of two ways:

  ✔ Convert the documents to HTML and save them as Web pages.

  ✔ Just publish the documents as Word files.

We've already talked about how to turn Word documents into HTML. Publishing them as native Word documents is easy to do as well, though. You can still add hyperlinks to make it easy for the readers to find their way around your document, but you'll also want to protect the document from changes. Just choose Tools⇨Protect Document and choose Comments. Enter a password, and no one can change the text without your permission.

If your company moves to Internet Explorer 4, you can use the Active Desktop to put hyperlinks to online documents right on the desktop screen. That way, employees are one click away from the corporate policy binder and cafeteria lunch menu at all times.

Creating an ad-hoc intranet for your small business is discussed in more depth in Chapter 14.

Insert Auto-Updating Charts into Reports and Presentations

Already have a chart or graph in one document that you'd like to use elsewhere? There's no need to re-create it from scratch — just use OLE to drop it in place in the document you're writing. If the source data changes and it affects the original chart, the copy will change automatically, too! Now *that's* a time-saver.

OLE stands for Object Linking and Embedding, and it is the standard way Windows documents share data. OLE can be a "cold" link (once you paste the data in a new document, its relationship to the old document is severed) or a "hot" link (if you change the original file, changes are automatically updated in the new one too). That's the kind we're using in this example.

To take a chart from Excel and drop it into Word, do this:

  1. **Open the Excel file with your nifty graphic and select the chart. Choose Edit⇨Copy.**

  2. **Switch to Word. Choose Edit⇨Paste Special.**

  3. **Click on the button marked Paste Link and click OK.**

That's it. Now you can test the link by returning to Excel and changing some of the data that effects the chart. The chart should change automatically. Switch back to Word — the new chart is changed, too.

See Chapter 11 for more exuberantly exciting details on adding OLE charts and spreadsheet data to other Office documents.

Add Visual Warnings to Your Spreadsheets

Often, the data you store in a spreadsheet needs to stay in a certain range. Say that you can only afford to pay an employee for a certain amount of overtime each pay period — Excel can flag the overtime cell if it exceeds whatever pittance you're paying. Let's say you're monitoring overtime hours and you want to flag any value greater than 10. Here's how to do that:

1. **Select the overtime cell.**

2. **Choose Format⇨Conditional Formatting.**

   The Conditional Formatting dialog box appears.

3. **Make sure that the dialog box reads "Cell Value Is," "Greater Than," and "10."**

4. **Click on the Format button and change the text color to red.**

5. **Click OK.**

If you had other constraints — like an upper and lower value — you can add other conditions using the Add button. One condition is enough for us, though. Experiment by putting different numbers in the cell and watch how the color changes.

Store Matching Letterhead and Envelopes in the Same File

Imagine storing a matching letter and envelope in a Word file. Think of the convenience; picture the hours you'll save every day; envision the long, carefree vacations it'll earn you. Well, maybe not.

But it *is* convenient to store your company's letterhead and matching envelope in the same Word file. That makes it easy to customize and print letters. You probably already have a letterhead template, so open it up. Then do this:

1. Choose Tools⇨Envelopes and Labels.

2. Fill in some text and then choose Add to Document. The envelope appears at the top of your letterhead.

3. Finally, copy the graphic from the letterhead and paste it into the envelope. You may need to resize the graphic so that it looks appropriate to the size of the envelope.

Add Mail Merge fields to the addressee part of the envelope, and you're, like, totally cooking.

Make a Template for Your Most Common Projects

If you create the same kind of project in Word often, you might want to save a template that contains just the formatting you use. Try this:

1. Choose File⇨New to start with a fresh document.

2. Choose Format⇨Style.

   The Style Sheet dialog box appears.

3. Pick an existing style — like Normal — and click on the Modify button. Change the style formatting (like Paragraph and Font settings) to suit your needs.

   Repeat for as many styles, like headings and captions, perhaps, as you need in your template.

4. When you're done, save the file as a new template.

When you need to invoke a style using the template, just place the cursor on the text you want to change and select the appropriate formatting from the drop-down Style picker in the toolbar.

Surf the Web without Starting a Web Browser

Most of the Office applications include a set of Web navigational tools in the toolbar. You can invoke them by right-clicking in the toolbar region and choosing Web. You can access Favorites, navigate forward and back, and type URLs directly into the toolbar.

Chapter 16

Ten Downloadable Extras to Get You Home Earlier

In This Chapter

▶ Ten useful pieces of software

*I*t doesn't take long to begin to see some of the chinks in Office 97's armor. Little problems here, occasional shortcomings there, and before you know it, you're calling your spouse to say, "I'll be home late and so would you please record *Babylon 5* for me because it's going to be the really cool one where Garibaldi gets his memory back after being 'programmed' to be a sleeper agent by the Psi Corp."

Todd's misguided opinion: Sounds just like the exciting dialog they write for the show, doesn't it?

Even if it's not a *Babylon 5* night, you might want to get home earlier anyway — and there is a veritable treasure trove of software on the Internet that can make Office work a bit smarter for you.

Office 97 Service Release

`http://www.microsoft.com/officefreestuff/office/`

Despite how much we like Office 97, we've gotta admit that it is far from perfect. Top of the list of complaints was the fact that the file format for Word 97 was different than for the previous version, and if you tried to save your work in the Word 6 format, it wasn't readable by older versions of Word. That bodes poorly for anyone who needs to share data with others who weren't as far-thinking and visionary as you and haven't already upgraded to Office 97 as well.

The Office 97 Service Release is Microsoft's answer, and you should make sure that everyone in your office gets it. Not only does it fix the Word file-saving bug, but it adds a lot of other little features to Office as well.

Wondering if elves — or perhaps the IS guys — installed the patch when you weren't looking? Choose Help⇨About in any Office application. If you see **SR1** after the name of the program, the patch is installed. If not, you need it.

Internet Explorer 4

```
http://www.microsoft.com/ie
```

Aw, come on — a new browser is going to get me home earlier? We know that's what you're saying. But it's true. Internet Explorer 4 (its friends call it IE4) is the newest Web browser from Microsoft. It has a lot of convenient new features and capabilities, like:

- The Active Desktop, which turns your main Windows screen into a Web page on which you can scatter Web stuff for quick and easy reference.

- An easy-to-get-to history list divided chronologically, which makes it easy to find sites you visited, say, on Tuesday.

- A new Explorer bar that displays your search results while you surf through them in the main window.

- A free Web page editor that you can use to create your company site — it has a lot of features, considering it's free.

- Enhanced security. You can change the level of protection that IE4 provides you based on general categories of sites.

In addition to those new features, IE4 has a bunch of new capabilities like Desktop components and Channels, which you can add to your own Web site. That way, IE4 users will say, "Wow, this dude is IE4-savvy. I think I'll buy his product." (But because older browsers ignore IE4 enhancements, just hope that Ted Turner isn't surfing with Netscape 2 when he's out looking for companies to acquire for obscene amounts of money.)

Rules Wizard

```
http://www.microsoft.com/OfficeFreeStuff/outlook/
```

Back in Chapter 5, we mention how handy it is to be able to let Outlook manage some of your mail for you automatically. You need Microsoft's Rules

Wizard for that, but once you have it, the fun never stops. After installing it, choose Tools➪Rules Wizard and configure it to do something. Follow these steps:

1. **Click New. A new Rules Wizard will start.**

2. **Choose a situation from the drop-down menu at the top.**

   For example, you might choose Move New Messages From Someone. This allows you to put messages from a specific address in their own folder.

3. **Click on each of the underlined words and provide the information that Outlook needs to effectively deal with your new rule.**

   The underlined words in the lower window are placeholders that you need to fill in.

4. **Step through the wizard and provide any more information you need, like possible exceptions to the rule. Give the rule a name and click Finish.**

5. **In the main Rules Wizard window, you can temporarily disable a rule by unchecking the box next to the rule. Or make sure it is checked, and it'll do its work behind your back.**

You can use the Rules wizard to corral e-mail arriving from a Web site into a specific folder — else it'll overwhelm your inbox. You can also set up a "kill file" to trash junk mail or messages from specific individuals that you know you don't want to read. Just have the rule automatically file the e-mail in the Deleted Items folder.

PrintMe for PowerPoint

http://www.microsoft.com/OfficeFreeStuff/powerpoint/

This handy little tool can save you hours of frustration when creating PowerPoint presentations. In a nutshell, this quick little download is a two-slide presentation that reproduces the color palette used by PowerPoint. Simply print the file and keep it handy when you're working with color slides. When you want to choose colors for a background or object, refer to the printout to confirm what it'll really look like when printed. That way, you won't be surprised by the difference between the colors onscreen and the color your printer spits out.

Export Graphic Shape Add-in

    http://www.microsoft.com/OfficeFreeStuff/powerpoint/

If you spend much time creating Web pages, you'll probably crave stock art. In particular, you'll wish there were an easy way to make buttons just like the ones in PowerPoint. Well golly, if you download the Export Graphic Shape Add-In, then you can steal buttons or other AutoShapes right out of PowerPoint and save them as GIF or JPG images.

After you install the Add-In, it appears as a small toolbar. Here's how it works:

1. **Select the object that you want to export.**

2. **Click the Export Shape button and give the file a name. If you want to automatically load the object in your graphics program as it saves, make sure the View Export button is pushed in before you save the image.**

You'll need to make the object pretty big — perhaps the size of the slide itself — or it'll be too small to use as a graphic.

Sales and Marketing Templates

    http://www.microsoft.com/OfficeFreeStuff/Word/

Microsoft Word is great, but the basic installation doesn't come with enough business-related templates. Microsoft has a few handy ones on their Web site, however, and they're free for the pickin'. The Sales and Marketing Templates is one of our favorites because it helps you create both brochures and press releases. (Sure, those fit together. The next template set will be holiday cards and traffic tickets.) After you install the templates, look for them in File⇨New⇨Publications.

Human Resources and Operations Templates

http://www.microsoft.com/OfficeFreeStuff/Word/

Another handy set of templates, this package includes an invoice, a weekly time sheet, a purchase order, and a company directory. After installation, you'll find the new templates in File⇨New⇨Other Documents.

You can customize a template to your own business needs and save it as a different template. If you do that, be sure that you choose File⇨New and edit the template. Then save it as a Document Template with a different name. Some documents (like the Invoice) are "protected" from change except in certain fields, however. To edit it, you'll need to choose Tools⇨Unprotect Document.

PowerToys

http://www.microsoft.com/windows95/info/powertoys.htm

They may not sound very professional, but Microsoft's PowerToys are a handy collection of Windows 95 add-ons that add a lot of new functionality to the operating system. In other words, they're things that Microsoft meant to put in Windows 95 but ran out of time because they were too busy making the task bar display that little animated *Click Here to Start* sequence.

PowerToys includes about a dozen utilities, but our favorites include the following:

- ✔ **TweakUI.** This is a new Control Panel applet that lets you fine-tune many aspects of the way Windows works that previously took a trip to the evil, musty Registry).

- ✔ **QuickRes.** Changes the resolution and color depth of your Windows display without rebooting. Great for switching rapidly to applications that demand a particular resolution.

- ✔ **Contents Menu.** Displays the contents of a menu without actually opening the menu. Hey, those quarter-second mouse-clicks add up!

Microsoft Camcorder

http://www.microsoft.com/officefreestuff/office/

This handy little utility lets you capture all the activity on the screen — with or without narrative audio — for training, demonstrations, and other multimedia applications. It's simple to use and saves movies in standard AVI format or as executable files that you just click on to run. As AVI files, you can embed Camcorder movies in Web pages, PowerPoint slides, and Word documents.

Use Movie⇨Preferences to configure your movie. In particular, you probably want to hide the Camcorder interface while you're recording the movie.

Avery Wizard

http://www.microsoft.com/OfficeFreeStuff/Word/

If you use standard, precut labels from Avery, this wizard helps you print professional-looking documents. It places a button in the toolbar, and you can also reach its features from File⇨New⇨Avery. Use the wizard by selecting the product number from the Avery box you are using. This template set is a real time-saver!

New Office AutoShapes

http://www.microsoft.com/OfficeFreeStuff/office/

Choose from 18 new shapes for PowerPoint, Word, Publisher, and Internet applications with this selection. The good news is that it's a handy collection. The bad news is that it's kind of a pain to use. After downloading, you'll find that it's an Excel file filled with shapes. Just select the shape you want to use, choose Edit⇨Copy, and then switch to the application you want, like Word, and paste it in.

Appendix

About the CD

*I*t's a Frisbee! It's a coaster! No, it's a CD with lots of goodies on it to help you get more out of Office 97.

System Requirements

Make sure your computer meets the minimum system requirements listed below. If your computer doesn't match up to most of these requirements, you may have problems using the contents of the CD. You need a CD-ROM drive, for example, because you can't hold the CD up to the light like a thin postal envelope to see what's inside.

- ✔ A PC with a 486 or faster processor.
- ✔ Microsoft Windows 95.
- ✔ At least 16MB of total RAM installed on your computer. For best performance, we recommend that you have at least 32MB of RAM installed, but that's good advice for almost any Windows 95 software.
- ✔ At least 55MB of hard drive space available to install all the software from this CD. (You'll need less space if you don't install every program.)
- ✔ A CD-ROM drive — double-speed (2x) or faster.
- ✔ A sound card. Not one of those greeting cards that play music — we mean an actual audio card for your PC.
- ✔ A monitor capable of displaying at least 256 colors or grayscale.
- ✔ A modem with a speed of at least 14,400 bps.

If you need more information on the basics, check out *PCs For Dummies,* 5th Edition, by Dan Gookin or *Windows 95 For Dummies* by Andy Rathbone (both published by IDG Books Worldwide, Inc.).

How to Use the CD

To install the items from the CD to your hard drive, follow these steps.

1. **Insert the CD into your computer's CD-ROM drive.**

2. **Click the Start button and click Run.**

3. **In the dialog box that appears, type** D:\SETUP.EXE.

   Most of you probably have your CD-ROM drive listed as either drive D or drive E under My Computer in Windows 95. Type in the proper drive letter if your CD-ROM drive uses a different letter.

4. **Click OK.**

   A license agreement window appears.

5. **Since we're sure you'll want to use the CD, read through the license agreement, nod your head, and then click the Accept button. Once you click Accept, you'll never be bothered by the License Agreement window again.**

   The CD interface appears. The CD interface is a little program that shows you what is on the CD and coordinates installing the programs and running the demos. The interface basically lets you click a button or two to make things happen.

6. **The first screen you see is the Welcome screen. Click anywhere on this screen to enter the interface.**

   Now you are getting to the action. This next screen lists categories for the software on the CD.

7. **To view the items within a category, just click the category's name.**

   A list of programs in the category appears.

8. **For more information about a program, click the program's name.**

   Be sure to read the information that appears. Sometimes a program might require you to do a few tricks on your computer first, and this screen will tell you where to go for that information, if necessary.

9. **To install the program, click the appropriate Install button. If you don't want to install the program, click the Go Back button to return to the previous screen.**

   You can always return to the previous screen by clicking the Go Back button. This allows you to browse the different categories and products and decide what you want to install.

   Once you click an install button, the CD interface drops to the background while the CD begins installation of the program you chose.

10. **To install other items, repeat Steps 7, 8 and 9.**

11. **When you're done installing programs, click the Quit button to close the interface.**

    You can eject the CD now. Carefully place it back in the plastic jacket of the book for safekeeping, or feed it to the dog. But remember that if Fido gnaws on it, you can't install any other software from the disc (and it's bad for his teeth anyway).

What's on the CD?

Here's a summary of the software on this CD. In general, we've given you easy access to many of the free things on Microsoft's Web site and shareware found elsewhere on the Internet. You can install just a few of the items or go for broke and install them all. Just remember that some of these applications may require a small fee to the author for continued use after you've fallen in love with the software.

Active Office, from Software Publishing Corporation: Quickly transform an Office document with compelling business graphics. Just a few clicks adds graphics and layout elements to any Office document.

At the Office — Christmas Edition, Corey Deitz: Fun, tongue-in-cheek screen saver and message taker that provides you with some clever office humor and fun during the holiday season.

CaBook, CaRedirect, CaPrint, CaSave from Ludek Mokry: Three more Outlook extension packages designed to help you get the most out of the address book, redirect e-mail messages to other users, print, and save, all using special extensions to Outlook's rules capabilities.

Excel Viewer 97, from Microsoft: Need to share worksheets with people who don't have Microsoft Excel 97 yet? The Microsoft Excel Viewer 97 lets anyone view page layout, copy, zoom, AutoFilter, and print files created with Microsoft Excel.

ExLife, from Ludek Mokry: Add additional filter rules functionality to Microsoft Outlook 97, including the ability to move, copy, delete, forward, reply, run a program, print, and save attachments based on filter rules criteria.

ExSign, from Ludek Mokry: Works with ExLife to add advanced e-mail signature capabilties to Outlook 97. Have different signatures for different services and message types.

Followup System 97, from pyz01: Keeps track of critical projects, the person or company responsible for project tasks, and the due date of the tasks so that you can easily see what assignments are coming due for critical projects. You can print reports of all tasks due by a due date, print individual reports for each person responsible for tasks, print individual reports by project, and print a list of all tasks in the system.

GIF Animator, from Ulead: Ulead makes some nifty graphic tools, and the GIF animator is a cool program that easily makes animated GIFs for your Web site. Using GIF Animator, you can combine images into animated buttons, icons, and ad banners for your Web site, and the program uses an intuitive "wizard-like" interface.

Home Budget, from Jim Porter: This Excel 5.0 spreadsheet has seven separate color pages, four of which are interactive. Created by an ex-stock-broker, this file includes pages for a Monthly Home Budget, a cost of waiting study of four people who had opposing views of when to start their IRAs, a savings planner to help with retirement planning and salary adjustments, plus information on tax-deferred investing and other issues.

Internet Explorer 4, from Microsoft: Internet Explorer 4 is Microsoft's newest Web browser that integrates Web browsing features right into the desktop. We think IE4 is pretty neat, particularly for some of its more subtle features. Check out the History bar, for instance — it lets you revisit Web pages based on a chronological list of when you went there. That makes it easy to go back to a place you found back on Tuesday, for example. IE4 also includes a good e-mail client and a great graphical Web page editor. Try it! You'll like it!

Microsoft Camcorder, from Microsoft: Let's say you're a trainer and you need to teach folks how to use Word. Perhaps you want to put a lesson on CD-ROM and distribute it throughout the company. How do you demonstrate how to use a complex feature? It would be really cool if you could just record the procedure as a short movie, right? Well, you can using Camcorder. Microsoft Camcorder lets you record everything you see on the screen, save it as a Video for Windows movie, and put it on disc for all to see.

My Bills 97, Version 2, from VisualWare: This Microsoft Access 97 database application allows you to create and maintain your bills and financial obligations, list and sort bills by categories, and identify and sort creditors and accounts by profile.

Office Toys for Word 97, from Merlot International: Office Toys is a unique collection of utilities for Word that can enhance your productivity. Office Toys offers file management tools right inside Word, better toolbars, im-proved spell checking, font previews, an improved style selector, and much more.

PaintShop Pro, from Jasc: One of the most full-featured shareware paint programs around, Paint Shop Pro is a neat tool for creating images from scratch or editing existing ones. We use PSP a lot just to convert an image into fewer colors or save it in another image format. PSP may very well be all the paint program you ever need.

Pastor's Helpmate 8.1, from Pinnacle Productions: Church data management application for MS Access 97. Church administrators can efficiently and effectively manage all their church data including membership, attendance, contribution, and group membership records.

Phone Book 97, from VisualWare: A Microsoft Access 97 database application that allows you to create and maintain an extensive phone list. List and sort numbers by categories. Identify and sort recipients by profile. Produce a complete set of reports.

Snapshot Viewer, from Microsoft: If you want to send an Access report to someone in e-mail, you're pretty much stuck sending the whole database. And not only can that get a little unwieldy to start sending through the ether, but the database might also have information in it that you don't want to distribute. Using the Snapshot Viewer, you can let others view your report from their Web browser or e-mail client. And with Snapshots, you can send a report though e-mail without sending the whole database. You need to install the Office Service pack from Microsoft's Web site in order to use this tool.

The Outlook Company Updater, from Jay Harlow: Here's a Microsoft Outlook 97 form that displays just company information and allows you to update other records in the Contacts folders from the same company. Rename the company or office location, for example, and all related contacts can be updated.

Word 6.0/95 Binary Converter, from Microsoft: One of the worst mistakes Microsoft made with Word 97 was the way the program saved documents in Rich Text Format (RTF) while using the .DOC extension. That made old versions of Word gag when trying to load these files. This patch "fixes" Word 97 so that you can save files as good old Word 6 documents and share them with the world.

Word Viewer 97, from Microsoft: Not everyone has Microsoft Word (no, really!), but you sometimes need to share documents you created in Word with those heathens. Word Viewer allows folks without Word to view — but not edit — anything you do in Word. Even better, the Word Viewer document is properly formatted, so they see it the way you intended. This version requires Windows 95 or NT, but there's another version for Windows 3.*x* users.

Word Viewer 97 (16-bit version), from Microsoft: Not everyone has Microsoft Word, but even worse, many folks don't even have Windows 95! What if you need to let them read a Word document? Well, it's time for the Word Viewer to the rescue. This 16-bit version works with older versions of Windows like 3.1 and Windows for Workgroups.

If You've Got Problems (Of the CD Kind)

If you encounter problems, the two likeliest causes are that you don't have enough memory (RAM) for the programs you want to use, or you have other programs running that are affecting installation or running of a program. If you get error messages like `Not enough memory` or `Setup cannot continue`, try one or more of these methods and then try using the software again:

- ✔ Turn off any antivirus software that you have on your computer. Installers sometimes mimic virus activity and may make your computer incorrectly believe that it is being infected by a virus.

- ✔ Close all running programs. The more programs you're running, the less memory is available to other programs. Installers also typically update files and programs. So if you keep other programs running, installation may not work properly.

- ✔ Have your local computer store add more RAM to your computer. This is, admittedly, a drastic and somewhat expensive step. On the other hand, adding more memory can really help the speed of your computer and enable more programs to run at the same time.

If you still have trouble with installing the items from the CD, please call the IDG Books Worldwide Customer Service phone number: 800-762-2974 (outside the U.S.: 317-596-5430). Don't call Dave or Todd at home unless it's really urgent and you have tickets to a Throwing Muses concert (for Dave) or a jazz concert (for Todd).

Index

Notes

Notes

Notes

Notes

Notes

Notes

Notes

IDG Books Worldwide, Inc., End-User License Agreement

READ THIS. You should carefully read these terms and conditions before opening the software packet(s) included with this book ("Book"). This is a license agreement ("Agreement") between you and IDG Books Worldwide, Inc. ("IDGB"). By opening the accompanying software packet(s), you acknowledge that you have read and accept the following terms and conditions. If you do not agree and do not want to be bound by such terms and conditions, promptly return the Book and the unopened software packet(s) to the place you obtained them for a full refund.

1. **License Grant.** IDGB grants to you (either an individual or entity) a nonexclusive license to use one copy of the enclosed software program(s) (collectively, the "Software") solely for your own personal or business purposes on a single computer (whether a standard computer or a workstation component of a multi-user network). The Software is in use on a computer when it is loaded into temp-orary memory (RAM) or installed into permanent memory (hard disk, CD-ROM, or other storage device). IDGB reserves all rights not expressly granted herein.

2. **Ownership.** IDGB is the owner of all right, title, and interest, including copyright, in and to the compilation of the Software recorded on the disk(s) or CD-ROM ("Software Media"). Copyright to the individual programs recorded on the Software Media is owned by the authors or other authorized copyright owner of each program. Ownership of the Software and all proprietary rights relating thereto remain with IDGB and its licensers.

3. **Restrictions on Use and Transfer.**

   (a) You may only (i) make one copy of the Software for backup or archival purposes, or (ii) transfer the Software to a single hard disk, provided that you keep the original for backup or archival purposes. You may not (i) rent or lease the Software, (ii) copy or reproduce the Software through a LAN or other network system or through any computer subscriber system or bulletin-board system, or (iii) modify, adapt, or create derivative works based on the Software.

   (b) You may not reverse engineer, decompile, or disassemble the Software. You may transfer the Software and user documentation on a permanent basis, provided that the transferee agrees to accept the terms and conditions of this Agreement and you retain no copies. If the Software is an update or has been updated, any transfer must include the most recent update and all prior versions.

4. **Restrictions on Use of Individual Programs.** You must follow the individual requirements and restrictions detailed for each individual program in the "About the CD" section of this Book. These limitations are also contained in the individual license agreements recorded on the Software Media. These limitations may include a requirement that after using the program for a specified period of time, the user must pay a registration fee or discontinue use. By opening the Software packet(s), you will be agreeing to abide by the licenses and restrictions for these individual programs that are detailed in the "About the CD" section and on the Software Media. None of the material on this Software Media or listed in this Book may ever be redistributed, in original or modified form, for commercial purposes.

5. **Limited Warranty.**

   (a) IDGB warrants that the Software and Software Media are free from defects in materials and workmanship under normal use for a period of sixty (60) days from the date of purchase of this Book. If IDGB receives notification within the warranty period of defects in materials or workmanship, IDGB will replace the defective Software Media.

(b) IDGB AND THE AUTHORS OF THE BOOK DISCLAIM ALL OTHER WARRANTIES, EXPRESS OR IMPLIED, INCLUDING WITHOUT LIMITATION IMPLIED WARRANTIES OF MERCHANTABILITY AND FITNESS FOR A PARTICULAR PURPOSE, WITH RESPECT TO THE SOFTWARE, THE PROGRAMS, THE SOURCE CODE CONTAINED THEREIN, AND/OR THE TECHNIQUES DESCRIBED IN THIS BOOK. IDGB DOES NOT WARRANT THAT THE FUNCTIONS CONTAINED IN THE SOFTWARE WILL MEET YOUR REQUIREMENTS OR THAT THE OPERATION OF THE SOFTWARE WILL BE ERROR FREE.

(c) This limited warranty gives you specific legal rights, and you may have other rights that vary from jurisdiction to jurisdiction.

6. **Remedies.**

   (a) IDGB's entire liability and your exclusive remedy for defects in materials and workmanship shall be limited to replacement of the Software Media, which may be returned to IDGB with a copy of your receipt at the following address: Software Media Fulfillment Department, Attn.: *Small Business Microsoft Office 97 For Dummies,* IDG Books Worldwide, Inc., 7260 Shadeland Station, Ste. 100, Indianapolis, IN 46256, or call 800-762-2974. Please allow three to four weeks for delivery. This Limited Warranty is void if failure of the Software Media has resulted from accident, abuse, or misapplication. Any replacement Software Media will be warranted for the remainder of the original warranty period or thirty (30) days, whichever is longer.

   (b) In no event shall IDGB or the authors be liable for any damages whatsoever (including without limitation damages for loss of business profits, business interruption, loss of business information, or any other pecuniary loss) arising from the use of or inability to use the Book or the Software, even if IDGB has been advised of the possibility of such damages.

   (c) Because some jurisdictions do not allow the exclusion or limitation of liability for consequential or incidental damages, the above limitation or exclusion may not apply to you.

7. **U.S. Government Restricted Rights.** Use, duplication, or disclosure of the Software by the U.S. Government is subject to restrictions stated in paragraph (c)(1)(ii) of the Rights in Technical Data and Computer Software clause of DFARS 252.227-7013, and in subparagraphs (a) through (d) of the Commercial Computer@ndRestricted Rights clause at FAR 52.227-19, and in similar clauses in the NASA FAR supplement, when applicable.

8. **General.** This Agreement constitutes the entire understanding of the parties and revokes and supersedes all prior agreements, oral or written, between them and may not be modified or amended except in a writing signed by both parties hereto that specifically refers to this Agreement. This Agreement shall take precedence over any other documents that may be in conflict herewith. If any one or more provisions contained in this Agreement are held by any court or tribunal to be invalid, illegal, or otherwise unenforceable, each and every other provision shall remain in full force and effect.

CD-ROM Installation Instructions

To install the items from the CD to your hard drive, follow these steps.

1. **Insert the CD into your computer's CD-ROM drive.**

2. **Click the Start button and click Run.**

3. **In the dialog box that appears, type** D:\SETUP.EXE.

   Most of you probably have your CD-ROM drive listed as either drive D or drive E under My Computer in Windows 95. Type in the proper drive letter if your CD-ROM drive uses a different letter.

4. **Click OK.**

   A license agreement window appears.

5. **Read through the license agreement and then click the Accept button. Once you click Accept, you'll never be bothered by the License Agreement window again.**

The CD interface appears. The CD interface is a little program that shows you what is on the CD and coordinates installing the programs and running the demos. The interface basically lets you click a button or two to make things happen.

For more information about the contents of the CD-ROM, and for more detailed installation instructions, see the appendix of this book.

IDG BOOKS WORLDWIDE
BOOK REGISTRATION

Register This Book and Win!

We want to hear from you!

Visit **http://my2cents.dummies.com** to register this book and tell us how you liked it!

🖋 Get entered in our monthly prize giveaway.

🖋 Give us feedback about this book — tell us what you like best, what you like least, or maybe what you'd like to ask the author and us to change!

🖋 Let us know any other *...For Dummies* topics that interest you.

Your feedback helps us determine what books to publish, tells us what coverage to add as we revise our books, and lets us know whether we're meeting your needs as a *...For Dummies* reader. You're our most valuable resource, and what you have to say is important to us!

Not on the Web yet? It's easy to get started with *Dummies 101®: The Internet For Windows® 95* or *The Internet For Dummies®,* 4th Edition, at local retailers everywhere.

Or let us know what you think by sending us a letter at the following address:

...For Dummies Book Registration
Dummies Press
7260 Shadeland Station, Suite 100
Indianapolis, IN 46256
Fax 317-596-5498

BUSINESS AND GENERAL REFERENCE BOOK SERIES FROM IDG

COMPUTER BOOK SERIES FROM IDG